Davis H Bays

The Doctrines and Dogmas of Mormonism Examined and Refuted

Davis H Bays

The Doctrines and Dogmas of Mormonism Examined and Refuted

ISBN/EAN: 9783337297817

Printed in Europe, USA, Canada, Australia, Japan

Cover: Foto ©Lupo / pixelio.de

More available books at **www.hansebooks.com**

THE

DOCTRINES AND DOGMAS

OF

MORMONISM

EXAMINED AND REFUTED

BY

ELDER DAVIS H. BAYS

St. Louis
CHRISTIAN PUBLISHING COMPANY

To My Devoted Wife
WHO, THROUGH A LONG AND SERIOUS ILLNESS,
NURSED ME BACK TO LIFE, AND ONLY FOR
WHOSE WATCHFUL CARE THESE
PAGES WOULD NEVER HAVE
BEEN WRITTEN,
THIS VOLUME IS AFFECTIONATELY DEDICATED

PREFACE.

THE only apology the writer has to offer for presenting this volume to the public, is the consciousness that such a work is needed. It is designed as an aid to those who care to become more thoroughly acquainted with the intricacies of Mormon theology, and especially those who have only been able to study it from the outside. With few exceptions those who have undertaken to "expose" Mormonism have dealt with the follies and "grosser crimes" of the system, and have paid little or no attention to the fundamental principles upon which the Church of the Saints is based.

No writer, so far as we are informed, has ever undertaken to analyze and refute, in a thorough, systematic manner, the doctrines and dogmas of Mormonism. In this volume we have endeavored to present the doctrines of the church as they are defined by its leading minds, together with the Biblical evidences adduced in their support, and then offer such evidences from scriptural and other sources as will, in the writer's opinion, overthrow the arguments presented, and prove the entire system erroneous.

Reared in the faith of the Saints from early childhood, and having been, for twenty-seven years, a zealous advocate and defender of its peculiarities, the writer has had rare opportunities for studying Mormonism from the *inside*.

The line of argument usually employed by writers and speakers to refute the Mormon dogma is of such a character as to render success almost impossible. They depend very largely upon the current belief that the prophet's general reputation for veracity was bad; and that the Book of Mormon was concocted from the old Spaulding Romance.

PREFACE

In this work we rely upon nothing of this kind. We have something far better, and upon which we may confidently rely.

We take up each proposition as it is presented by its friends, and then proceed to answer and refute their arguments in a fair, straightforward manner, demonstrating the fallacy and erroneousness of the entire system, from a purely Biblical and philosophical point of view.

Containing, as the work does, full proof-texts and historical references upon every question discussed, it is a complete hand-book of ready reference, and is admirably adapted to the use of clergymen and others who may have the questions to meet, as well as a source of reliable information to the general reader.

The work, in both its design and mode of argument, may truthfully be said to be original and altogether unique, and contains much valuable matter never before published.

In collecting data for the work, I have been placed under obligations to a number of the leading scholars of the country, prominently among whom may be mentioned President James B. Angell, of the University of Michigan; Ira Maurice Price, Ph.D., Associate Professor of Oriental Languages and Literatures, of the University of Chicago; Charles H. S. Davis, Ph.D., M. D., of Meriden, Conn., Dr. Chas. E. Moldenke, of New York, Specialist in Egyptology and Archeology, and Pres. W. R. Harper, of the University of Chicago. To these gentlemen, together with many others who have rendered valuable aid, the writer hereby tenders his expression of thanks.

In the hope that this volume may be the humble means of reflecting needed light upon the themes discussed, and that it may accomplish the good for which it is intended, and without stopping to offer apologies for its many defects, we send this little book out into the world upon its mission of mercy and love.

D. H. BAYS.

TABLE OF CONTENTS.

CHAPTER I.

INTRODUCTORY.

A remarkable claim—Marvelous if true—No middle ground—Either true or false—Apostle Pratt states the case—Origin of Mormonism—Joseph's vision—Churches all wrong—Their teachers corrupt—The angel Moroni—Hidden plates revealed—*Urim* and *Thummim*. 17

CHAPTER II.

Martin Harris and the stolen manuscript—Oliver Cowdery—His part in the work—Church organized—The Spaulding Romance—Deposited in Oberlin Library—Old theory abandoned—Sidney Rigdon not one of the originators—Book of Mormon, its purport—The American Bible—Apostles chosen—The First Presidency—The Patriarch—Other officers—Mormon intolerance—Doctrines of the Church. 21

CHAPTER III.

The Mormon House—Its internal garnishment—Visions, dreams, etc.—All deceptive—Spiritual gifts—Were they to be perpetuated?—Mormonism affirms—It must prove—The apostolic commission—Its obligations perpetual—The signs promised were limited—The church perpetuated—Gates of hell shall not prevail against it. 35

CHAPTER IV.

Casting out devils—The Saints try it—Devils are obstinate—Epilepsy and insanity—A modern instance—Great trial to the faithful—Unknown tongues not necessary—Conditions have changed—An unknown tongue impossible—A tongue and its interpretation—Missionaries cannot speak in tongues—1 Cor., twelfth chapter—1 Cor., thirteenth chapter—Tongues shall cease and prophecies fail—A rule—Gifts for Gentiles—Take up serpents. . . 45

(7)

CHAPTER V.

Deadly things—Joseph's claim—Was he poisoned?—The case examined—Hair came out—Claim unsupported—Healing the sick—The writer's experience and disappointment—Then and now—Discouraged—A Mormon subterfuge—Bible miracles and latter day pretensions. 62

CHAPTER VI.

Other claims—The Adventists—Free Methodists—Dr. Dowie—The Church of Rome—Their miracles lack authentication—The Church at Corinth—Spiritual gifts were for edification—Utah Church and its miracles—The sick healed—Cases cited—Are they genuine?—The Reorganized Church—Excellent moral character of its membership—Claims to miraculous powers—Tested by a simple rule—Miracles no longer necessary. 70

CHAPTER VII.

The Mormon Church a unique structure—Divided into many factions—Which is right?—King Strang—His kingdom—The Mormon idea of an apostolic church—Its officers—Apostle's Kelley's rule for testing churches. 75

CHAPTER VIII.

The Reorganized Church deficient—The patriarch omitted—Only nine apostles—An argument examined—Polygamy and highway robbery—A corrupt tree—A bitter fountain—Duties of an apostle defined—Brighamite and Reorganized churches agree—The whole system is unscriptural. 83

CHAPTER IX.

Apostles in the primitive church—The apostolic office is ambassadorial, not executive—Ambassadors in the church now are unnecessary and impossible—Mr. Kelley's rule applied—Apostolic succession. 91

CHAPTER X.

Nuts to crack—To the law and to the testimony—The Bible recognizes no First Presidency in the church—No Patriarch, no High Priests—From another standpoint—An elder is a Melchizedek priest—May give the Holy Spirit by the laying on of hands. 101

CHAPTER XI.

Church and kingdom synonymous—The church from John to the calling of the twelve without apostles—From 1830 to 1835 without apostles—Only elders—Fact and theory—Bible church and Mormon church compared—Branch president—Mr. Kelley's test applied to Mormon coin—Weighed in the balance and found wanting. 106

CHAPTER XII.

Foundation of the church—Various opinions on Matt. 16: 18—Upon this rock—What rock?—Joseph Smith's view—Apostle Smith examined—Revelation the foundation of the Mormon Church—The writer's heresy—Christ the rock, the foundation. . 112

CHAPTER XIII.

The spiritual house—Christ the chief corner-stone—In types—Pillar of fire—The smitten rock—The question settled—No other foundation but Christ—Book of Mormon and the rock—Joseph Smith vs. Joseph Smith—Witnesses in the balances—Summary. . 124

CHAPTER XIV.

Priesthood and preachers—Ministers must be called by revelation—Joseph was like Moses—Joseph and Oliver ordained to the Aaronic priesthood by an angel—Ordained by Peter, James and John to the Melchizedek priesthood—Questioned by President Smith of the Reorganized Church—His view criticised—How priesthood is conferred—Angels do not officiate at ordinations—Who ordained Moses, Melchizedek or Christ?—Christ the only Melchizedek priest. 132

CHAPTER XV.

Priesthood—What is it?—Webster vs. Kelley—Mormon definition erroneous—Joseph's revelation on priesthood—Handed down from father to son—Isaiah lived in the days of Abraham—Moses ordained by his father-in-law, Jethro—Abraham ordained by Melchizedek—A table of dates and ordinations—Gad ordained Jeremy 1120 years before the prophet was born. . . 144

CHAPTER XVI.

Apostles, then and now—How called?—What is an apostle?—Called by Jesus personally—Not ordained by the laying on of hands—

How were the apostles qualified?—Endued with power from on high—Mormon apostles—How called?—Chosen by Oliver Cowdery, David Whitmer and Martin Harris—Names of the twelve apostles. 151

CHAPTER XVII.

Joseph's apostles—How qualified—Tarry at Kirtland—Dedication of the Kirtland temple—House filled with angels—Questions and answers—Jesus did not appear—The Reorganized Church—When organized, and by whom—Of whom composed—Seven apostles chosen—Their names—Chosen by a committee of three—The lesser ordains the greater—Can a stream rise above its fountain?— Apostasy of Apostle Briggs—Repudiates his own revelation— Three of the seven apostles reduced to the ranks—Ells and Derry chosen by a committee of three—Apostle Derry resigns—Summed up. 158

CHAPTER XVIII.

The Book of Mormon—What is it?—History of a Jewish colony— Written on metallic plates—Plates discovered near Palmyra, New York—Joseph's account of the discovery—New revelation— Orson Pratt's view—All authority lost in the great apostasy— Restored by an angel—Joseph's key to the revelation of St. John —The man-child is the priesthood—Mr. Pratt answered—A monstrous claim. 165

CHAPTER XIX.

Is a new revelation necessary?—The great apostasy—Did it annul all existing authority?—The great Jewish apostasy—Authority not destroyed—Devout Zacharias—John the Baptist—The old kingdom and the new—Authority transferred—The latter day apostasy—How does it affect the Mormon Church?—Joseph's church apostatized—Church rejected of God—The Reorganized Church the result of apostasy—The Church of Christ transmitted from the times of the apostles. 172

CHAPTER XX.

A marvelous work and a wonder—An untenable claim—From President Blair—His comments on Isaiah 29—Mr. Kelley's points of identity—Ariel—Old and new—Book to be taken out of the ground. 182

CHAPTER XXI.

The land shadowing with wings—Is it North and South America?—Common ground—Ariel is Jerusalem—It shall be as Ariel—The Ariel of the West—A race exterminated—Their History—The land shadowing with wings is Egypt, not America—Views of Ira Maurice Price, Ph. D. 189

CHAPTER XXII.

The book that is sealed—Isaiah, chapter twenty-nine—The words of a book—Presented to Prof. Charles Anthon—A woe pronounced against Jerusalem—The city where David dwelt—Inspired translation—Different rendering of Isaiah twenty-nine—Quotation from—Comments—A safe rule—Isaiah twenty-nine relates to the destruction of Jerusalem—Ten propositions—No prophecy concerning a book—A question of exegesis and history—The prophecy of Isaiah concerning the destruction of Jerusalem literally fulfilled—Revolt of the ten tribes—Israel and Judah—The Assyrian captivity—A strange work. 194

CHAPTER XXIII.

The Babylonian captivity—Nebuchadnezzar—Siege of Jerusalem—Raised forts against the city—Terms of Isaiah's prophecy—Jeremiah records its fulfillment—The nations that fight against Mount Zion—Become as the dream of a night vision—Have all passed away—Wise and prudent men—The blindness of all Israel—The Chaldean army besieges Jerusalem—Josephus describes it—Downfall of the Jewish kingdom—A marvelous work and a wonder. 207

CHAPTER XXIV.

Professor Anthon and Martin Harris—The "words of a book"—Joseph Smith's transcript presented to the Professor—Read this, I pray thee—I cannot read a sealed book—Joseph Smith, not Martin Harris, made the statement—Times and Seasons for May 2, 1842—Mr. Kelley states the case—The Professor could not decipher the characters—Characters were Egyptian, Chaldaic, Assyrian and Arabic—Self-contradictory—Correctly translated—Professor Anthon's statement—Contradicts Mr. Harris—No other witnesses—The statements compared—Smith-Harris testimony incompetent. 220

CHAPTER XXV.

The testimony of the three witnesses—A remarkable document—Apostle Pratt's view—An immense conclusion—The witnesses not deceived—The testimony is true or they are impostors—The line is drawn by Mormon authority—Are the witnesses unimpeachable?—Direct and indirect evidence—The Mormon Church—Authority depends upon the veracity of these witnesses—An admission—A negative proposition—How established—An illustration. 237

CHAPTER XXVI.

The three witnesses—Did they see an angel?—Impeaching the witnesses—Seven counts in the indictment—Eight witnesses—Testimony unimportant—Their defection from the prophet in Missouri—Stick to their original story—The three witnesses did not recant—Reasons for adhering to the original story—Afraid to expose the fraud—Better die with a lie on their lips than to divulge the secret—The touch of angelic hands in holy ordination—How could they forsake the prophet?—If I had seen the angel—A visit to David Whitmer—Did the witnesses reaffirm?—A letter from Martin Harris. 244

CHAPTER XXVII.

They did not see the angel—The reasons given—Egyptology little understood in 1830—Under the light of recent discoveries—The veil removed—Book of Mormon written in Egyptian—Orson Pratt's testimony—Testimony of Martin Harris—Were the characters on the plates Egyptian?—Fac-simile of the characters—Genuineness verified by Mormon authority. . . . 254

CHAPTER XXVIII.

The characters are not Egyptian—The testimony of scholars—Mr. Kelley's fac-simile—Submitted to scholars for examination—Explanatory letter—President James B. Angell's reply—A moral, not a linguistic question—Characters fraudulent—Chas. H. S. Davis, M. D., Ph. D.—Characters put down at random—Resemble nothing, not even shorthand—Not an Egyptian letter or character in it—A letter from Jerusalem—Dr. Charles E. Moldenke—The plates of the Book of Mormon a fraud—Egyptian and Arabic side by side—Is ridiculous and impossible—Characters bear no resemblance to Egyptian or Assyrian—Testimony of the witnesses compared—Scholarship vs. ignorance—Conclusion of the whole matter. 260

CHAPTER XXIX.

The Doctrines of Mormonism—What the Saints believe—The only way to be saved—Erroneous exegesis—Faith towards God—Repentance from dead works—Works of the law—Must leave them—Cannot perfect the believer—Character of the Hebrew letter—Hebrews 6: 1, 2 paraphrased—The doctrine of baptisms—Divers washings of the law—Baptize—Born—The difference—The law of life—The law of sin and death—Summary. . . 277

CHAPTER XXX.

The laying on of hands—Is it an ordinance of the Gospel ?—Neither Christ nor the apostles enjoin it—Not a principle of the doctrine of Christ—Peter and John give the Holy Spirit—Paul at Ephesus—Classed among apostolic miracles—Not necessary to salvation—It is of Hebrew origin—The scape-goat—Sins laid upon the goat—Sins of the world laid upon Christ. 291

CHAPTER XXXI.

Testimony of the Book of Mormon—Does it teach the laying on of hands ?—Contains the fullness of the Gospel—The first Nephite Church—Alma the first high priest—No laying on of hands—One faith and one baptism—First appearance of Christ—His Doctrine—Taught his disciples—He neither taught nor practiced the laying on of hands—Holy Spirit received without it—Nephite twelve disciples did not teach the doctrine—Its practice—Not an instance in the Book of Mormon—It is mentioned but once—Faith, Repentance, Confession and Baptism—More than this cometh of evil—Joseph and Oliver received the Holy Spirit without the laying on of hands—Resurrection of the dead and eternal judgment—Leaving the principles of the doctrine of Christ—What is meant by it?—Conclusion. . . . - 303

CHAPTER XXXII.

Mormon polygamy—Was Joseph Smith its author?—Became public soon after the prophet's death—Joseph's power over his people—An illustration—"Thou shalt give heed to all his words"—Doctrine and Covenants accepted—Polygamy practiced before Joseph's death—Questioned only by the Reorganized Church—The son guards the good name of his father—Polygamy a gradual growth—Book of Mormon condemns the doctrine—Early suspicions—Charged with polygamy in 1835—Article on marriage—Does not exclude the practice—One man one wife—One woman but one husband—John C. Bennett—The secret wife system—Trouble between Smith and Bennett—The Nauvoo Legion—A sham battle. 318

CHAPTER XXXIII.

Side-lights—A. H. Smith on polygamy—Those certificates—Dr. Bennett's apostasy—He divulges the secret wife system—Joseph denies—Hyrum Brown cut off from the church—Hyrum Smith denies—Denials examined—Priesthood and polygamy—Testimony of William Marks—Joseph Smith knew polygamy existed—A thus saith the Lord would have stopped it—Joseph alone responsible. 331

CHAPTER XXXIV.

Revelation on celestial marriage—Joseph Smith its author—A house of order—If any man marry him a wife—For time and all eternity—Passing the angels and the gods—Then shall they be gods—All manner of sins and blasphemies shall be forgiven—Shedding innocent blood the unpardonable sin—Abraham's wives—Sarah and Hagar—Isaac and Jacob—David and Solomon—Sealed on earth and sealed in heaven—Emma Smith—Must accept the celestial law or be destroyed—If a man espouse a virgin—If he espouse another he is justified—If he have ten virgins given him—The original wife—She must procure other wives for her lord, or be destroyed—Will reveal more hereafter—Mrs. Stenhouse—Celestial law, indeed!—Joseph must have written it. . 344

CHAPTER XXXV.

Sprang from the same root—Shedding innocent blood—Evil and obscene practices—Who was their author?—Fruit of the Mormon tree—History of the polygamy revelation—What Emma Smith says about it—Interviewed by her son—What her statement proves—Her testimony does not agree with that of Elder Marks—Brigham Young's testimony—A copy of the revelation preserved by Brigham—Published in 1852—The Laws and Fosters—Nauvoo Expositor destroyed—The prophet arrested—Affidavits of Ebenezer Robinson and wife—Hyrum Smith taught them polygamy. 359

CHAPTER XXXVI.

Bearded the lion in his den—Alexander and David Smith in Utah—Deny that their father was in polygamy—Brighamites respond—Smith-Littlefield controversy—Positive proof that Joseph Smith had plural wives—Testimony of David Fullmer—Thomas Grover's letter—Certificate of Lovina Walker—Affidavit of Emily D. P. Young—Affidavit of Leonard Soby—What Z. H. Gurley says of Mr. Soby—Testimony of Mercy R. Thompson—She was sealed to Hyrum Smith—Her letter to President Smith—His view of the case—He accounts for the origin of polygamy—Summary. . 372

CHAPTER XXXVII.

The gathering—A new Jerusalem promised—Western Missouri the land of Zion—Independence the central spot—Temple to be built— Saints begin to gather—Established in Zion—A dark cloud arises —Driven from Jackson County—Zion in possession of the enemy —The redemption of Zion—How it is to be accomplished—A parable—Zion's camp—Baurak Ale—The Lord's warriors—Start for Zion—Meet a superior force—A narrow escape—A terrible storm —A new revelation—Army to disband—Wait for a little season— Cholera in the camp—Tried as Abraham—I will fight your battles—Shall find grace and favor in the eyes of the people—Let my army become very strong—Far West—The Mormon war—Resist the militia—Several killed—Exterminating order of Gov. Boggs— Joseph and the leaders arrested—Mormons driven from the State —The whole gathering scheme a failure. 391

CHAPTER XXXVIII.

Prophecies of Joseph Smith—Were they fulfilled?—The rebellion of South Carolina—President Jackson and the Nullifiers—The great rebellion—War of 1861-5—The prophecy analyzed—Unfulfilled—Letter to R. N. E. Seaton—Bloodshed, famine and earthquakes—A desolating scourge—Letter to John C. Calhoun—Dire things predicted—The prophet grows eloquent—The whole prediction a failure. 423

CHAPTER XXXIX.

A letter to Elder T. E. L.—Modern revelation—Apostles and prophets—Church organization—Its various officers—Two Priesthoods —"Those abominations"—Early Christians—A charge repelled— Those idolatrous Israelites—No new revelation necessary—The "basic idea of Mormonism"—An important question—The New Testament a perfect guide—Five pointed questions—Six reasons examined—The Bible a detector—A mere scrapping of incidents— The whole system wrong—Conclusion. 438

THE DOCTRINES AND DOGMAS OF MORMONISM.

CHAPTER I.

INTRODUCTORY.

A remarkable claim—Marvelous if true—No middle ground—Either true or false—Apostle Pratt states the case—Origin of Mormonism—Joseph's vision—Churches all wrong—Their teachers corrupt—The angel Moroni—Hidden plates revealed—*Urim* and *Thummim*.

IN order to a correct understanding of Mormon theology it becomes necessary to briefly state the ground upon which it is based.

Mormonism sets up a claim which, if true, is simply marvelous. But if, on the other hand, it is false, it will at once be stamped as the most daring fraud, the most unscrupulous effort to deceive and mislead the unwary and credulous that was ever attempted at any period of the world's history.

It will doubtless be conceded by all classes that no middle ground can, by any possible means, be taken upon this question. Mormonism is either absolutely true or unquestionably false. Its advocates claim it to be a system revealed directly from heaven by the personal ministry of angels, who conferred authority upon Joseph Smith and Oliver Cowdery by the "laying on of hands."

There can be no possible chance for mistake or deception in this matter, so far as the originators of the scheme are concerned. Upon this point Mr. Orson Pratt, one of the original twelve apostles, chosen under the direction of Joseph Smith, and declared in Mormon history to be the St. Paul of the nineteenth century, says:

"This book," referring to the Book of Mormon, "must be either *true* or *false*. If true, it is one of the most important messages ever sent from God to man. . . . If false, it is one of the most cunning, wicked, bold, deep-laid impositions ever palmed upon the world, calculated to deceive and ruin millions who will receive it as the word of God." (O. Pratt's works, Divine Authenticity of the Book of Mormon, page 1).

Under this view of the case, then, it becomes our duty to inquire whether this claim be true or false— whether it is supported by competent testimony.

In treating this subject it is the intention of the writer to state every proposition to be discussed, when possible to do so, in the language of the friends and advocates of the system, and thus avoid all controversy respecting premises.

Likewise every statement of fact shall be supported by Mormon authority, when practicable, or from other sources whose authenticity cannot be successfully controverted.

It is not the purpose of the writer to make war upon people who honestly believe in the doctrines of Mormonism, but to present, rather, what appears to be good and valid reason for believing that the system had its origin in fraud and deception.

We shall state as briefly as may be the entire ground upon which the system is based, and then proceed to examine each point under the light of such facts as are attainable.

ORIGIN OF MORMONISM.

Joseph Smith, founder of the Mormon hierarchy, was born in Sharon, Windsor County, Vermont, December 23, 1805.

When about ten years of age he removed with his father's family to Palmyra, Ontario County, New York. Here began his remarkable career as a religious teacher. He was confessedly illiterate, but nature had endowed him with a clear, strong brain, and by sheer force of his intellectuality he was from the very beginning of his career a leader

At about the age of fifteen he professed to have seen a remarkable vision. Two personages, he declares, stood above him in a "pillar of light." "One of them," he says, "spoke to me, calling me by name, and said, 'This is my beloved Son; hear him.'" Joseph then asked the Lord, for such he declared the personage to be, what church he should join.

Concerning the answer which he received, Mr. Smith says:

"I was answered that I should join none of them, *for they were all wrong;* and the personage who addressed me said that all their creeds were *an abomination in his sight;* and that the professors were *all corrupt.*"

The above quotation is from Tullidge's Life of Joseph the Prophet, pages 3 and 4, published by the Reorganized Church of Latter Day Saints at Lamoni, Iowa. This shows the light in which the founder of Mormonism viewed all other churches and creeds. The churches were all wrong, their creeds an abomination, and their teachers and professors all corrupt.

Surely, according to "Joseph the Prophet," the world was in a most deplorable condition.

Three years later Joseph had another interview which lasted all night, but this time it was the angel Moroni who appeared. The angel told Joseph that "God had a work for him to perform"—that "there was a book deposited, written upon gold plates, giving an account of the former inhabitants of this continent"—and that deposited with these plates were "two stones in silver bows," by means of which the book must be translated. (See Tullidge's History, pages 9 and 10.)

Here follows an interval of just four years to a day. During this time Joseph was seemingly on very intimate terms with the angel Moroni—said angel being none other than the departed spirit of the prophet Moroni, who wrote the closing book of the Book of Mormon, and who "hid up unto the Lord" the plates containing the record of his people.

(See Book of Mormon, chapter 4, page *532.)

Remembering exactly where he had "hid up" these plates, he of course experienced no difficulty in directing Joseph to the very spot where he had concealed them over 1400 years before. After four years of careful training under the tutelage of Moroni, Joseph was permitted to take the treasure from its long concealment and begin the translation of the sacred record by means of the "two stones set in a silver bow," otherwise known as the "*Urim* and *Thummim*."

---

*Note.—The copy of the Book of Mormon from which I quote is known as the "Palmyra edition," the first ever printed, and the page number will not, therefore, agree with subsequent editions, but book and chapter I think are the same.

CHAPTER II.

OLIVER COWDERY.

Martin Harris and the stolen manuscript—Oliver Cowdery—His part in the work—Church organized—The Spaulding Romance—Deposited in Oberlin Library—Old theory abandoned—Sidney Rigdon not one of the originators—Book of Mormon, its purport—The American Bible—Apostles chosen—The First Presidency—The Patriarch—Other officers—Mormon intolerance—Doctrines of the Church.

ABOUT this time an individual appeared upon the scene who performed a very conspicuous and important part in the development of the Mormon scheme. This man was Oliver Cowdery, a gentleman of considerable scholastic polish.

He made the acquaintance of Joseph Smith some time after he had commenced the pretended translation of the plates, assisted by one Martin Harris, a farmer of some means, who had become interested in the story concerning the angel and the plates. Harris wrote for Joseph till they had produced one hundred and sixteen pages of manuscript, which Harris was permitted to take with him to his home. This MS., it is charged, was stolen from Harris by an enemy, supposed to be his wife. This so interrupted the work of translation that no further work was done till Oliver Cowdery made the acquaintance of the young prophet, when the work was commenced anew.

"Two days after the arrival of Mr. Cowdery," says Joseph, "I commenced to translate the Book of Mormon, and he commenced to write for me, which having continued for some time, I inquired of the

Lord through the *Urim* and *Thummim*, and obtained the following revelation." (Tullidge's History, page 35).

Then follows a lengthy revelation, from which is excerpted the following:

"Behold, thou art Oliver, and I have spoken unto thee because of thy desire; therefore treasure up these words in thy heart. . . . And behold, I grant unto you a gift, if you desire it of me, to translate even as my servant Joseph." (Ibid, pages 36 and 37).

I thus particularly refer to the circumstance of Oliver Cowdery's association with Joseph Smith in the very rise of Mormonism, for the purpose of correcting an error which for some unaccountable reason has become well-nigh universal. Except by those acquainted with the facts connected with the early stages of its development, it is generally believed that Sidney Rigdon was the chief abettor of Joseph Smith in concocting the Mormon scheme.

The usual debater undertakes to trace the Book of Mormon to the Spaulding romance through Sidney Rigdon.

Nothing can be more erroneous, and it will lead to almost certain defeat. The well-informed advocate of Mormonism wants no better amusement than to vanquish an opponent in discussion who takes this ground. The *facts* are all opposed to this view, and the defenders of the Mormon dogma have the facts well in hand. I speak from experience.

As a matter of fact, Sidney Rigdon was an earnest and able advocate of the Reformation contemporaneously with Alexander Campbell, and pastor of a church at Mentor, Ohio, at the very time Joseph

Smith and Oliver Cowdery were propagating Mormonism in New York and Pennsylvania. Sidney Rigdon had never heard a Mormon sermon, nor had he ever seen a copy of the Book of Mormon till he was presented with one by Oliver Cowdery and Parley P. Pratt in the fall of 1830. It is an historical fact that Mr. Rigdon became a convert to the new religion through the preaching of these gentlemen during the visit referred to above.

Mr. Rigdon's large influence and pursuasive eloquence carried with him a great number of his admirers in that section of Ohio, which unquestionably gave the first decided impetus to the Mormon delusion. An eloquent speaker, and a gentleman of more than ordinary attainments, he soon became a recognized power in the propagation of the new faith.

Success of the efforts put forth in this section of Ohio was doubtless the prime cause of the settlement at Kirtland a short time afterwards, and which in its turn led to the building of the Kirtland temple.

In order to the successful-refutation of the Mormon dogma it is not at all necessary to connect Sidney Rigdon with Joseph Smith in its inception. In fact, such a course will almost certainly result in failure; and the principal reason why it will fail is because it is not true. Truth is always better than error, and is much more easily maintained.

THE SPAULDING ROMANCE.

In this connection it may be well to remark that another error, closely allied to the above, and co-extensive with it, is that which relates to what is popularly known as the Solomon Spaulding romance, out of which, it has been uniformly urged, the Book of Mormon was concocted by Joseph Smith and Sidney Rigdon. If it be true that the Book of Mormon is nothing more than a revamped edition of the old Spaulding romance, then it follows that the former must possess at least a few of the characteristics of the latter. Necessarily there would be a similarity in design, or a correspondence between the names, neither of which is true.

The long-lost Spaulding story has at last been unearthed, and is now on deposit in the library of Oberlin College at Oberlin, Ohio, and may be examined by anyone who may take the pains to call on President Fairchild, of that institution.

In a letter to Joseph Smith, of Lamoni, Iowa, dated at Honolulu, Sandwich Islands, March 28, 1885, Mr. L. L. Rice, in whose possession the original Spaulding story had been resting for forty-four years —from 1839 to 1885—says:

"There is no identity of names, of persons or places, and there is no similarity of style between them. . . . I should as soon think the book of Revelation was written by the author of 'Don Quixote,' as that the writer of this manuscript was the author of the Book of Mormon."

The writer has examined a certified copy of this remarkable document, and to say he was surprised is to express it moderately. Instead of exhibiting the qualities of a scholarly mind, as we had been led to believe it would do, quite to the contrary, it bears every mark of ignorance and illiteracy, and is evidently the product of a mind far below the average, even in the ordinary affairs of life. A twelve-year-old boy in any of our common schools can tell a better story and couch it in far better English. The Spaulding story is a failure. Do not attempt to rely upon it—it will let you down.

The entire theory connecting Sidney Rigdon and the Spaulding romance with Joseph Smith in originating the Book of Mormon must be abandoned. We have something better. All Mormon history and biography agree in connecting Oliver Cowdery, a man the equal of Sidney Rigdon in point of scholastic attainments and personal polish, directly with Joseph Smith in every stage of the development of Mormonism.

It was Oliver Cowdery—not Sidney Rigdon—who assisted in the so-called translation of the plates. It was he who helped to prepare the book for the press; and he it was, doubtless, who expected to share the profits arising from its sale. It was Cowdery, not Rigdon, who was in the woods with Smith when the angel—John the Baptist—is said to have laid his hands upon their heads and ordained them to what they call "the Aaronic Priesthood." It was Oliver Cowdery who was the first to receive baptism at the hands of Joseph Smith, and who in turn baptized the prophet. It was Oliver Cowdery who ordained Joseph Smith by the "laying on of hands," to be the "first elder of the church," and who in turn ordained Oliver to be the "second elder of the church;" and it was Oliver Cowdery who assisted Joseph in the organization of the church at Seneca, Fayette Co., N. Y., April 6, 1830.

In order to verify the above statement of facts, the reader is referred to Tullidge's History, pages 35, 43, 44, 75 and 77. But no intelligent Latter Day Saint will deny these statements. Thus it will be seen that Sidney Rigdon had absolutely nothing to do with originating Mormonism.

THE FOUNDATION.

That the whole Mormon superstructure is founded upon the Book of Mormon, no one will perhaps attempt to deny. If that book is *true*, then the authority of the Mormon Church is established beyond the possibility of reasonable doubt. But if it is *false*, then Mormonism may justly be branded as the most stupendous fraud of the ages, and its advocates are left without even the shadow of truth upon which to base their claim to divine authority.

The divine authenticity of the Book of Mormon must, therefore, be sustained by the testimony of competent witnesses, or Mormonism is a failure. Can its claims be sustained by the evidence offered in its support? If not, then the book and the system built upon its claim to be a divine revelation must go down together. In order to properly test the claims of the book we must first understand just what these claims are.

THE PURPORT OF THE BOOK OF MORMON.

The Book of Mormon is represented to contain a detailed account of three separate colonies which settled upon the great American Continent, the first coming from the tower of Babel, the other two from Jerusalem. The most important of these was that led by one Lehi, and with which the Book of Mormon principally deals.

This Lehi, a prophet, left Jerusalem, according to

the narrative, "in the commencement of the first year of the reign of Zedekiah, king of Judah" (B. of M., page 1), in the year 600, B. C.

It describes the wanderings of the little band through the wilderness on foot till they reached the borders of the Red Sea, and their sojourn upon the banks of a large stream, which *flows into the Red Sea*. From this point they traveled in a south-southeasterly direction, till finally they came to the sea called "Ireantum."

Here they build a ship, and, under the direction of the self-appointed Nephi, the youngest of four brothers, sail for the "promised land;" but where the promised land was located, or in what direction, the record does not inform us.

The book relates circumstantially the wanderings of the colony in the great wilderness in the promised land, till they finally settle somewhere in the interior. Dissension finally arises, and Nephi, with his two younger brothers, Jacob and Joseph, separated from their elder brethren, Laman, Lemuel and Sam. Henceforth they were two separate peoples, known as "Nephites" and "Lamanites." The book gives a very full account of the numerous wars and contentions between the two races, till the Nephites became extinct, in the year A. D. 420, leaving the entire Continent in possession of the Lamanites, from whom our American Indians are said to be descended.

Instead of keeping their records on papyrus, as did the Hebrews in every age, they were written on "plates of brass," and in the *Egyptian*, instead of the *Hebrew* language. This is a very important point, and should be borne in mind.

For a more extended account the reader is referred to Tullidge's History, pages 45-64.

The Book of Mormon, professedly written by a succession of prophets, stands to the inhabitants of Ancient America in the same relation that the Bible sustains to the Israelites. It is in fact the American Bible. The validity of this remarkable claim will be thoroughly examined under the proper head.

APOSTLES CHOSEN.

Having thus briefly sketched the rise of the Mormon hierarchy, let us now proceed to notice the different stages of its development. When first organized the church consisted of but six members. The new doctrine rapidly spread into the neighboring States, and among the accessions to the new church were such men as Sidney Rigdon, Parley P. Pratt, Brigham Young, Orson Pratt, Heber C. Kimball, Orson Hyde and others.

It now became necessary, in the opinion of this modern seer, to effect a more complete organization of the church. Joseph, having conceived the idea of an apostolic church, received a "revelation" appointing three men who were to choose the twelve apostles for the church of the new dispensation.

At a meeting called for the purpose at Kirtland, O., Feb. 14, 1835, the "Twelve" were chosen in the following manner:

"The three witnesses [to the Book of Mormon], namely, Oliver Cowdery, David Whitmer and Martin Harris, united in prayer; they were then blessed by the laying on of the hands of the Presidency, and then proceeded to make choice of the Twelve." (Tullidge's History, page 150.)

On page 154 of the same work, in giving the apostolic charge, Oliver Cowdery says:

"Have you desired this ministry with all your hearts? If you have desired it, you are called of God, not of man, to go into all the world."

Continuing this charge to these apostles, Mr. Cowdery says:

"Remember, you are not to go to other nations till you receive your endowment. Tarry in *Kirtland* until you are endowed with power from on high." (Ibid, page 157.)

We cite the above in order to call attention to the marked difference between the Lord's method of calling twelve apostles and that employed by Joseph Smith, and shall give special attention to it in the proper place.

THE FIRST PRESIDENCY.

Not only was there a "quorum" of twelve apostles, but another "quorum" of vastly more importance was called into existence, known as the "First Presidency."

This body of dignitaries is a triumvirate, consisting of a "chief apostle and high priest, with two associate counselors." This is the highest official executive body in the church.

There is also another triumvirate of lower grade, composed of the "Presiding Bishop" and his two counselors. The Bishop has charge of the finances of the church, and should be a literal descendant of Aaron. But in the event that such descendant can not be found, a person of some other lineage may be chosen, as shown in Joseph's "revelation on priesthood," as follows:

"The bishoprick is the presidency of this [Aaronic] priesthood, and holds the keys of authority of the same. No man has a legal right to this office, to hold the keys of this priesthood, except he be a literal descendant of Aaron. But as a high priest of the Melchisedek priesthood has authority to officiate in all the lesser offices, he may officiate in the office of bishop *when no literal descendant of Aaron can be found.*" (Tullidge's History, page 217; also Doctrine and Covenants, Sec. 68, Par. 2, page 199.) The italics are mine.

But you may ask, How is it possible at this late day to determine this difficult question of Aaronic lineage?

To ordinary mortals this would, I confess, prove an insurmountable barrier; but Joseph was a man of resources, and this matter of lineal descent was a trifling affair. You must bear in mind the fact that Joseph was in possession of that magical "*Urim* and *Thummim,*" by means of which he had access to the fountains of all knowledge. Appealing to this, the question was soon settled. A PATRIARCH must be appointed whose duty and privilege it shall be to determine the lineage, not only of the man whose privilege it is to "hold the keys of this priesthood," but of any and every man who may be curious to know from just which of the twelve patriarchs of old he might be descended.

THE PATRIARCH ANOINTED.

Accordingly "my servant Joseph Smith, Sen.," was duly consecrated to the patriarchate of the church. The particulars of this unprecedented transaction are given by Tullidge, as follows:

"The interesting episode of anointing and blessing the first patriarch of the church, with the marvelous manifestations which then occurred, is spoken of by Joseph as follows:

"We then laid our hands upon our aged father Smith, and invoked the blessings of heaven. I then anointed his head with the consecrated oil, and sealed many blessings upon him. The presidency then in turn laid their hands upon his head, beginning at the eldest, until they had all laid their hands upon him, and pronounced such blessings upon his head as the Lord put into their hearts,—all blessing him to be our Patriarch, to anoint our heads, and attend to all duties that pertain to his office." (Tullidge's History, page 161.)

This remarkable ceremony took place in the unfinished temple at Kirtland, Ohio, Jan. 21, 1836.

On Feb. 28, 1835, two weeks after the twelve apostles were chosen, and at the same place, "The Apostles of the Seventies" were in part called and ordained. (Ibid, page 160.)

OTHER OFFICERS.

Then follows the "Quorum of High Priests," the bishop and his "two associate counselors," elders, "priests," teachers and deacons. As completed, the organization stands thus:

1. The First Presidency; 2. The Patriarch; 3. Twelve Apostles; 4. Seventies; 5. High Priests; 6. Bishops; 7. Elders; 8. Priests; 9. Teachers; 10. Deacons.

The above officers are named in the order of their importance, and comprise the entire official force of the Mormon Church. No church organization short of this will pass muster with any Latter Day Saint as the Church of Christ. Wm. H. Kelley, one of the twelve apostles of the "Reorganized Church of Jesus Christ of Latter Day Saints," in his work entitled "Presidency and Priesthood," after an exhaustive argument to prove the above organization to be strictly Biblical (see p. 83), clinches his argument with the following:

"After having made diligent search among all the societies and organizations extant, with your guide [the Bible] in hand, where do you find amidst them all, my friend and reader, an institution in exact accord with the pattern of Christ's Church? Ah, echo answers, Where?

Yet one established according to this plan is all that God has ever deigned to acknowledge as his. What will you do? Throw away your guide, and join the daughters of the old mother, or some institution of men? You cannot afford to do this." (Presidency and Priesthood, pages 188 and 189.)

Again:

"Tired and discouraged, perhaps, you are ready to exclaim: With guide in hand, I have surveyed the whole of Christendom, and I have failed to find an organization in harmony with it, or anything approximating it. I want to be saved! I must join something or I am lost! Hold, sir! The daughters of 'Mystery, Babylon' cannot save you; neither any institution of man." (Ibid, pages 190 and 191.)

In the foregoing extracts we have the very essence and spirit of the Mormon theology.

The sentiment is that expressed by Joseph Smith, and is entertained by every branch and faction of the Mormon Church in every part of the world. It is the spirit by which its ministry is controlled, although for prudential reasons they do not always declare it so plainly and bluntly as does Mr. Kelley.

Of all religions extant to-day, Mormonism is the most exclusive and intolerant. How unlike the religion founded by Christ! How unlike the spirit of Mormon intolerance was that which characterized the teachings of the world's great Law-giver! He could say: "He that is not against us is for us," but Joseph Smith says, substantially, that "We are against every man and every church, because they are *all wrong;* their creeds are an *abomination*, and their teachers *all corrupt.*"

Among ecclesiastical bodies the Mormon Church is the Ishmael of the nineteenth century. Its hand is against every man and every church. It tolerates nothing which is not purely Mormon in its origin and tendencies.

THE DOCTRINES OF THE CHURCH.

The doctrines of Mormonism are characterized by peculiarities as remarkable as they are, in many respects, erroneous. Briefly stated, they are as follows:

"(1) Faith in God. (2) Faith in Jesus Christ. (3) In the Holy Ghost. (4) Belief in the doctrine of repentance. (5) In baptism. (6) In the laying on of hands. (7) In the resurrection of the dead. (8) Eternal judgment. (9) The Lord's Supper. (10) The washing of feet. These, together with . . . the endowment of the Holy Ghost as realized and enjoyed in the testimony of Jesus,—such as faith, wisdom, knowledge, dreams, prophecies, tongues, interpretation of tongues, visions, healings," etc.— (Presidency and Priesthood, pages 83 and 84).

Mr. Kelley might have included in the above three other points of doctrine, peculiarly Mormon, and without which the list is by no means complete, namely: the "law of tithing," the "gathering of the saints," and "baptism for the dead."

Having presented what may fairly be termed the groundwork of Mormonism, I shall now proceed to a careful examination of the material entering into both its foundation and superstructure. The laws of construction require us to begin at the foundation and build upward; but, quite to the contrary, if we undertake to tear down and remove a useless and dangerous structure, we usually begin at the top and work downward; and as the work in hand is destructive rather than constructive, we shall adopt the latter method.

CHAPTER III.

THE MORMON HOUSE—ITS INTERIOR GARNISHMENT.

The Mormon House—Its internal garnishment—Visions, dreams, etc.—All deceptive—Spiritual gifts—Were they to be perpetuated?—Mormonism affirms—It must prove—The apostolic commission—Its obligations perpetual—The signs promised were limited—The church perpetuated—Gates of hell shall not prevail against it.

THE Latter Day Saints have constructed what they are pleased to call a "spiritual house," whose foundation is in fact the Book of Mormon, and whose essential frame-work is the various officials, from the "First Presidency" down to the deacon—with "spiritual gifts" for its internal garnishment. The advocates of Mormonism confidently assure us that this very remarkable structure is in perfect accord with the pattern left by the great Architect over eighteen centuries ago.

When an architect submits the plan for a building of specific dimensions, he usually submits therewith specifications setting forth the kind of materials to be used in its construction.

The *quality* of the materials of which the building is constructed is of as much importance as that the structure shall be of the required dimensions. A failure in this regard would be as fatal to the builder as if he had changed the style of architecture, or the dimensions of the building. It must likewise be borne in mind that the interior construction and finish are of as much importance as any other part of the work.

To the casual observer the edifice may have a very imposing appearance, but when examined by an expert and compared with the plans and specifications, it may be found woefully wanting in many important particulars as to both foundation and superstructure. And so it is with the spiritual house called the church.

The important question, then, for us to consider is this: Does the Mormon structure fill the bill? Does it strictly accord with the plans and specifications? We shall see.

The edifice must be constructed in every particular *exactly* according to the divine plan. Its interior adornments must be of the *kind* and of *the quality* called for in the contract, or it will not be accepted.

Reader, did you ever carefully inspect the interior of this unique specimen of spiritual architecture? If not, just take a little stroll with me through its spacious corridors and numerous apartments. Remarkable as it may appear, this building has but one door—BAPTISM—and you can enter by no other. This admits you to the main hall. Here on the right is a room called "WISDOM." It contains a few pieces of bric-a-brac—somewhat attractive, but of very little practical value. The next one we enter has the word "KNOWLEDGE" written over the entrance. Upon entering this room you are conscious of a keen sense of disappointment. While the walls are hung with a few fairly good productions, the larger portion of the specimens exhibited are of inferior grade.

The first room on the left, here, is denominated "DREAMS." This apartment is delightful. At once upon entering it you are carried away into that blissful fairy-land, where all is quiet and peace, and where nothing is impossible. Dream on! dream on! How delightfully realistic! Never aroused from this blissful slumber, you would never know sorrow—would never weep. But ah! "life is real, life is earnest," and sooner or later we must face its stern realities and taste the bitter as well as the sweet.

Here is another large room furnished almost exactly like that we have just left—"VISIONS." The effect may be pleasing, but O, how delusive! Nothing substantial—nothing real about it all. "All is vanity and vexation of spirit." But here is another—"SPIRITUAL GIFTS." Perhaps this will be more satisfactory. It is said to be the exact duplicate of one of the most marvelously beautiful apartments in a very ancient building, designed by the most skillful architect the world ever knew. But, alas! when you come to examine its furnishings the heart is faint with disappointment. You had every reason to expect, from representations made to you before entering, that every article in this room would be of purest gold of the most dazzling brightness. But on applying every known test—the most potent of which is experience—you turn away in sorrow and disgust. Instead of pure gold, you find the merest dross. Instead of the divine luster, you find only the tarnishment and rust pertaining to things earthly and impure. Disappointment meets you at every turn, and with bowed head and sad heart you seek the nearest exit, and make your way out into heaven's bright, refreshing sunlight, to seek relief from the disappointment and gloom which had overwhelmed you like a flood because of falsehood and deception.

SIGNS, OR SPIRITUAL GIFTS.

Covet earnestly the best gifts." (1 Cor. 12: 31).

This injunction of the apostle is regarded by Latter Day Saints as being equivalent to a divine promise to perpetuate the miraculous gifts of the Holy Spirit to every age of the world, and that Christians may, therefore, prophesy in the sense of foretelling important events, speak in unknown tongues, interpret tongues, see visions, heal the sick, etc., as in the days of Christ and the apostles. But the Scripture upon which they chiefly rely to prove this position is the following:

"Go ye into all the world and preach the gospel to every creature. He that believeth and is baptized shall be saved, but he that believeth not shall be damned. And these signs shall follow them that believe. In my name shall they cast out devils; they shall speak with new tongues; they shall take up serpents; and if they drink any deadly thing, it shall not hurt them; they shall lay hands on the sick, and they shall recover." (Mark 16: 15-18).

It is the boast of Latter Day Saints that no man living can possibly *disprove* or in any way invalidate their claim upon this point. In the first place the burden of proof lies with *them*. They affirm the perpetuity of these miraculous powers, while we simply deny. The man who affirms must *prove* what he affirms. It is entirely sufficient to meet an affirmative proposition with a bare denial. When affirmative evidence has been introduced, the negative may offer such evidence in rebuttal as may be deemed necessary. Thus it will be seen that we are under no obligation to *disprove* any affirmative proposition.

In this issue Mormonism has affirmed something, and has offered testimony to prove it—is in fact the plaintiff in an action before the civilized world, and asks for judgment on the ground that the testimony of its witnesses sustains the allegation. Their petition sets up a claim that certain jewels—spiritual gifts—at one time in the possession of a woman of great distinction—the Church of Christ—rightfully belong to said plaintiff—the Mormon Church. St. Mark is the chief witness. He was likewise one of the executors of the will under whose provision the jewels were bequeathed to the woman. Now, does the testimony of Mark declare that these jewels were to be transmitted and delivered to persons claiming to be the legal heirs of said woman, who lived more than seventeen centuries after her death? Whether it does or not a careful examination of the testimony will determine.

With this text, as with nearly all others relied upon to establish the claims of Mormonism, the question is purely one of exegesis. While I am by no means vain enough to imagine that we shall be able to finally and forever settle this disputed question, yet I do indulge the belief that we shall be able to show the Mormon exegesis to be erroneous, and hence incompetent to sustain their contention.

Let us now proceed to carefully analyze the terms of the commission quoted from Mark's testimony, and note the result.

"Go ye into all the world."

Who go into all the world? The disciples—*the eleven*. No one else is addressed, and hence, *no one else is included*. This seems conclusive.

"*Go ye.*" Go where? "Into *all the world.*" Does this mean the disciples thus addressed—the eleven—were to go into every inhabited portion of the globe? Certainly not, for their labors were confined almost exclusively to a small portion of southwestern Asia and that portion of continental Europe bordering on the Mediterranean Sea.

"Go ye and preach." Preach what? *The Gospel.*

Go when? "After Pentecost, and continue to preach the Gospel during your natural lives." This was all they could do.

Go to whom? "To every creature within your reach." What shall be the result? "He who hears *you*, and receives the message which *you* declare, shall be saved. But he who hears you, and believes *not* the Gospel which you teach, shall be damned."

So far we find nothing in the language of Mark to indicate that the promised "signs" were to extend to future ages; but on the contrary they were clearly intended as a necessary means to a desired end, and that end was *the establishment of the church of Christ* among the nations of the earth.

"And these signs shall follow."

Here is a promise; but to whom does it extend? Are there no limitations? Let us see. "And these signs shall follow *them that believe.*" Follow them that believe what? Why, the Gospel, to be sure. "And these signs shall follow them that believe the Gospel?" Preached by whom? Why, by the disciples, of course, for none others were authorized. Analyzed, the proposition stands thus: "And these signs shall follow them that believe the Gospel preached by the disciples." Just that, and nothing more, is affirmed.

This analysis shows most conclusively that the promise of miraculous powers was limited to the lifetime of the first disciples—the eleven, and those upon whom they had laid their hands. No amount of sophistry and false reasoning is competent to show that the promises contained in the apostolic commission were ever intended to extend beyond the lifetime of the apostles.

While the Great Commission to preach the Gospel and administer its ordinances was general, extending, under proper conditions, to every age and every nation under the heavens, the "signs," or miraculous gifts of the Holy Spirit, were confined, as we have already shown, to the times of the apostles. While these miraculous powers were limited to the apostolic age, the obligation to "preach the Gospel to every creature," along with the "conditions upon which sinners are accepted under the Gospel," as provided in the commission, was made perpetual.

And right here is where the Saints make another serious, I might say fatal, blunder. They insist, with characteristic pertinacity, that the commission was a document wholly temporary in its character, while the "signs" were intended to be perpetual. It seems to me that any reasonable person, unbiased by preconceived opinion and fundamental error, ought, at a glance, to see the absurdity and unscripturalness of this position. If authority to preach the Gospel *ceased with the apostles*, then most certainly the Church of Christ must cease to exist as soon as the persons composing it at the time of the death of the last apostle were all dead; and if this be true, then what becomes of the declaration of Christ: "Upon this rock I will build my church, *and the gates of hell shall not prevail against it?*" (Matt. 16:18).

In order that the "gates of hell"—the powers of darkness—should not prevail against the Church of Christ, *authority* to minister in Gospel ordinances *must be perpetuated.* As the apostles could not themselves personally deliver the divine message, committed to them in the Great Commission, to all people, they very wisely, and doubtless by the command of God, set apart other faithful men to the work, and clothed them with authority to preach the Gospel and baptize penitent believers into the name of Jesus Christ. That such ministers—elders, or bishops, deacons and evangelists—were ordained by the apostles is perfectly clear, as the following shows:

"And from Miletus he sent to Ephesus, and called the *elders of the church*. . . . And now, behold, I know that ye all, among whom I have gone preaching the kingdom of God, shall see my face no more. . . Take heed therefore unto yourselves, and to all the flock, over which the Holy Ghost hath made you *overseers*, to feed the church of God, which he hath purchased with his own blood." (Acts 20:17, 25, 28).

"And when they had ordained them *elders* in every church, and had prayed with fasting, they commended them to the Lord, on whom they believed." (Acts 14:23).

For this cause left I thee in Crete, that thou shouldest *set in order* the things that are wanting, *and ordain elders in every city*, as I had appointed thee. . . . For a *bishop* [elder] must be blameless, as the steward of God, . . . holding fast the faithful word as he hath been taught, that he may be able by sound doctrine both to exhort and to convince the gainsayers." (Titus 1:5, 7, 9).

To Timothy Paul says:

"This is a true saying, If a man desire the office of a bishop [or elder], he desireth a good work. A bishop then must be blameless, the husband of one wife, vigilant, sober, of good behavior, given to hospitality, *apt to teach*. For if a man know not how to rule his own house, how shall he *take care of the church of God?*" (1 Tim. 3:1, 2, 5).

Continuing, the apostle gives the following instructions concerning deacons:

"Likewise must the deacons be grave, not doubletongued, not given to much wine, not greedy of filthy lucre. . . . And let these also be proved; then let them use the office of a deacon, being found blameless." (1 Tim. 3:8, 10).

" And the saying pleased the whole multitude: and *they* [the congregation] chose Stephen, a man full of faith and of the Holy Ghost, and Philip, and Prochorus, and Nicanor, and Timon, and Parmenas, and Nicolas, a proselyte of Antioch; whom they set before the apostles: and when they had prayed, they laid their hands on them." (Acts 6:5, 6).

Two of these deacons (as the seven are generally conceded to have been), Stephen and Philip, afterwards became very prominent evangelists, rendering great service to the church.

"And Stephen, full of faith and power, did great wonders and miracles among the people." (Acts 6:8. See also chapters 7 and 8).

Besides the elders and deacons of the church, there were also men known as *evangelists* (see Eph. 4:11), whose duties correspond very nearly to those of the apostles, even performing great miracles, as in the cases of Stephen and Philip. These men were often co-laborers with the apostles, and were very efficient ministers of Christ.

Of this class may be mentioned such men as John Mark the traveling companion of Paul and Barnabas (Acts 12:25; 15:37); Luke, the evangelist and "beloved physician," who also traveled with Paul (Acts 16:12; 20:5; Col. 4:14; 2 Tim 4:11).

Along with these may also be mentioned Timothy, Titus, Barnabas, Judas and Silas (Acts 15:22), and many others.

These men possessed authority to preach, baptize, set in order the churches, *ordain other ministers*, and perform any and all duties pertaining to the Christian ministry in order to the perpetuation of the Church of Christ.

Thus it will be seen that this whole question depends upon " the statutes in such cases made and provided;" and as no divine statute can be found which provides for the *establishment* and *perpetuation* of the apostolic office, and for the continuation of miracles beyond the time of the apostles, we may, therefore, very justly conclude that no such thing was ever intended.

As the divine code makes no provision for perpetuating the apostolic office in the church, or for the extension of miraculous powers beyond their time, if any such powers be claimed in this age by people pretending to be divinely commissioned, that claim must be supported by the same class of incontrovertible evidence as that offered by the apostles of Christ. Otherwise it must be rejected.

CHAPTER IV.

CAST OUT DEVILS.

Casting out devils—The saints try it—Devils are obstinate—Epilepsy and insanity—A modern instance—Great trial to the faithful—Unknown tongues not necessary—Conditions have changed—An Unknown tongue impossible—A tongue and its interpretation—Missionaries cannot speak in tongues—1 Cor., twelfth chapter—1 Cor., thirteenth chapter—Tongues shall cease and prophecies fail—A rule—Gifts for Gentiles—Take up serpents.

"*In my name shall they cast out devils.*" Did any Mormon prophet, priest or king, ever cast out a devil—a real, genuine, live devil? Of course they will say, "Yes, many of them." But who among them has the ability to determine the presence of a devil, if, indeed, there be such a thing to-day as demoniacal possession? During my forty years of experience and observation among Latter Day Saints, I have never known a man among them, from Joseph Smith down through the ranks of apostles, high priest and Seventy—and I have personally known them all—who could distinguish, if, indeed, such distinction in fact exists, between demoniacal possession and epileptic fits. Epilepsy is usually regarded as evidence *prima facie* of the presence of one or more devils, and frequent efforts are made to cast them out. In fact I confess to having, in connection with others, undertaken the job myself; but his satanic majesty was uniformly obstinate, and persistently refused to be cast out; and so the unfortunate sufferer continued to have fits right along, just the same as ever.

These latter day devils not infrequently manifest their presence in the form of insanity, and I have never yet known a single instance where this kind of a "devil" was cast out. Many such cases are now being cared for in that modern and humane institution known as the asylum for the insane. A very striking instance of this kind occurs to me which I will relate, and I do so with all due deference to the feelings of the unfortunate man's friends. It is perhaps the most remarkable instance of the kind on record, and this is my apology for presenting it.

David H. Smith, a posthumous son of Joseph Smith, Jr., and brother of President Joseph Smith, of Lamoni, Iowa, when first I knew him, some thirty-five years ago, was a young man of rare mental endowments, with a brilliant future. A poet of no mean ability, and regarded as the modern "sweet singer of Israel," he at once became the idol of the Reorganized Church.

By "revelation" through his brother Joseph, he was early called to a seat in the "quorum of the First Presidency." (See Tullidge's History, page 715.) Shortly after his elevation to this exalted position, he began to develop unmistakable signs of insanity. These symptoms continued to grow more alarming, notwithstanding the repeated administrations by anointing and the laying on of hands.

The entire denomination, by appointment, at two different times observed a day of fasting and prayer especially for his recovery, but all to no purpose. The unfortunate young man continued to grow worse, till he was finally taken to the insane asylum at Elgin,

Ill., where he has been kindly cared for during the past eighteen or twenty years.

I hope to be pardoned for thus alluding to the circumstances of this sad case, as there is no intention to wound the feelings of anyone. I refer to it merely to show that when there is anything seriously the matter, the laying on of hands to heal the sick is a poor, miserable failure.

This case was a source of severe trial to the faith of many, and no wonder. "If," they would reason, "David was in reality called of God by revelation to be Joseph's counselor, why would the Lord permit him to become insane?—why can he not be healed?" And it will be conceded that these are very pertinent questions.

UNKNOWN TONGUES.

"*They shall speak with new tongues.*"

The advocates of Mormonism maintain that the "new tongues" here alluded to means unknown tongues, and that such tongues are to constitute one of the distinguishing characteristics of the Church of Christ in every age. Does it follow that because those under the ministry of the apostles could speak in unknown tongues it is therefore necessary for Christians to do so now? This question may be satisfactorily determined by ascertaining whether there exists any actual necessity for their presence in the church to-day.

If the conditions are found to exist now that existed in the time of the apostles, then we may reasonably conclude that the power to speak in unknown tongues is as necessary now as then. But on the other hand, if conditions have changed—if conditions which existed then do not exist to-day, then it will be just as reasonable to conclude that "unknown tongues," as a "spiritual gift," are wholly unnecessary in order to the accomplishment of the purposes for which they were then intended. This brings us to inquire, *Have the conditions changed?*

To this question there can be but one answer, and that is, Conditions have materially changed. At the beginning of the Christian era the world lay enwrapped in the somber robes of ignorance and superstition. Educational facilities were confined to the wealthy. There were no schools to which the common people had access. Languages of the neighboring nations were not taught in colleges and universities, and these unlettered Galileans were commanded to preach the Gospel to every nation, kindred, tongue and people. How could they do it? How could they reach the people? was the burning question of the times.

God had provided a means, and that means was none other than "the gift of tongues" (see 1 Cor. 12:10), and the only possible means of accomplishing the divine purpose.

But how is it to-day? Ignorance and superstition have vanished before the advancing civilization of the ages; colleges and universities flourish in every civilized nation of the globe. In these institutions of learning are taught every written language and tongue employed by men. Besides this, the tongues and dialects of perhaps every nation or tribe of earth are understood and spoken. By this means, then, the Gospel may now be preached to every nation and tongue under the whole heavens. My Mormon friends, have conditions changed? Honestly answer, and then decide as to whether "tongues" are necessary to-day.

Adequate means to the accomplishment of an end is all that is necessary. More is superfluous, and may prove a hindrance rather than a means of advancing the end in view. To aid in preaching the Gospel to peoples of foreign tongue was *the prime object* of this divine gift. Wherever the end sought can be accomplished by the employment of ordinary means, the extraordinary or supernatural becomes absolutely unnecessary, and may therefore be dispensed with.

In this age of the world to speak in an unknown tongue is simply impossible, for the very excellent reason that *an unknown tongue does not exist*. Somebody understands it, and in it can declare the saving power of the Gospel of Christ. With these undisputed and undisputable facts before him, what well-informed man can still honestly declare that the gift of unknown tongues is still necessary in order to preach the Gospel to "every creature?"

Every man, in order to teach, must be qualified; and the principal qualification necessary to preach the Gospel to every creature in apostolic times was that pertaining to language—they must be able to speak in the language, or tongue, of the people to whom they were to go. Therefore the apostles were commanded to "tarry at Jerusalem" until they should be qualified by a special endowment with "power from on high." Accordingly, they waited till the day of Pentecost, when they received the promised induement, and were able *to speak in unknown tongues*.

On that memorable occasion there were assembled "devout men out of every nation under heaven," namely: "Parthians, and Medes, and Elamites, and the dwellers in Mesopotamia, and in Judæa, and Cappadocia, in Pontus, and Asia, Phrygia, and Pamphylia, in Egypt, and in the parts of Libya about Cyrene, and strangers of Rome, Jews and proselytes." (Acts 2: 5, 9, 10).

Now, let it be remembered, these disciples were all Galileans, and yet every man, it mattered not what his nationality, heard the Gospel "in his own language, . . . in his own tongue" (verses 8 and 9). No need for the disciples to assure these people that they could speak in "unknown tongues," and no one asked for proof. Here was an oral and ocular demonstration of the fact—no possible chance for mistake or doubt here—the evidence was overwhelming and conclusive. Unsought by the people and wholly unexpected by them, evidence of a character absolutely indisputable was offered by divine power.

Let Mormonism produce such evidence as this, and the world will bow in reverent acknowledgment of its divine authority. But Mormonism never has produced, and, we may safely say, it never can produce such evidence.

It is not sufficient for some old woman or some weak-minded man to arise in a congregation of English-speaking people and deliver some strange jargon and call it an unknown tongue to be "interpreted" by some other person equally weak or unscrupulous. This will never do. Sensible people want something better—something more convincing. To illustrate the uncertainty of these "tongues" and "interpretations," even among Latter Day Saints themselves, I will relate an incident which came under my own observation.

At the Semi-Annual Conference of the Reorganized Church, held at Galland's Grove, Shelby Co., Iowa, Sept. 20, 1877, during an evening prayer service, "the gifts" were enjoyed to a remarkable degree, and a sister (whose name is withheld for the reason that she had been the fourth polygamous wife of Lyman Wight, of Texas, one of Joseph Smith's apostles), arose in the large audience and spoke in tongues. On resuming her seat Elder Alfred Jackson gave the "interpretation." Upon resuming his seat, and after a verse had been sung, Elder Ingvert Hansen arose and said: "Brethren, if you will pray for me I will try and give you the interpretation of Sister J.'s tongue, for the Spirit says to me that Bro. Jackson did not give it." Whereupon Bro. Hansen proceeded to give the "interpretation" of the "tongue." Comment is useless.

Now, to conclude on this point, I think I am perfectly safe in saying that no Mormon missionary, foreign or otherwise, ever preached the Gospel to congregations of foreign tongue, except as he had first learned to speak such language or tongue. Having sat, during a period of twenty-seven years, as a member of general conferences, I am in a position to know whereof I affirm.

Missionaries are always selected with reference to their fitness for the work to be performed; and to be able to speak the language of the people to whom they are sent is always considered a necessary qualification.

Hence, a Frenchman is sent to France, a German to Germany, a Welshman to Wales, and so on. English-speaking people have been sent to the Society group and other islands of the Pacific, but in such cases the speaker reaches the people through the medium of an interpreter, and never through the "gift of tongues."

These missionaries must learn the language of the people, just as do the missionaries of other churches. One of the missionaries, writing from Papeiti, Tahiti, says:

"Mrs. Case did a good work in setting in order the Sunday-school, following Sr. Devore's plan of carrying on the work. She had a very great deal of writing to do on the Sunday-school books of questions and answers, also about six weeks' work, making a complete copy of the *Tahitian English Dictionary*. I hope for the benefit of *those who come to do labor here* that the good brethren who have taken away *the only copies of said book obtainable*, will remember to *please return them to the mission.*"—*The Saints' Herald*, for Feb. 3, 1897, page 72.

If these people possess the same powers that were conferred upon the apostles and primitive saints, what need have they for a "Tahitian English Dictionary?" Why not reach these poor heathen in the *same way*, if they have the "same power," as did the apostles? *i. e.*, speak to them *in their own language*. Why consume precious time in learning the language of the natives, when an old-fashioned apostolic enduement is so easily attainable, and far more effective in reaching the desired end?

The fact that these "inspired" missionaries must learn the language of the people to whom they are sent is proof positive that *they cannot speak in unknown tongues*. If these people would perform what they so liberally advertise, it would inspire confidence in their claim, and secure the respect and esteem of an intelligent public, and assure their success. But this they never have done, and this they never can do.

> Empty claims are empty things,
> And empty heads oft make them;—
> Empty bubbles all they seem,—
> The TRUTH will surely break them.

But I think I hear some faithful saint in objection saying: "This cannot be true—the claim to divine power is not all an empty dream; it is no illusive phantasm, but real, and based upon a divine promise. These signs *shall* follow them that believe. The preaching of the Gospel, the signs that were to follow, and the salvation of the believer, were all placed upon the same footing, and where one ceases the other must fail. The signs were to follow *whenever* and *wherever* the Gospel is preached and obeyed." Not so fast, please, my good brother. This is the very question in controversy; and the correctness of your position must be *proved*, not assumed. Before such a claim can be accepted, it must be supported by some clear, direct statement of Scripture, or by actual and ocular demonstration. Can you produce such testimony?

"Yes," continues the objector, "I think such a statement may be found in Paul's first letter to the church at Corinth. Let me read it for you:

"'Now concerning spiritual gifts, brethren, I would not have you ignorant. Ye know that ye were Gentiles, carried away unto these dumb idols, even as ye were led. Wherefore I give you to understand, that no man speaking by the Spirit of God calleth Jesus accursed: and that no man can say that Jesus is the Lord, but by the Holy Ghost. Now there are diversities of gifts, but the same Spirit. And there are differences of administrations, but the same Lord. And there are diversities of operations, but it is the same God which worketh all in all. But the manifestation of the Spirit is given to every man to profit with all. For to one is given by the Spirit the word of wisdom; to another the word of knowledge by the same Spirit; to another faith by the same Spirit; to another the gifts of healing by the same Spirit; to another the working of miracles; to another prophecy; to another discerning of spirits; to another divers kinds of tongues; to another the interpretation of tongues: But all these worketh that one and the selfsame Spirit, dividing to every man severally as he will.' (1 Cor. 12: 1-11).

"Here," continues our friend, "we have an apostolic letter exhorting the Corinthians to be not ignorant concerning 'spiritual gifts;' and he shows them that they must be charitable. In the 13th chapter he informs them that they might have the gift of prophecy, and be able by faith to remove mountains, and yet be lost if they have not charity. He then devotes the next chapter to giving them proper instructions with respect to the use of these gifts. Beginning with this injunction Paul says:

"'Follow after charity, *and desire spiritual gifts.*' (Chap. 14, verse 1.)

"Certainly the apostle would not have been so particular to give them this instruction had he not intended these gifts to continue. Why would he exhort them to desire spiritual gifts—to *covet them earnestly*—if he knew they were to pass away?"

This seems a perfectly honest, as well as a very pertinent question, and we shall try to answer it in the same spirit of candor in which it is propounded; for we desire the truth, the whole truth, and nothing but the truth.

In order to correctly understand the Scriptures it is important to observe four things, namely:
1. Who is speaking or writing;
2. To whom the language is addressed;
3. What the principal subject, and
4. What the environments.

With these points properly considered, we shall find little difficulty in arriving at the exact truth. In the case under consideration, 1. Paul is speaking; 2. The Corinthians are spoken to; 3. The "spiritual gifts" are spoken of, and 4. The environments detrimental to progress in Christian life.

The epistle is addressed to Gentile Christians—a people who had but recently been converted from the worship of "those dumb idols" (chapter 12: 2), and, ignorant of the true God, they were constantly inclined, from force of old habits, to follow after their old teachers, "even as they had been led."

These facts may serve as a key to unlock the door of mystery, and enable us to understand more clearly the purport of the apostle's letter.

These Gentiles were weak and vacillating—were mere children, in fact, and were in constant need of a teacher. "These signs," primarily, were intended to "confirm the word" (see Mark 16: 20), and none needed this confirmation more than the church at Corinth. Hence Paul's letter of instruction and encouragement.

These miraculous powers seem to have been of especial service in establishing the Gospel among the Gentiles; as, for example, Cornelius and his household "spake in tongues and magnified God" (Acts 10: 46).

These powers were conferred upon another Gentile church—the Ephesian (Eph. 2: 11), by the laying on of Paul's hands, who "spake with tongues and prophesied" (Acts 19:6). Also concerning the church at Rome Paul said: "For I long to see you, that I may impart unto you some spiritual gift, to the end ye may be *established*." (Rom. 1: 11).

From the above we learn two important facts:

1. The "spiritual gifts" were more particularly bestowed upon the Gentile churches; and

2. That the prime object was to *establish them in the truth* as it was revealed by Christ.

That these gifts of the Holy Spirit were intended to continue with the church at Corinth till they had reached mature manhood in Christ, there is little room to doubt; and there is no intimation that they ever ceased from among them until the church itself became extinct. But because this is probably true, it affords no guarantee for the assertion that they were to be perpetuated.

But, quite to the contrary, the apostle informed the church at Corinth that these miraculous gifts should cease, as I shall now undertake to prove. He says: "But covet earnestly the best gifts; and yet shew I unto you a more excellent way." (1 Cor. 12: 31).

The apostle at once proceeds to describe this "more excellent way" in the following forceful and most beautiful manner:

"Though I speak with the tongues of men and of angels, and have not charity, I am become as sounding brass or a tinkling cymbal. And though I have the gift of prophecy, and understand all mysteries, and all knowledge; and though I have all faith, so that I could remove mountains, and have not charity, I am nothing.

"And though I bestow all my goods to feed the poor, and though I may give my body to be burned, and have not charity, it profiteth me nothing.

"Charity suffereth long, and is kind; charity envieth not; charity vaunteth not itself, is not puffed up, doth not behave itself unseemly, seeketh not her own, is not easily provoked, thinketh no evil; rejoiceth not in iniquity, but rejoiceth in the truth; beareth all things, believeth all things, hopeth all things, endureth all things." (1 Cor. 13: 1-7).

More excellent is this way than all things besides, and why? Because men may possess any and all the spiritual gifts, even including great faith—nay, *all* faith—without which it is "impossible to please God" (Heb. 11: 6); yet if they have not CHARITY, it profits them nothing. Possessing all the "spiritual gifts," yet without charity, they must be finally lost. Hence, the saying of Jesus:

"Many will say unto me in that day, Lord, Lord, have we not *prophesied* in thy name? and in thy name have *cast out devils?* and in thy name have done *many wonderful works?* And then I will profess unto them, *I never knew you:* depart from me, ye that work iniquity." (Matt. 7: 22, 23).

Destitute of that principal Christian grace, CHARITY, and although pleading in self-justification their possession of miraculous powers, yet it will be said unto them, "Depart from me, ye that work iniquity." They had not LOVE, and "*love is the fulfilling of the law.*"

Thus charity is contrasted with all spiritual gifts, and Paul singles out *love* as the *summum bonum*.

"Charity never faileth: but whether there be *prophcies*, they shall fail; whether there be *tongues*. they shall cease; whether there be *knowledge*, it shall vanish away." (Verse 8).

Here we have a positive declaration; the spiritual gifts of which he had been writing were to cease, and he particularly names that of *prophecy*, which was regarded as the greatest among them all. Love, you will doubtless have observed, is not named as a "spiritual gift." Why is this? Doubtless because in charity, or *love*, we have the sum of them all.

Of the nine spiritual gifts named in the twelfth chapter, but one was permanent—FAITH. All others were to vanish—pass away.

"And now abideth faith, hope, charity, these three; but the greatest of these is charity." (Verse 13).

Why was faith retained? Why was it not dismissed along with the other gifts? Evidently because it is the means to an end.

All men are required to become godly; that is, become like God. "God is love," and without love men cannot become like God. Without faith we could not love; without love we can never dwell with God, "for God is love." "Hence Faith, the means, is in order to Love, the end."—*Drummond*.

That this is just what the apostle meant; that the miraculous powers with which the early churches were so liberally endowed were to cease when the object for which they were given had been accomplished—that is, when men had become *established*— no better proof can be offered than the universally conceded fact that *they have ceased*.

Prophecy declared they should cease, and history records the *fact* that they *did cease*. What better evidence of the divine purpose can be offered? To say, as do the Saints, that they ceased because of the accident of apostasy, is to impugn both the wisdom and the foreknowledge of God. Latter Day Saints say these miraculous powers ceased because of apostasy. This we most positively deny, and challenge the Saints to *prove* what they assert.

After telling the Corinthians that prophecies should fail, tongues should cease and knowledge, as they had received it through these gifts, should vanish away, he proceeds to tell them *why* it was to be so, and *when* it should occur. Of this he says:

"For we know in part, and we prophesy in part. But *when* that which is perfect is come, *then* that which is in part shall be done away."

Here, as in every other case, the claim for the continuity of the gifts of the Spirit, as it is urged by the Saints, depends entirely upon their exegesis of the text just quoted.

Their argument to prove that the "signs" were to continue is based upon a peculiar and, as it appears to me, erroneous construction of the words, "When that which is perfect is come." Nothing is perfect but Christ, they tell us, and when the perfect Christ comes the second time, *then*, and not till then, the spiritual gifts were to cease.

If their premise be correct, the conclusions will be admitted; but the premise is wrong. In the first place we admit, nay, we urge the fact that *Christ is perfect*. Christ being perfect, any law that emanated from him must also be perfect. The Gospel law was given by him. Therefore the gospel law *is perfect*, and hence the declaration of James concerning "*the perfect* law of liberty" (Jas. 1: 25), in contradistinction to the "law of sin and death," concerning which Paul says:

"For the law of the spirit of life in Christ Jesus hath made me *free* from the law of sin and death." (Rom. 8: 2).

The apostle here speaks of this law as having emanated from Christ, and calls it "the *law* of the *spirit of life*," and declares that it had made him *free*. James calls this same law "the *perfect law* of liberty."

Evidently, then—and it is a fact not to be denied—the law of Christ was perfect. These Corinthians had not yet brought themselves under complete subjection to this law, and hence they were not free. They saw as but "through a glass darkly"—in fact, they were but mere children, having a very imperfect conception of the beauties and grandeur of the Gospel they had formally received.

Paul wishes to encourage them to understand that as soon as they were able to bring themselves into perfect harmony with the "spirit of the law of life;" when that "perfect law of liberty" had made them *free*, as it had made him free; when the *perfect law* of liberty had come to them in all liberating power as that in which it had come to him, *then* prophecies and tongues, for their instruction and confirmation, would be no longer needed, and should therefore cease.

As children they saw "through a glass darkly;" but when they should become men grown up in stature to the full "measure of the stature of Christ" (Eph. 4: 13) they should see *face to face*. Then, "whether there be prophecies, *they shall fail.*" *Then*, "whether there be tongues, *they shall cease.*"

If it shall be urged that the foregoing views are

erroneous, and that the "signs" or "spiritual gifts" are still in the Church of Christ, then we *demand* of those making such claim that they produce the only evidence of which the case is susceptible, namely, perform the works in open daylight, in the presence of an unbelieving public, as did the apostles of Christ.

SERPENTS.

"*They shall take up serpents.*"

There can be but one possible use for the exercise of this "gift," or "sign," and that is to prove a divine apostolic call. We have but one recorded instance of its employment—that of the apostle to the Gentiles, and this resulted in many conversions. The saints might secure similar results by the performance of similar works. But can they perform the works? Far from it! and, wisely, they never attempt such a thing. I have known a number of persons who were bitten by poisonous serpents, but not in a single instance was the victim willing to risk his faith. A pint of good brandy was always preferable, and far more effective.

As a matter of fact, the average Mormon preacher is as much afraid of snakes as are ordinary mortals. He would not risk the bite of an adder or the sting of an asp for the possible salvation of the whole nation. His faith is very strong, but he takes no chances.

CHAPTER V.

DEADLY THINGS.

Deadly things—Joseph's claim—Was he poisoned?—The case examined—Hair came out—Claim unsupported—Healing the sick—The writer's experience and disappointment—Then and now—Discouraged—A Mormon subterfuge—Bible miracles and latter day pretensions.

"*If they drink any deadly thing it shall not hurt them.*"

Latter Day Saints, like all sensible people, avoid deadly poisons. Instances are of record, however, where it is claimed deadly poisons were administered without serious results, but in no single instance has such a claim been verified by competent testimony. Here is a case in point.

Early in May, 1832, while Joseph Smith, Sidney Rigdon, and Newell K. Whitney were returning by team from Independence, Mo., to Kirtland, Ohio, at a point "between Vincennes, Ind., and New Albany, near the falls of the Ohio," the team ran away, and "in their efforts to escape from the coach, Mr. Whitney was so unfortunate as to sustain a compound fracture of the bones of one of his limbs," and they were compelled to put up at a wayside "tavern," where they remained four weeks.

"Here," says Mr. Smith's historian, "occurred quite a marvelous episode. The Anti-Mormons, it appears, attempted to poison the prophet, as a means of cruelly testing whether the 'signs' followed the Mormons. Joseph says:

"'One day, when I arose from the table, I walked directly to the door and began vomiting most profusely. I raised large quantities of blood and poisonous matter, and so great were the contortions of my muscular system, that my jaw was dislocated in a few moments. This I succeeded in replacing with my own hands, and I then made my way to Brother Whitney (who was on his bed) as speedily as possible. He laid his hands on me, and administered to me in the name of the Lord, and I was healed in an instant, although the effect of the poison had been so powerful as to cause much of the hair to become loosened from my head.'" (Tullidge's History, pages 141, 142).

Several points of objection may be urged against the probable truthfulness of this statement, and which tend to destroy its force. Among these are the following:

1. No proof is offered to show that poison of any character had been administered to Mr. Smith by Anti-Mormons or anybody else—he only suspects something of the kind.

2. That it was done to "cruelly test whether the 'signs' followed the Mormons," is simply a wild assertion without a thing to support it.

3. No analysis of the alleged "blood and poisonous matter" was ever made by a competent person to determine the fact that poison had been administered, and yet this is the only means, in this case, of determining the presence of poison.

4. The mere fact that Mr. Smith turned sick while at the dinner table is incompetent to establish

the fact of poison, as this effect may be produced in various ways.

5. The fact that Joseph soon recovered from this sudden attack of nausea after Whitney laid his hands on him, does not prove, nor even tend to prove, that Mr. Smith was healed, because that would be the natural result of "profuse vomiting."

6. It is a fact that God never does things by halves, and it seems remarkably strange that the Lord would heal his own prophet, and do it "in an instant," and yet allow the poison to have such a powerful effect upon him as to cause the hair to fall from his head. Why did not the remedy save the prophet's hair?

7. But perhaps the most serious objection to this alleged case of healing arises from the following consideration, namely: If Joseph Smith had in fact been poisoned, either by an enemy or by accident, and if Mr. Whitney's administration by the laying on of hands, as a matter of fact, actually healed Joseph Smith, as claimed, then why in the name of common sense did not the combined effort of Joseph Smith and Sidney Rigdon heal Newell K. Whitney's broken leg? Why lay by at a public house, among enemies who sought their lives, waiting for Whitney's leg to get well by the slow processes of nature, when there was a prophet of God present who possessed such marvelous power? *Why was it thus?* Can any Latter Day Saint answer?

Viewing it from the standpoint of honesty and common sense, the whole thing looks like a fraud— an effort to deceive. The evidence does not support the proposition affirmed, and must therefore be rejected.

HEAL THE SICK.

Last, but by no means least, among the "signs" that should follow the believer was, "They shall lay hands on the sick, and they shall recover."

Little was known at that age of the world concerning the science of medicine. Physiology had not yet been born. The action of the heart was little understood, and it remained for Harvey to discover the circulation of the blood.

Physicians of that day were powerless to contend with the malignant forms of disease which then afflicted humanity. To be able to do what the most skilled physicians failed to accomplish gave the apostles a prestige not otherwise attainable. The power to heal every manner of disease was a "sign"—a positive proof—to all those who obeyed the Gospel as preached by those unlettered fishermen that the God whom they preached had power to heal the soul as perfectly and as completely as the body. One they could believe because the other they had seen and felt.

The apostles, in substance, said to the people, "If you will believe the Gospel, and obey all its demands, you shall have power to lay your hands on the sick, just as you have seen us do, and *they shall recover.*" Believing, the people obeyed, and obeying, they received. Hence the concluding declaration:

"And they [the disciples] went forth, and preached everywhere, the Lord working with them, and confirming the word with signs following." (Mark 16:20).

Had the signs failed to follow the obedient believer, or had they seemingly followed only at long intervals, the faith of the believer would have been destroyed rather than confirmed. The unquestionable fulfillment of the promise must be the rule—not the exception. To witness a seeming instance of healing among Latter Day Saints is the exception, not the rule. I feel perfectly safe in saying that on the average not more than one case in a hundred could be regarded as even seemingly successful.

While in charge of the Southwestern Mission, including Texas, western Louisiana, Arizona and New Mexico, I kept a record of all administrations to the sick, noting time, place, the name of patient, the nature of the malady, by whom assisted, and the results. At the close of the year I found myself unable to report a single instance of healing in the entire mission. This was in 1878-9.

You can only imagine my feelings of disappointment and regret with this record staring me in the face, especially when many of those to whom I ministered had been brought into the church under my ministry. Often, very often, indeed, I would feel discouraged and sick at heart. I knew I was doing my best, and I had every reason to believe the people were honest. I had told them the "signs" should follow, but I was made to realize they did not, and was amazed that the new converts did not manifest greater signs of disappointment; but most of them surmounted the difficulty, and for aught I know are still in the church.

That the signs promised did follow those who received the teachings of the apostles of Christ there seems little room to doubt; but that they follow the honest believers in Mormonism, I have every reason in the world to deny.

When Latter Day Saints are asked to prove their

ability to work miracles as did the apostles, they evade the issue by quoting the language of Christ to a class of wicked Jews:

"A wicked and adulterous generation seeketh after a sign; and there shall no sign be given unto it but the sign of Jonas." (Matt. 16: 4).

This is a mere subterfuge on the part of Latter Day Saints. Neither Christ nor the apostles ever sought to evade the inquiries of an honest seeker after the truth in this manner. It is a tacit confession of inability to perform what they advertise. Besides this, the most wicked Pharisees did not question the *fact* that a miracle had been performed. They acknowledged the miracle, but attributed it to satanic power. (See Matt. 9: 32-34; 12: 22-24.)

Not so to-day. That a miracle has been performed by any modern apostle or prophet is denied by thoughtful Christian people everywhere, and no reasonable demand for proof should be treated lightly by those pretending to possess such powers, and any attempt to evade the issue can only be regarded as an unmanly effort to shirk the responsibility the claim involves.

When pressed further on this point they again quote the words of Christ:

"He that doeth the will of my Father which is in heaven shall *know* of the doctrine," and then invite you to test the matter by joining the Mormon Church, assuring you that by so doing you may get the proof that what they teach is true. This is but another ingenious effort to dodge the issue. If you make the effort and do not receive what you had been led to expect—as you certainly will not—you are told it is because you lack faith—that you must persevere and not allow the devil to cheat you out of the promised blessing.

You continue to strive, believing it is all your own fault that you do not receive "the gifts," until finally you either convince yourself that you have received a "testimony" and become established in the faith, or, discouraged and disheartened, turn away in disgust.

How utterly unlike the apostolic method is all this! No such evasions were necessary then, nor would they be now if Mormonism possessed the powers claimed for it. St. Paul, when withstood by Elymas the sorcerer, who sought to "turn away the deputy from the faith," was able to say in the name of the Lord:

"O full of all subtilty and mischief, thou child of the devil, thou enemy of all righteousness, wilt thou not cease to pervert the right way of the Lord? And now, behold, the hand of the Lord is upon thee, and *thou shalt be blind*, not seeing the sun for a season." (Acts 13: 8-11.)

No faith on the part of this sorcerer was necessary for Paul to perform this wonderful miracle. Nor yet was faith on the part of the recipient of the blessing required when Peter raised Dorcas from the dead.

"But Peter put them all forth, and kneeled down and prayed; and turning him to the body said, Tabitha, arise. And she opened her eyes: and when she saw Peter she sat up. And he gave her his hand, and lifted her up, and when he had called the saints and widows, presented her alive. And it was known throughout all Joppa, and many believed on the Lord." (Acts 9: 40-42).

Here was a miracle performed by an apostle of Christ, that defied contradiction, and the result of it was, "many believed on the Lord." In this case two very important facts appear. First: No faith by any one except Peter himself was necessary to the performance of this stupendous miracle; and, secondly: Being absolutely unquestionable, it was the direct means of many conversions.

When any latter-day apostle shall duplicate these miracles, then, and not till then, shall he be able to maintain the claim of Mormonism to miraculous powers.

CHAPTER VI.

OTHER CLAIMS.

Other claims—The Adventists—Free Methodists—Dr. Dowie—The Church of Rome—Their miracles lack authentication—The Church at Corinth—Spiritual gifts were for edification—Utah Church and its miracles—The sick healed—Cases cited—Are they genuine? The Reorganized Church—Excellent moral character of its membership—Claims to miraculous powers—Tested by a simple rule—Miracles no longer necessary.

NOT only does every branch and faction of the Mormon Church, polygamous or otherwise, pretend to have power to work miracles, but this power is claimed by others, only in a somewhat modified form, perhaps. The Seventh Day Adventists get revelations through the "visions" of Mrs. Ellen G. White, of Battle Creek, Michigan; and the "Come-Outers," or "Saints," as they prefer to be called, under the leadership of the late Elder Warner, of Michigan, and the Free Methodists, under Superintendent Roberts, all urge, as a proof of their divine mission, that the sick are healed among them by the anointing and "laying on of hands," not to mention Dr. Dowie, of Chicago, and a score of other so-called divine healers.

It is a well known fact in history that the Church of Rome has ever claimed the power to work miracles. Indeed, her claim to such power is thoroughly attested, so far as mere interested human testimony is capable of such attestation. But who believes her miracles genuine? Nobody. The entire Protestant world is a unit in the rejection of her claim to miraculous powers.

The most remarkable thing about this whole affair is found in the fact that not one of these churches will admit the miracles of the other—neither can convince the other of its divine authority. To the thinking mind the question very naturally arises: Do any of them possess the powers claimed? No sooner is the question asked than the answer comes with irresistible force that no such power is possessed by any of them, their pretensions to the contrary notwithstanding. No valid reason for the existence of such powers has ever been given.

If, indeed, such powers are necessary to-day, God, having lost none of his power, would certainly demonstrate their existence in an unmistakable manner, as in former times. The fact that there is no satisfactory proof of their existence amounts to very strong presumptive evidence that they are wholly unnecessary to the salvation of a fallen race. In fact, it is nowhere stated that such powers were ever necessary to salvation. Tongues, interpretations and prophecy —that is, *teaching*—were, in the apostles' time, a necessary means of edification, as appears from the testimony of Paul:

"For he that speaketh in an unknown tongue speaketh not unto men, but unto God: for no man understandeth him. . . . But he that prophesieth speaketh unto men to *edification* and exhortation and comfort.

"Even so ye, forasmuch as ye are zealous of spiritual gifts, seek that ye may excel to the edifying of the church.

"How is it, then, brethren? when ye come together, every one of you hath a psalm, hath a doctrine, hath a tongue, hath a revelation, hath an interpretation.

Let all things be done unto edifying." (1 Cor. 14: 2, 3, 12, 26).

Thus the church at Corinth, composed of people of different tongues, were urged to covet such gifts as were necessary to their excellence " to the edifying of the church," and to do this "tongues" and "interpretations" must be employed. But when a church is composed of people all speaking the same language, or where the minister can speak the different languages of those present, "the spiritual gifts" are not necessary to the "edifying of the church."

Spiritual gifts, then, are clearly to edify and *not to save.* If not to save, and as the church may be edified without them, their employment is superfluous.

Perhaps no people have ever been more boastful of miraculous powers than are the leaders of the church at Salt Lake City; and yet their vicious and corrupt practices have seldom been equaled, and perhaps never excelled. The following shows what wonderful things they claim to have done:

"HEALING OF ONE BORN BLIND."

. . "So the mother took another of her daughters and put her upon his knee [that of an unbeliever], and said, 'Sir, is that child blind?' And after he had examined her eyes, he said, '*She is.*' 'Well,' said the mother, 'she was *born blind:* and she is now four years old, and I am going to take her to the elders of our church for them to anoint her eyes with oil and lay their hands upon her; and you can call again when you have time, and see her with her eyes open.' . . 'Well,' said he, 'if she does ever see, it will be a great proof.'

"Accordingly, the mother brought the child to the

elders, and Elder John Hackwell anointed her eyes, and laid his hands upon her, only once; and the Lord heard his prayer, so that the child can now see with both of her eyes as well as any other person. For which we feel thankful to our heavenly Father, and are willing to bear testimony of it to all the world.

"Yours in the Kingdom of God,
"GEORGE HALLIDAY.

"P. S.—We, the father and mother of the child, do here sign our names to the above, as being true.
"WILLIAM BOUNSELL.
"ELIZABETH BOUNSELL.
"*No 12 Bread Street, Bristol, England, Nov. 25, 1849.*"

The above, with over a score of other similar cases, covering a variety of ailments, including leprosy, are recorded in the work from which this is taken. (See O. Pratt's works, Divine Authenticity of the Book of Mormon, No. 5, page 71.)

Mr. Pratt was at the time an apostle of the Utah Church and in charge of the English mission, and the parties to the alleged healing were members of the same church.

Who can believe that a people who did not hesitate for a moment to violate every commandment of the Decalogue could possibly be blessed with such marvelous power, while at the same time they are denied to the peace-loving and virtuous? The very claim is a burlesque on Christianity, and is alike repulsive to man and dishonoring to God. It cannot be true.

If to be found anywhere within the domain of Mormonism, these "spiritual gifts" might, with a greater show of reason, be expected among the people of the Reorganized Church, whose membership, I am glad to say, are as a rule honest and law-abiding people, and the purity of whose lives no man may truthfully question. I speak of this as the merest matter of justice to the membership of that church. But do they possess supernatural powers?

With forty years of acquaintance with Mormonism in its various phases, common honesty impels me to say I have never known a single instance of miraculous power. I have witnessed, it is true, what I was at the time willing to call a miracle, because, like all others who believe in such things, I wished to have it so; but never have I witnessed anything which would bear the test of intelligent scrutiny, or be confirmed by candid, sober second thought.

When, some years ago, I began a careful review of the entire ground upon which Mormonism is based, a simple rule assisted me very much in the solution of this vexed question. The rule was to accept nothing as miraculous which may be accounted for upon natural or scientific principles. This led me out of the woods. When tried by this simple rule no pretended miracle would stand the test.

Respecting this question, then, I no longer ask myself if these miraculous gifts are attainable by Christians to-day, but rather, are their presence in the Church of Christ, or their possession by the individual, necessary for the formation and development of Christian character?

Since the Scriptures nowhere declare that spiritual gifts, or power to work miracles, are in any sense necessary to the formation of true Christian character, or essential to the salvation of any man in any age, we shall certainly be perfectly safe in maintaining that their presence in the church is altogether immaterial, if not absolutely unnecessary. With this point satisfactorily settled, there exists no reason for concern.

CHAPTER VII.

CHURCH ORGANIZATION.

The Mormon Church a unique structure—Divided into many factions — Which is right?—King Strang—His Kingdom—The Mormon idea of an apostolic church—Its officers—Apostle Kelley's rule for testing churches.

HAVING disposed of that part of the subject which relates to the "signs," or "spiritual gifts," let us now pass to a careful consideration of the organic structure of the Mormon Church.

As between the different factions of the church which have arisen since the death of Joseph and Hyrum Smith, in June, 1884, there exists no difference with respect to the organization of the church, with one single exception, namely, that of James J. Strang, late of Beaver Island, Lake Michigan, who inaugurated a slight change.

Although claiming to be the legal successor to Joseph Smith, as "prophet, seer, and revelator," he skillfully avoided the triumvirate known as the "First Presidency," and assumed the modest title of king.

This, of course, he had a perfect right to do. Being a "prophet, seer, and revelator," all he had to do was to get a new revelation authorizing the change, and no man in the kingdom dare question its validity. This done, the question was settled. Strang organized the "Kingdom of God," and of course there could be no kingdom without a king—and Strang was the king.

Perhaps few of my readers are aware that a kingdom, pure and simple, with all the appurtenances thereunto belonging, was once established, and for several years flourished in the United States, almost immediately under the shadow of the folds of "Old Glory;" yet such is the case.

It is difficult to conceive how any intelligent man with the Bible in his hand could originate such a system of church government as that announced by Joseph Smith and Oliver Cowdery, and then have the effrontery to declare it to be an exact reproduction of the apostolic form of government.

And it is equally strange that intelligent people can, by any specious method of reasoning, be induced to accept such a system as being strictly Biblical; and yet such is the case. It is not so much a matter of astonishment, however, in the case of those who have been schooled in Mormon theology from infancy. The very essence of the delusion has been infused into every fiber of brain and body, and is hard to eradicate; yet such persons may reason themselves out of it, if happily they are able to so far break away from early traditions as to allow themselves to reason.

It is the boast of all Latter Day Saints that theirs is absolutely the only church in existence whose organization is exactly in accord with the plan laid down in the New Testament. With one accord they echo the sentiment of Joseph Smith's angel Moroni, who solemnly declared the churches were *all wrong*, their creeds an *abomination*, and their teachers all *corrupt*.

This unholy charge against every church and every creed in all Christendom should be repelled in the most decided manner, for the reason that it is not true in fact, and is wholly unchristian in sentiment, yet it is perfectly in keeping with the spirit and tone of Mormon theology.

Corruption, indeed! Where, under the broad canopy of heaven, did there ever exist a people calling themselves Christian, who were more intolerably corrupt than the people who composed the different factions which grew up out of the wreck of the first Mormon Church after the death of the Smiths at Carthage, Ill., in 1844? Let those who live in glass houses beware how they cast stones.

I shall endeavor to so completely overthrow the entire Mormon superstructure as to render its reconstruction absolutely impossible—show most conclusively, notwithstanding their boastful claim, that their organization is not only unscriptural, and therefore untenable, but that it stands without a parallel in the history of the ages.

We shall now proceed to a critical examination of their claims upon this point, and review the scriptural texts upon which they rely for support.

That there may be no controversy respecting the positions taken, I shall let their own writers state them. Wm. H. Kelley, one of the twelve apostles of the Reorganized Church, and a recognized authority in matters of doctrine, concerning church organization has this to say:

"In the New Testament there is a history given of the foundation of the Church of Christ in the times of the apostles. It sets forth the class of officers belonging thereto, and defines their duties." (Presidency and Priesthood, page 49).

Mr. Kelley then proceeds to name each officer which the Mormon creed prescribes as being necessary to the complete organization of the Church of Christ, as follows:

"(1) A chief apostle and high priest, with two associate counselors.

(2) A quorum of twelve apostles.

(3) Seventy elders.

(4) Elders.

(5) Bishops.

(6) Priests.

(7) Teachers.

(8) Deacons.

(9) High priests, evangelists and pastors in their proper places and order." (Presidency and Priesthood, page 226. See also pages 42, 53 and 83).

The writer then proceeds:

"In the light of the above facts, can any organization, however proud and haughty in its claims or large its members, not having these God-sent and heaven-inspired officers, be the Church of Christ?" (Ibid, page 45).

Here we have the whole thing in a nutshell. No church, except organized according to Mr. Kelley's "pattern," can by any possible means be the Church of Christ.

The antithesis of this proposition would be that any church organized according to this pattern must be the Church of Christ. Under this view of the case, will Mr. Kelley inform us just which of the seven or eight Mormon churches having such organization is the genuine church? There are the Brighamite Church, the Josephites, the Strangites, the Rigdonites, the Whitmerites, the Brewsterites, and the Hedrickites, to say nothing of the half-dozen defunct organizations, among which was that led by William B. Smith, brother of the prophet.

Mr. Kelley, as a matter of course, will tell us that the Reorganized Church (the Josephites) is the only genuine, simon-pure, Mormon Church, while the Brighamites declare in the most vehement manner that "young Joseph" is an apostate, wholly without authority, and that the true church is found only in Salt Lake City. This very question has been a bone of contention among the different factions of the Mormon Church ever since the death of Joseph Smith.

Of one thing we are morally certain, and that is, they cannot all be the Church of Christ, for the reason that the Apostle Paul declares, "Christ is not divided." Mr. Kelley devotes 107 pages of his book to the task of proving that the Protestant churches are in a hopeless state of division, and utterly without authority, to say nothing of the 82 pages devoted to the church of Rome. He refers more particularly to the different Baptist organizations as illustrative of the perniciousness of division, and says:

"But which Baptist church is the one standing in the true line of succession? This is not agreed upon by the Baptists themselves, and there are many Baptist churches; yet this is the important thing to men interested in knowing the true way." (Ibid, page 132).

All the different Mormon churches named above claim to stand in "the true line of succession" from Joseph Smith; and all that is affirmed of the Baptist churches will apply with equal force to the half-dozen or more Mormon churches now extant. Using Mr. Kelley's language, changing only the name of the church, we may very properly ask the pertinent question:

"Which Mormon church is the one standing in the true line of succession? This is not agreed upon between Mormons themselves, and there are many Mormon churches; and yet this is the important thing to men interested in knowing the true way."

How does your logic suit you, Mr. Kelley? When applied to your case, don't you think it proves just a little too much for the safety of your own position?

This defender of Mormonism thus continues:

"Again this writer [D. B. Ray] has the courage to assert that 'no man can be in the church or kingdom of Jesus Christ who is not in that kingdom which has the succession from the apostolic age.'" (Ibid, page 133).

Let us again make an application of Mr. Kelley's logic. That gentleman has the "courage to assert" that no man can be in the Church of Christ who is not in that church or kingdom having in its organic structure "God-sent and heaven-inspired" apostles, prophets, and so on, and yet all Mormon churches are so organized. The logic of this position is clearly this: The church having this particular organization is the Church of Christ. All Mormon churches are so organized. Therefore, *all* Mormon churches are the churches of Christ.

If Mr. Kelley's logic is sound, would not ordinary prudence dictate that the Reorganized Church and the Utah organization shake hands across the bloody chasm, kiss and make up, and join their forces in a common cause against the "old mother" and all her "daughters?" "A house divided against itself cannot stand."

If the division of Methodists, Baptists, and other denominations, into separate and distinct organic bodies, proves such churches to be without authority, as the advocates of Mormonism aver, then a like condition existing among Latter Day Saints will prove all Mormon churches equally unauthorized. The mere fact that a church may set apart twelve men and dub them "apostles" cannot be accepted by sensible, thinking people as proof that such a body is the Church of Christ.

Even were we to admit the peculiar organization advocated by Latter Day Saints to be the correct one, we should still be left in doubt as to which of them is right, for they have never been able to settle the question satisfactorily among themselves. But the question which more vitally concerns us at present is this: Does the Mormon Church, in its organic form, harmonize with that described in the New Testament? Mr. Kelley, as do all Latter Day Saints, insists that there must not be a thing omitted nor a single point added—it must be in "*exact* accord with the pattern."

A good physician should not refuse to take the medicine he prescribes for others when afflicted with the same disease; and Latter Day Saints cannot, therefore, refuse to be governed by the rule prescribed for the government of others. If the church organization described by Mormon writers, and uniformly, and sometimes eloquently, urged by its preachers, shall be found to be in perfect harmony with the Bible, then I am free to admit that the Mormon Church is right, and everybody else is wrong.

But, on the other hand, if they have either too much or too little, then they are in error, and should as frankly confess it.

In seeking to determine this important question we must be goverened by a rule upon which there is perfect agreement between the parties to the controversy. Defenders of the Mormon faith and doctrine can certainly have no ground of complaint if we ask them to submit to a rule of their own making—one by which they propose to test the claims of every other church. Mr. Kelley furnishes an excellent rule, to which I think the reader will most heartily subscribe, as follows:

"To avoid imposition in finance, there is put in circulation a money test, by which the holder of money is enabled to determine whether there is tendered to him true or false coin. When every mark or figure on a coin or bill tendered in exchange harmonizes with the detector, it is pronounced good money. But if there is anything found on the coin or in the bill, *not to be found in the detector*, or if there is something *left out* of the coin or bill *that is found in the detector*, it is rejected as *spurious*.

"The New Testament contains the history of the formation of the primitive church; hence *it is the test or detector* by which *all church* organizations, claiming to be the true, are to be tried. . . . Then friend, seeker, take the New Testament in your hand as your *guide* and *test* by which to try systems. . . . Do not lose sight of the detector, or you will be in danger of being imposed upon by something man-made and spurious. *The counterfeiter is abroad in the land.*" (Presidency and Priesthood, pages 49 and 50). The italics are mine.

With this rule for our guide let us lay the Mormon system beside the "detector," and see if it is able to stand the test.

CHAPTER VIII.

PATRIARCH OMITTED—APOSTLES WANTING.

The Reorganized Church deficient—The patriarch omitted—Only nine apostles—An argument examined—Polygamy and highway robbery—A corrupt tree—A bitter fountain—Duties of an apostle defined—Brighamite and Reorganized churches agree—The whole system is unscriptural.

HAVING already given the list of officers necessary to a properly organized church, from the Mormon point of view, it is unnecessary to reproduce it here.

It is a remarkable fact that when preaching to the world—and that means everything not Latter Day Saints—they uniformly omit any reference to the First Presidency, the Patriarch, and High Priests. You will no doubt have observed that Mr. Kelley omits the Patriarch from his list of church officials, but for what reason he fails to mention that important functionary does not appear, unless it be from a consciousness that no such officer is mentioned in the New Testament; and yet no Mormon Church is complete in its organization without that dignitary, as we have already shown.

Two remarkable deficiencies have ever existed in the Reorganized Church, which may, with propriety, be mentioned in this connection, namely:

1. While the church has existed nearly forty-seven years, yet it has never had a full "quorum" of Twelve Apostles—the number usually being from seven to ten.

2. It has never had, in all these years, a Patriarch;

and as the duty of that official is "to confer blessings" upon the members of the church, their loss can never be estimated.

These defects in the organic structure of the church cause more or less uneasiness and comment upon the part of some of the leading men, and their fears were not removed till April 15, 1894, when President Joseph Smith received the following revelation, in which the Lord is represented as saying:

"It is not expedient in me that the Quorum of the Presidency and the Quorum of the Twelve Apostles shall be filled, for reasons which will be seen and known unto you in due time."—Doctrines and Covenants, sec. 122, par. 4, page 353.

Concerning the appointment and consecration of a Patriarch, the revelation continues:

"For the same reasons in me that it is not expedient to fill the quorums of the First Presidency and the Twelve, who are apostles and high priests, it is not expedient that a Patriarch for the church should be indicated and appointed."—Ibid, page 358.

This shows that the Patriarch is still regarded as a necessary part of the church machinery, and that the only thing in the way was a question of expediency.

The Patriarchate was carefully kept in the Smith*

---

*NOTE.—Since the above was written, a revelation was received by President Joseph Smith, at Lamoni, Iowa, April 9, 1897, appointing his brother, Alexander H. Smith, to the Patriarchate of the Reorganized Church. Following is the language of the revelation:

"Thus saith the Spirit of your Lord and Savior Jesus Christ: Your fastings and your prayers are accepted and have prevailed.

"Separate and set apart my servant Alexander H. Smith to be a counselor to my servant, the President of the church, his brother; and to be *Patriarch* to the church, and an evangelical minister to the whole church." (Minutes of General Conference, Lamoni, Iowa, April 6-16, 1897, page 28.)

family. It was first conferred upon the prophet's father, Joseph Smith, Sr., and later upon his elder brother Hyrum, who held the office at the time of his death. The position was a lucrative one, the Patriarch receiving, it is said, one dollar for each "blessing sealed upon the head" of the faithful.

In order to prove their form of organization to be strictly Biblical, Latter Day Saints quote two passages of Scripture, as follows:

"And God hath set some in the church, first apostles, secondarily prophets, thirdly teachers, after that miracles, then gifts of healing, helps, governments, diversities of tongues." (1 Cor. 12:28).

"Wherefore he saith, When he ascended up on high he led captivity captive, and gave gifts unto men.

"And he gave some apostles, and some prophets, and some pastors and teachers; for the perfecting of the saints, for the work of the ministry, for the edifying of the body of Christ: till we all come in the unity of the faith, and of the knowledge of the Son of God, unto a perfect man, unto the measure of the stature of the fulness of Christ: that we henceforth be no more children, tossed to and fro, and carried

---

Patriarch Smith enjoys the unique distinction of being the only ecclesiastic to hold three offices at the same time, namely: A member of the "First Presidency," a "Patriarch," and "*an evangelical minister to the whole church*," the last named office being a new creation, authorized by this new revelation. When will the official list be completed?

The same revelation—par. 4—also sets apart "my servants I. N. White, J. W. Wight [son of apostle Lyman Wight, of Texas], and R. C. Evans," to the apostleship, thus completing the organization of the "Quorum of Twelve."

With the appointment of Bishop E. L. Kelley as a counselor *pro tem.* to President Smith, the organization of the church is completed for the first time during its entire existence.

about with every wind of doctrine, by the sleight of men and cunning craftiness, whereby they lie in wait to deceive." (Eph. 4: 8, 11, 12).

It is maintained by Latter Day Saints that these Scriptures prove:

1. That God set in the church "apostles and prophets," as a necessary part of its organic structure.

2. That inspired apostles and prophets were designed to continue in the Church of Christ in every age of the world.

3. That these inspired persons are necessary to the "work of the ministry"—that is, to preach the Gospel and administer its ordinances—in every age.

4. That the apostles and prophets are a necessary safeguard against every form of fraud and deception.

If the Scriptures quoted sustain the above views, then Christians everywhere should accept them. But if they do not, Latter Day Saints should renounce the heresy at once. Let us now review the ground of this claim and see if it be tenable.

1. While 1 Cor. 12: 28 affirms that "God set some in the church," and names apostles and prophets, among others, it does not intimate that such officers are a necessary part of the church organization; in fact, it does not even call them "officers" of the church, nor does any other Scripture so declare. Nothing is here, then, to show that apostles and prophets were a part of the official and organic structure of the church.

2. Ephesians 4: 11-14 declares that Christ gave "gifts" unto men, and among other things he gave some apostles and prophets, but there is not one word about the *office* of apostle and prophet, much less a

provision to continue such "offices" in all ages of the world.

3. That inspired apostles and prophets are neces- to preach the Gospel and administer its ordinances is an assumption wholly unwarranted by the facts, and can be regarded only as the idle fancy of a brain disordered by a false theology; and even Mormons themselves are forced to admit that *elders* may perform all the duties necessary to induct "foreigners and strangers" into the "commonwealth of Israel."

4. Which of the divine writers is so bold as to declare that the presence of apostles and prophets in the church is a safeguard against cunning and craft, fraud and deception? No such thought is suggested by the text quoted.

That we may not be "tossed to and fro by every wind of doctrine," and thus be safe from the wiles of the cunning and crafty, is conditioned on the fact "that we henceforth *be no more children*," but instead be full-grown men—men so fully developed as to fill "the measure of the stature of Christ." That the presence of apostles and prophets is no safeguard against fraud and deception will more fully appear as we proceed.

If apostles and prophets were designed as a means of protection against fraud—to prevent the possibility of being "carried about with every wind of doctrine," then how does it come that the Mormon Church has developed a greater amount of fraud, and its membership have been "tossed to and fro," and carried about with "winds of doctrine" such as have never disturbed any other church or people? Will somebody answer?

For instance, under the guidance of the "twelve

apostles" set in the church organized by Joseph Smith and Oliver Cowdery, was developed that pernicious, soul-destroying "wind of doctrine" known as polygamy, but which is known among its devotees by the euphonious title of "Patriarchal marriage." Instead of preventing the iniquity, these modern apostles, under the eye of Joseph Smith, if not by his sanction and authority, were the instigators and teachers of the abomination.

Who but these so-called apostles introduced and taught that damnable doctrine of human sacrifice known as "blood atonement," as it has been known to exist in Salt Lake City?

Who but these same men made their ignorant dupes believe that "Adam is our God and our father, and the only God with whom we have to do?"

Who but these self-styled apostles and prophets taught their credulous followers that it was perfectly legitimate to despoil their enemies and rob the hated "Gentiles?" This delicate operation was modestly called "consecration," and King Strang was entitled to one-tenth of all such "consecrations." The writer speaks from observations made during more than a year's residence among them on Beaver Island, and was present when Strang was assassinated by two of his followers.

The list of unholy doctrines and practices might be extended indefinitely, but we desist. Enough has been said to show that the presence of so-called apostles in the church affords no guarantee of purity, either in doctrine or practice.

If it be true that "a corrupt tree cannot bring forth good fruit," or that "a bitter fountain cannot send forth sweet water," then, what must be said of the tree that has yielded such an abundant harvest of corrupt fruit, or of the fountain from which has flowed the bitter waters of vice and corruption, as those exhibited under the different phases of Mormonism? Testing the system by this infallible rule, there can be but one conclusion reached, namely, the fruit being *evil*, the tree must have been corrupt; the stream being bitter, the fountain must have been *impure*.

From the foregoing it will be seen that Mr. Kelley is evidently in error when he affirms that the passages of Scripture under consideration "provide for the existence and *necessity for the continuation* of an inspired ministry," including apostles and prophets. No such provision is made, and no such necessity is shown to exist.

Of the duties of an apostle, the late Orson Pratt, of the Utah Church, says:

"One of the important duties required of an apostle is to ADMINISTER THE SPIRIT. . . The ordinance through which the Spirit is administered is the LAYING ON OF HANDS. (See Acts 8 and 19, and Hebrews 6.)

"To the apostles were entrusted three very important ministrations for the salvation of man:

"First. *The ministration of the word.*

"Second. *The ministration of the baptism of water.*

"Third. *The ministration of the baptism* of the Spirit." (O. Pratt's works, The Kingdom of God, part 1, page 7.)

"These offices were *created*, set, established by the Almighty in the priesthood, to receive occupants for the government and guidance of the church." (Presidency and Priesthood, page 43).

Thus it will be seen that the two principal Mormon

Churches agree both as to the existence and duties of apostles in the church to-day.

Several serious objections may be urged against the last quoted statement, among which may be named:

1. No such "offices" as those mentioned were ever "created," and hence never received "occupants" for the "*guidance* of the churches."

2. Such offices never having been created could not have been, and in fact were not, *established* in the Church of Christ.

3. Never having been established, it is impossible for them to continue.

4. No officer, it matters not how high, was ever set in the church for its "government and guidance." The Gospel, "the perfect law of liberty," was ordained for the "government and guidance of the churches," and the officers were only its ministers.

That "the universe is governed by law," is as true of the spiritual and divine, as it is of the physical world.

I have diligently searched the Scriptures to find where, when and by whom such officers as those named by Mr. Kelley were "created" and "set" in the church established by Christ, and I am bold to declare that *no such system can anywhere be found in the Bible.* It is clearly and unmistakably modern in its origin, and purely and absolutely Mormon in its inception—"created" and foisted upon the public by Joseph Smith and Oliver Cowdery as a new revelation. It is a fraud and a deception, and has not even the shadow of support in the Word of God.

CHAPTER IX.

Apostles in the primitive church—The apostolic office is ambassadorial, not executive—Ambassadors in the church now are unnecessary and impossible—Mr. Kelley's rule applied—Apostolic succession.

In the face of the foregoing facts the Saints will no doubt continue to insist that apostles and prophets are a part of the constitutional organic structure of the church.

That God set apostles in his church, none are disposed to question; but that apostles were a part of its official, organic structure, is most emphatically denied; and those who affirm as much are required to establish their contention by the production of competent evidence—such evidence as will establish the fact beyond the possibility of reasonable doubt.

AMBASSADORS.

The twelve apostles were, in their official character, *ambassadors;* and were representative, rather than executive or judicial, officers, and as such were not a part of the internal organism of the body spiritual. Now, if we shall be able to establish this view by competent testimony, we shall have gained a point both material and relevant to the controversy, whose importance will be recognized at once. Then to the task let us hasten.

Although having the privilege to minister in Gospel ordinances, if the apostles were ambassadors, they were not necessarily executive officers of the Church

(91)

of Christ by virtue of their apostleship. Bearing directly upon this question the apostle Paul says:

"For Christ sent me not to baptize, but to preach the Gospel." (1 Cor. 1:17).

To baptize is the function of an executive officer, while preaching the Gospel is the duty of a representative official. Hence, Paul was specifically a representative of Christ. The same is true of all the apostles.

The specific duty of the eleven, as set forth in the commission, was to "preach the Gospel." Incidentally they might baptize, but their commission did not require them to do so. They *must* preach Christ, but others might do the baptizing. A Paul may plant, while an Apollos may water. While Paul was not obliged to baptize, yet he says: "Woe is me if I preach not the Gospel."

If the office of the apostles was ambassadorial, it will doubtless readily be granted that they are at once removed from the domain of the executive and judicial, except in a manner purely ex-officio.

What is true of one is true of a class. Hence, if one apostle was an ambassador, all were. The only thing necessary to a fair settlement of this question will be to determine whether the apostles were ambassadors in the proper sense of that term. But first, what is an ambassador? Webster defines the word thus:

"The minister of the highest rank, employed by one prince or state at the court of another to manage the public concerns of his own prince or state, and representing the power and dignity of his own sovereign."

The apostle is "a minister of the highest rank," as

declared by all New Testament writers, and was employed by the "Prince of Peace" to represent his "power and dignity" at the courts of all the princes of earth. The apostolic credentials were unquestionable. They bore the insignia of divine approval in signs and miracles of an incontestable character.

These facts alone declare in terms not to be misunderstood, that the apostles were the ambassadors of Christ; but fortunately we are not left to inference for the determination of this question, for we have the express declaration of the Apostle Paul upon this point, as follows:

. . . "God was in Christ, reconciling the world unto himself, . . . and hath committed unto us the word of reconciliation."

To whom was the word of reconciliation committed? Specifically to the apostles. (See Matt. 28: 19, 20; Mark 16: 15-18).

"Now then *we* [the apostles] *are* AMBASSADORS *for Christ*, as though God did beseech you by us: we pray you in Christ's stead, be ye reconciled to God." (2 Cor. 5: 19, 20).

Thus we have the proof that an apostle is an ambassador, and in his letter to the Church at Ephesus, Paul gives further assurance of this when he says, "I am an ambassador in bonds" (Eph. 6: 20).

This point, then, may be regarded as authoritatively settled. *The apostles of Christ were his ambassadors.*

The question now arises as to whether an ambassador is necessary either to the existence of a government or to its perpetuation. No one possessing ordinary intelligence would think of asserting that an ambassador is necessary to the existence of any form of government, however desirable such a dignitary might be regarded.

As well may we argue that the presence of our ambassador at the court of St. James is necessary to the existence of the government of the United States, as to declare the presence of apostles—ambassadors—in the Church of Christ is necessary to its existence. This government could recall every ambassador now representing the American people at foreign courts without interfering in the least with the constitutional form of its government. What is true of an earthly government, in this regard, may also be affirmed of the Church of Christ. Hence, the removal of the apostles from the church could in no possible manner interfere with, or change, the constitutional form of its government.

Viewing the question from this standpoint, it becomes clear that neither apostles nor prophets are in the least necessary to the existence and perpetuity of the Church of Christ, and may be dispensed with, therefore, without interfering with its utility.

But suppose we look at the question from another point of view, and test the argument by another Mormon rule. Most writers on the subject agree that the apostolic office expired with St. John; but the Saints deny this, and maintain that the office was never abolished, and that it did not expire with the apostles. To sustain this view they introduce what is considered a most potent argument—unanswerable, in fact—and which is employed in different forms by most of their leading speakers and writers, to prove that the apostolic office was to be perpetuated in the church. The argument consists in applying the well-known rules of civil government to church affairs. Mr. Kelley states the case thus: "The removing of the officer does not destroy the office, any more than the death of the President of the United States destroys the office which he holds. When the President dies, or is removed from office, or his term of office expires, *by due process of law* another may be appointed to fill the same office. The office remains, although the President is dead, and to have a government proper, another must take his place. So it is in all the essential offices of the government. This is true of the kingdom of God, or Church of Jesus Christ." (Presidency and Priesthood, page 45).

This is conceded to be a good and perfectly safe rule, and will aid us in determining the validity of the Mormon claim.

Mr. Kelley informs us that "all the *essential* offices of the government" are filled and perpetuated " by due process of law," and makes the rule applicable to the offices of the church. By this we are led to understand that all *essential* offices of the church are provided for in the organic law, the same as in all civil governments, and all offices not so provided for, are merely provisional and temporary, and designed to cease when their temporary purposes have been served.

Does the organic law of the Church of Christ make provision for the filling of the apostolic office upon the death or removal of the officer? If so, where may such law be found? Who filled St. Peter's chair after his death? and by what "due process of law" was his successor appointed? Who succeeded James and John in the apostolic office? and by virtue of what law, and by whom were such successors made apostles? Who was St. Paul's successor? and by what "process of law" was he created an apostle? Will some latter-day apostle or prophet answer?

Biblical annals afford but one instance of attempted apostolic succession, namely, the appointment of Matthias to fill the place of Judas, the traitor. This case is remarkable in more than one respect. It serves to raise the question of succession, but fails to reveal any *law* by which any subsequent vacancy in the apostolic college should be filled, if indeed such vacancy was to be filled. A careful reading of the account (Acts 1: 15-26) shows clearly that the eleven were governed, not by anything which the Master had taught them respecting this matter, but rather by their own conception of what ought to be done under the circumstances. Jesus had chosen *twelve*, and they were of the impression that this number should be kept good. This view seems to have been confirmed in their minds by the apparent applicability of certain Scriptures to the suicide of Judas, and the appointment of another to take his place.

The action of the eleven, in forming what is deemed by some as a precedent, was doubtless prompted by an exegesis of what they seemed to think was a prophecy relating directly to the question they were then considering. This fact, and not that they were governed by any law then in existence, was their only authority for this remarkable transaction.

There is not even an intimation that they were directed by the Holy Spirit in the matter. As a matter of fact, the Spirit had not yet been given by which it had been promised they should be guided into "all truth." Hence, it is by no means certain that the choosing of Matthias by "lot" was ever accepted and approved of God, but the circumstances tend rather to support the opposite view of the case. Matthias sank as utterly from view as did the individual whom he had, by *accident*, been chosen to succeed.

It may be unpopular to say so, but the writer does not believe the Scriptures referred to by Peter, who seems to have presented the matter to the meeting, has any reference whatever to Judas Iscariot or the betrayal of Christ. Detached from their contexts, and applied after the event supposed to be described had transpired, such an interpretation might seem feasible; but when taken in connection with the contexts, and read and applied before the event had transpired, no such thought could possibly be suggested. No Jew—not even the apostles themselves—previous to the betrayal of Jesus, would have ever dreamed of making any such application of the texts. But this is merely suggestive.

If we allow the correctness of the application of the Scriptures quoted, and that the apostles were acting under some pre-arranged plan in the divine economy, then we are confronted with the undeniable fact that this remarkable transaction on the part of the eleven cannot form a precedent for any future action of a similar character, for the reason that no possibility exists for the subsequent duplication of the tragic events which rendered such action possible, or in any sense necessary. That which is impossible of reproduction can never form a precedent.

Another very important point is brought to view by a careful examination of this case, namely: In making the selection, the apostles recognized the fact, and urged it as a necessary qualification, that to be an apostle one must be chosen who had been with Christ from the beginning, and the two men selected, Joseph and Matthias, to one of whom the lot must fall, had been with Jesus "from the baptism of John, unto that same day that he was taken up from them," and that such persons only could "take part of this ministry and apostleship," and "be a witness with us of his *resurrection*." (See verses 22-25).

To be an apostle of Christ, then, these eleven understood that the following qualifications were absolutely necessary:

1. That the individual must have seen Christ. "Am I not an apostle? *Have I not seen Jesus Christ our Lord?*" (1 Cor. 9: 1. See also Luke 1: 2; Acts 10: 41; 1 Cor. 15: 5-8; 2 Pet. 2: 16).

2. That he must have been with Christ from the "*beginning.*" Paul's apostleship was questioned on this ground. Instead of being a witness he had been a persecutor from the beginning, and hence was not acknowledged as an apostle of Christ until he was able to produce the "seal of his apostleship;" his miracles were unquestionable.

3. He must have been a "witness of his resurrection."

Those who regard this event as a precedent will find but little in it to encourage them in the belief of latter-day apostles. Who among them will dare say that he has seen Christ? and who declare he is a witness of his resurrection? And yet these are qualifications absolutely requisite to the apostleship, according to the so-called precedent. But to return to Mr. Kelley's rule.

Every form of government designed to be permanent has a fundamental law or constitution, providing for not only the different offices, but also for specific rules by which such offices shall be filled when vacated by death or removal from office.

Thus the Constitution of the United States "creates" the office of President. It likewise provides permanent and specific rules by which the President shall be elected and installed in his office. Each department of the government is provided for in like manner.

And now, in pursuance of this excellent rule, will Mr. Kelley, or any other defender of this Mormon dogma, take the New Testament, the "guide," the "detector," urged by Mr. Kelley with so much earnestness, and which contains the only constitution of the Church of Christ, and show us:

First. Where does the fundamental law of the church provide for the office of apostle?

Second. Where may we find the law which "creates" the office of prophet?

Third. What portion of the divine law provides for the *manner* of filling said offices when vacated by death or removal from office?

Fourth. Are these officers elected or appointed?

Fifth. If elected, how? If appointed, by whom?

Sixth. What are the duties of apostles and prophets, respectively?

Mr. Kelley has assured us that their duties are "clearly defined" in the New Testament; perhaps he will be kind enough to explain. These questions are important and come strictly within the rule, and the advocates of the system should meet them fairly and squarely

Now let the advocates of this unprecedented, unheard-of organization of theirs show us good authority for their claim—give us chapter and verse in support of their position, or cease to ask an intelligent public to accept a dogma so palpably absurd.

CHAPTER X.

NUTS TO CRACK.

Nuts to crack—To the law and to the testimony—The Bible recognizes no First Presidency in the church—No Patriarch, no High Priests—From another standpoint—An elder is a Melchizedek priest—May give the Holy Spirit by the laying on of hands.

"To the law and to the testimony: if they speak not according to this word, it is because there is no light in them." (Isa. 8: 20.)

This is a favorite text with all ministers of the Mormon Church, and is quoted to remind you that every church, both in organization and doctrine, must be in accord with the "pattern" given in the Bible in every minute particular. Suppose we apply this divine injunction to their church organization, and see how it will work.

Will some of those sticklers for "the law and the testimony" tell us where the New Testament describes the process of calling and setting apart a few of the officers of the Mormon Church?

For instance, where does it say anything about the "First Presidency," consisting of "a chief apostle and high priest, with two associate counselors?"

It will be interesting to know something about when Jesus called the "Patriarch" and "set" him in the church; and a short biographical sketch of that dignitary would be very interesting reading. Who will volunteer the information?

Will some zealous defender of the Mormon theology tell us when and for what purpose Christ placed "High Priests" in his church? It might be well at the same time to give us a little information concerning the consecration of "Patriarchs" and "High Priests."

It will be interesting to know when the Savior "created" the office of "priest" and "established" it in his church, and for what purpose. What is the duty of a priest?

Come, brethren, "to the law and to the testimony." Will your system bear the test of the rule you have given us?

The questions are full of interest alike to the uninitiated and the experienced, and we hope some one interested in the defense of Mormon theology will undertake a solution of the problem. But none better understand the difficulty of this task than do the advocates of this heresy. The leaders in thought among them well know that no support for such an absurdity can be found in the Word of God.

Mr. Kelley devotes eighty-four pages of his book to the task of proving the "First Presidency" dogma, but, as even the most casual reader of the Bible must know, failed most signally. That gentleman enjoys the distinction of being the only man who ever essayed the defense of this creation of Mormonism in print. While his courage is certainly commendable, his judgment must be deprecated.

Thus it will be seen that the faithful application of Mr. Kelley's rule excludes the possibility of apostles in any church in modern times, as the organic law of the Church of Christ makes no provision for the continuation of such office. If the organic law makes no provision for the perpetuation of the apostolic office, it proves that such office was not intended by the Law-giver to be continued. As Mr. Kelley assures us that all "*necessary*" offices are provided for in the law, and since no provision is made for the continuation of apostles and prophets in the church, such officers can only be regarded as unnecessary, and being unnecessary, the apostolic office *expired with the beloved disciple*. Nothing can be plainer.

FROM ANOTHER STANDPOINT.

Reasoning from another but kindred premise the same conclusion may be reached. Suppose we try it.

Such officers only as are necessary to administer the laws of either church or state are to be regarded as essential to its existence or perpetuation. More than this would be superfluous, and therefore unnecessary. This proposition is so clearly evident that it may not be disputed.

As already shown by the quotation from Mr. Pratt, the greatest apostle of Mormonism, the most important duty assigned to an apostle is to "ADMINISTER THE SPIRIT" by "THE LAYING ON OF HANDS."

It follows as a logical sequence that if this duty may legally be performed by any person other than an apostle, the presence of such officer would be wholly superfluous and hence unnecessary. If the apostle is the only official empowered to perform the laying on of hands, and if the laying on of hands be a divine requirement, then the presence of an apostle is an absolute necessity. But, on the other hand, if the laying on of hands is divinely imposed, which is by no means admitted, and if it can be accomplished by one not an apostle, then the apostle is an official absolutely nonessential. I shall now introduce a little evidence from Mormon sources to prove that to minister in the laying on of hands is not confined to the apostleship by any means, but that officials of inferior grade may perform that office.

There are in the Mormon Church what they erroneously call "two priesthoods," namely, the "Melchizedek and the Aaronic." Any officer "holding the Melchizedek priesthood," as the saying goes among the Saints, may officiate in all the ordinances of the church, including the "laying on of hands for the gift of the Holy Ghost."

The "First Presidency," the "Twelve," the "Seventy," the "High Priests," the "Bishoprick," that is, the "Presiding Bishop and his two counselors," and the Elders, descending in the order named, are all described as "holding the Melchizedek priesthood," while the minor offices, namely, those of priest, teacher and deacon, come under the head of the lesser, or "Aaronic priesthood."

From a work called the "Doctrine and Covenants," a book of Joseph Smith's revelations, I quote the following:

"There are, in the church, two priesthoods, namely: the Melchizedek and the Aaronic, including the Levitical priesthood. . . . The office of an *elder* comes under the priesthood of Melchizedek. Melchizedek priesthood holds the right of presidency, and has *power and authority over all the offices in the church*, in all ages of the world, to administer in *spiritual things*.

"The *high priest* and *elder* are to administer in spiritual things, agreeably to the covenants and commandments of the church; and they have a *right* to officiate in *all these offices of the church* when there are no higher authorities present. The elder has a right to officiate in his stead when the high priest is not present." (Doctrine and Covenants, sec. 104, par. 1, 2, 3, 6, 7, pages 289, 290).

The *elder*, then, may officiate in *all the offices of the church* the same as a high priest. He is authorized also to perform any office which the seventy may perform—in fact, the only difference between them is the seventy must travel under the "direction of the twelve," while the elder is under no responsibility of "traveling in all the world." (See par. 41-43).

An elder may, therefore, "ADMINISTER THE SPIRIT by the LAYING ON OF HANDS." Hence, as an elder is authorized to perform all the offices necessary to induct people into the church and regulate the affairs thereof, no office higher than this is at all necessary.

This unscriptural array of church dignitaries can only serve to encourage selfish aspirations to place and power.

Thus it is made clear, Latter Day Saints themselves being the witnesses, that apostles and prophets, seventies and high priests, are in no sense a necessary part of the organic structure of even the Mormon Church, and may be discarded with impunity.

CHAPTER XI.

CHURCH AND KINGDOM.

Church and kingdom synonymous—The church from John to the calling of the twelve without apostles—From 1830 to 1835 without apostles—Only elders—Fact and theory—Bible church and Mormon church compared—Branch president—Mr. Kelley's test applied to Mormon coin—Weighed in the balance and found wanting.

As already shown by the testimony of Mr. Pratt, of the Utah Church, and Mr. Kelley, of the Reorganized Church, the terms "Church of Christ" and "Kingdom of God," are used interchangeably. If we concede such use of the terms to be correct, we are thereby furnished with another very strong argument against the arrogant claims of Mormonism. Concerning the kingdom of God, Jesus, when teaching the Pharisees, said:

"The law and the prophets were until John: since that time the kingdom of God is preached, and every man presseth unto it." (Luke 16:16).

Here we have it plainly stated that the "kingdom of God" had its inception with John. If the terms "Kingdom of God" and "Church of Christ" are synonymous, then the Church of Christ had existed from the beginning of John's ministry to the calling of the twelve, without either apostles or prophets.

Since the church existed from the beginning of John's ministry to the calling of the twelve without either apostles or prophets, it follows as a necessary sequence that neither was an essential part of its official membership.

This, however, is ancient history, and may be questioned by our Mormon friends, and so we shall come down to a period of later date for a little history relative to this matter, the authenticity of which no Latter Day Saint will care to deny.

"The Church of Jesus Christ of Latter Day Saints," was organized with *six members*, "at Fayette, Seneca Co., N. Y., Tuesday, the 6th day of April, 1830." (See Tullidge's History, page 75).

This church, Mr. Kelley informs us, was "regularly organized," at the above time and place. Query—How many apostles were included in this organization with *six* members? At the time this organization was effected, another important event occurred, namely, the ordination of Joseph Smith and Oliver Cowdery to the "Melchizedek priesthood." The prophet himself, concerning the ordination, says:

"I then laid my hands upon Oliver Cowdery and ordained him an *elder* of the Church of Jesus Christ of Latter Day Saints, after which he ordained me also to the office of an *elder* of said church.' (Ibid, page 75).

Thus it will be seen that the highest officer in the church at the time of its organization was an elder. These two elders—Joseph and Oliver—at the time of organizing the church, "confirmed," by the *laying on of hands*, all persons who had previously been baptized, as the history of the event shows. Under the ministry of persons holding the office of an elder, and nothing higher, the Mormon Church flourished and continued to grow till Feb. 14th, 1835, when the twelve apostles were chosen.

If the church could exist and flourish from April 6, 1830, to Feb. 14, 1835, without apostles, why could it not continue to exist, and flourish, and grow, from 1830 to 1897?—and if that length of time, why not forever? Why cumber the church with apostles, when the elders may perform the work assigned to an apostle?

But, on the other hand, if apostles, prophets, high priest and seventy are really necessary to its proper organization, then the church constituted April 6th, 1830, with *elders only*, could not have been the Church of Christ, and its members, including Joseph Smith and Oliver Cowdery, were still "foreigners and strangers to the commonwealth of Israel."

Which horn of the dilemma will our Mormon friends take? Either is fatal to their cause. Viewed from this standpoint it appears conclusive that apostles and prophets are superfluous and unnecessary.

THE "TEST" APPLIED.

The Mormon Church does not have in fact what is claimed for it in theory, as will abundantly appear as we proceed. Several officers which the Saints insist must be in the church in order to its complete organization, are not to be found in their church as it actually exists.

Allowing, for the sake of the argument, that prophets, seventies, evangelists, elders, bishops and pastors, are separate and distinct ranks of ministers, which is by no means conceded, then the Mormon Church organization evidently comes far short of the "pattern," as appears from the following comparison:

THE BIBLE ORGANIZATION.	THE MORMON ORGANIZATION.
1. Apostles.	1. *The First Presidency.*
2. *Prophets.*	2. *The Patriarch.*
3. Seventy.	3. The twelve apostles.
4. *Evangelists.*	4. The Seventy.
5. *Pastors.*	5. *High Priests.*
6. Elders.	6. Elders.
7. Bishops.	7. Bishops.
8. Teachers.	8. *Priests.*
9. Deacons.	9. Teachers.
	10. Deacons.

The titles in italics in the Bible list represent officers named in the Bible which are not found in the Mormon Church; while the titles in the Mormon list in similar type represent officers in the Mormon Church which are not found in the Bible.

Thus it may be seen that *three* officers, namely, that of *prophet, evangelist* and *pastor,* named in the Bible, and also in Mr. Kelley's list, are positively not to be found in any Mormon Church in existence. There is no official in all Mormondom known as a *prophet.* It is true that Joseph Smith, Jr., and the present Joseph Smith are called " prophets," and are so considered, but I wish it distinctly understood that the *office* was that of the " *Frist Presidency,*" and not that of a prophet. I repeat it with emphasis: The office of prophet does not exist in the Mormon Church.

The same is true of the evangelist and pastor. No man living ever saw a Mormon "evangelist." He simply does not exist, and never did. Those doing evangelistic work are usually apostles, seventies, high priests or elders, but *evangelists,* never.

Who ever heard of a Mormon " pastor?" Nobody. Such an officer does not exist even in name. The minister having charge of a church is the "president of the branch," and usually holds the office of an elder, although other officers may officiate, as "branch president," but as *pastor*, never.

On the other hand, *four* offices, namely, the "first presidency," the "patriarch," the "high priest," and the "priest," found in the Church of the Saints, and urged as absolutely essential to the existence of the Church of Christ, are not to be found in the New Testament—the "guide"—as every intelligent Bible reader is perfectly aware.

I am somewhat at a loss to see how the advocates of the Mormon heresy can stand before an intelligent public and defend a system abounding in heretical dogma with any hope of success. Yet upon mature reflection it may not seem so strange after all. As a matter of fact, they do not present the intricacies of the system—they say nothing that would seem untenable to the investigator.

I am unable now to recall a single instance of any minister ever presenting this heresy to his audience. From force of habit, rather than from design, I am inclined to believe, the "first presidency," "patriarch," and "high priests" are kept well in the background, presenting only that for which a show of support may be found in the Bible, and thus avoid a defense of this clearly untenable doctrine.

"To the law and to the testimony." If the "law" here means the law of Christ as found in the New Testament, and if the "testimony" has reference to the testimony or the apostles of Christ, then we ask, where does the *law* speak of a "first presidency," or the *testimony* of the apostles declare for the "patriarch" and "high priest" in the Church of Christ? "Ah! echo answers, Where?"

DISTINGUISHING MARKS.

Let us make a careful application of Mr. Kelley's "money test" to the Mormon "coin or bill," and see whether it be genuine. Says Mr. Kelley:

"When every *mark* and *figure* on the coin or bill tendered in exchange *harmonizes with the detector*, it is pronounced good money. But if there is anything found on the coin or bill *not to be found in the detector*, or if there is something *left out of the coin* or bill, that *is found in the detector*, it is regarded as *spurious.*"

On the Mormon coin, as shown in the foregoing parallel lists, we have discovered *four* distinct and very important "figures" not found in the "detector," and *three* clearly defined "marks" which the "detector" requires, that are *not found on the coin*. Tried by Mr. Kelley's "test," the money is most certainly *spurious*. Mr. Kelley's position is absolutely unique—he places a bank-note detector in the hands of the president of the bank, and then deliberately proceeds to pass a counterfeit bill on the cashier.

Surely, "the counterfeiter is abroad in the land."

Tried by the infallible rule, tested by the touchstone of eternal truth, the organic structure of the Mormon Church is shown to be a failure and a fraud.

One thing only remains to be done—write in flaming letters the Belshazzaran inscription, "WEIGHED IN THE BALANCES, . . . AND FOUND WANTING," and nail it above the door of the Mormon superstructure, that he who runs may read.

CHAPTER XII.

FOUNDATION OF THE CHURCH.

Foundation of the church—Various opinions on Matt. 16: 18—Upon this rock—What rock?—Joseph Smith's view—Apostle Smith examined—Revelation the foundation of the Mormon Church—The writer's heresy—Christ the rock, the foundation.

"Upon this rock I will build my church, and the gates of hell shall not prevail against it." (Matt. 16: 18).

The Church of Christ, as a spiritual superstructure, must rest upon a solid, permanent foundation. The above text declares that the church was to be built upon a specific rock—"upon *this* rock I will build my church." What is this particular rock upon which the Savior declared he would build his church?

Upon this question three separate and distinct views are advanced, namely:

First. The church of Rome maintains that St. Peter was the "rock" upon which Christ declared he would build his church, because "Peter" means rock. "Thou art Peter—a rock—and upon this rock—Peter—I will build my church." Hence the dogma of Papal succession from St. Peter.

Second. Another class of theologians—the Latter Day Saints—take unique 'ground upon this question and affirm that "*revelation*" is the rock. They seem to derive this view from what Christ said to Peter, namely:

"Blessed art thou, Simon Bar-jona: for flesh and

blood hath not *revealed* it unto thee, but my Father which is in heaven." (V. 18.)

This revelation, they tell us, is the rock upon which Jesus declares he will build his church. But they have something much stronger than this upon which their faith is based,—a more recent revelation. Here is what "Joseph the prophet" says about it:

"Christ was baptized by John to fulfill all righteousness; and Jesus in his teachings says, 'Upon this rock I will build my church, and the gates of hell shall not prevail against it.' What rock? *Revelation*. . . . I know what I say. I understand my mission; . . . God Almighty is my shield." (Tullidge's History, pages 414, 415.)

On the preceding page the prophet assures us that this is no mere opinion, but that he speaks authoritatively, saying:

"Now I will give my testimony. I care not for man. I speak boldly and faithfully, *and with authority*."

In a volume to which I do not now have access—"The Times and Seasons," the official organ of the church, published at Nauvoo, Illinois, and in Vol. 5, if I mistake not—the statement is more authoritative and emphatic than the above quotation from Tullidge, and is as follows: "Verily, thus saith the Lord, it is revelation."

From the prophet the elders of every grade took their cue, and from the beginning until now they talk about being built upon the "rock, revelation," and few of them have the courage to preach anything else, for in so doing they would run up against a "thus saith the Lord" of Joseph Smith, and in the Mormon Church that has ever been a dangerous business.

Any man having the independence to question the correctness of an opinion backed by a "thus saith the Lord" of the prophet is considered on the high road to apostasy. The writer understands this from experience.

Some twenty years ago apostle T. W. Smith wrote a pamphlet which was published by the Reorganized Church at Plano, Illinois, entitled, "The One Body," in which he undertook to prove that the apostles are the *foundation* of the church, and that the "rock" Jesus referred to in his conversation with the apostles was "revelation." After quoting Eph. 2: 20, Mr. Smith says:

"It is here assumed by some that the church is to be built upon the *teachings* of apostles and prophets, and not that *apostles and prophets* are to always be present as the *foundation of the existing church*." (One Body, pages 6, 7.)

Promising to show the fallacy of the position which he creates, (for it is extremely doubtful if any scholar ever assumed such a position) Mr. Smith proceeds as follows:

"So the Church of Christ, including the foundation [apostles] and the corner-stone [Christ], is built upon a rock; but what is the rock? . . . Thou art Peter, and upon this rock I will build my church. . . . What rock? Peter? No; for Peter was one of the foundation stones, for he was an apostle, and could not be the rock on which the foundation is built. . . . Well, then, was it upon Christ? No; for he was the corner-stone, or head of the corner. Well, then, perhaps on the truth that Peter uttered. . . . Hardly; for while this is a cardinal principle in the Gospel, yet it is not the main one. . . .

What then? Blessed art thou, FOR, or because, it was not REVEALED by flesh and blood, but by the Father; that is to say, Peter received this knowledge of the character of Christ by divine revelation." (Ibid, page 7.)

We have permitted apostle Smith to tell his own story in his own way; and this is the position of the Reorganized Church in particular, and of Mormon churches in general.

Mr. Smith's whole argument is based upon an assumed premise, namely, that the apostles and prophets are *the foundation of the church.* Not a word in Eph. 2: 20 about apostles being the foundation. In the next place he assumes that Christ himself was built upon the rock, thus reducing the Alpha and Omega of the Christian Church to the common level of fallible man. Such a method of reasoning can hardly be dignified by the term argument.

In what follows we shall show the utter fallacy and groundlessness of apostle Smith's positions. Not only does he undertake to defend the pet theory of Mormonism, but he positively declares that Christ is not the rock upon which the church was built, and upon which it still must rest.

This set me to thinking, and I investigated the foundation question most thoroughly. I had not yet learned to doubt that "revelation" was the rock—the foundation,—but I felt sure that apostle Smith's view was fundamentally and radically wrong. The investigation showed me that not only was T. W. Smith wrong, but that the entire church was in error, and had ever been. At first I was appalled by the discovery.

I could no longer preach that "revelation" is the

rock when everything pointed to Christ as being the "sure foundation." But who was I that I should stand up against "the authority of the priesthood?" What right had I to question the uniform teachings of an "inspired ministry" and a "thus saith the Lord" of the prophet Joseph? What was I to do? I could no longer preach the heresy, however much it might be required of me, and to remain silent would be to convict me, in the court of my own conscience, of moral cowardice.

After much prayerful consideration and a fruitless struggle to render myself subservient to the "powers that be," the voice of conscience said to me, Be true to yourself, to your manhood, and to your own convictions of right. Stand by the truth if the heavens fall. This decided me. A burden was removed and my course was now clear.

President of the Southeastern Kansas District—which then, as now, included Southwestern Missouri—I was expected to preach the opening sermon of the conference. I did so, "Upon this rock I will build my church," serving as the text.

To the consternation and chagrin of most of the ministers present, I exposed both horns of the heresy, and established beyond controversy or reasonable doubt the fact that CHRIST was the rock—the *foundation* upon which his church was built, and that both "revelation" and "apostles and prophets" were excluded from the foundation of the Church of Christ, whatever might be the foundation of others.

I soon discovered that I had cast a stone into a hornets' nest, but I was fully assured that I had only cast a Gospel stone, and that others must follow, even if, in their fury at being disturbed, the hornets should sting me.

Through The Saints' Herald and from the pulpit the controversy went on for years, till the entire church was aroused to the importance of the question. In the meantime I had been taken to task by many of the leading men of the church, among whom were to be numbered President W. W. Blair, of the "First Presidency," and ex-apostle Charles Derry—but now only a high priest—who insisted that my views were heretical, and the source of dissension and discord in the church, but when asked for the proof of my heresy they were only able to refer me to the declaration of Joseph Smith already quoted.

Confident of the righteousness of my cause, and the ultimate triumph of truth over error, I resolved to force the issue to a final adjudication, and accordingly gave notice through The Saints' Herald, the official organ of the church, that on the third day of the ensuing General Conference (1880) I should formally call up the vexed question for final action. Meanwhile many converts had been made to the "new departure," and I stood not alone in the contest. At the appointed time the question was called up, and the preliminary struggle began. For some reason the conference did not seem willing to act upon it, and after consuming half the business session in an effort to have the question settled, further consideration was cut off by the prevalence of a motion to refer the matter to the "General Assembly," by which is meant an assembly of all the "Quorums" in the church, from the "First Presidency" down to the deacons. This "General Assembly" is the tribunal of last resort, and is convened only in cases of great importance. Although several cases have been referred to that august body, the "Assembly" has never been convened in the history of the Reorganized Church, and perhaps never will be.

There the question was left, and there it is likely to remain. Viewing this seeming defeat in the light of a decided victory, I have never ceased to declare that Jesus, the Christ, is the Rock and the Foundation of the Christian's hope.

If this position be the right one; if Christ is the Rock, then it follows, as night the day, that a church built upon any other foundation cannot be the Church of Christ.

The founder of Mormonism declares, as we have seen, that the "rock" upon which his church is based is "REVELATION." The Book of Mormon is declared by every class and shade of the Mormon priesthood to be the greatest revelation of the ages. Being the greatest, from the Mormon standpoint, and so directly connected with the birth of Mormonism, it may very justly be termed the foundation of the Mormon Church. Syllogistically presented, the proposition would stand thus:

Revelation is the foundation of the church.

The Book of Mormon is a revelation.

Therefore the Book of Mormon is the foundation of the church.

Perhaps the advocates of this revelation dogma may not be willing to frankly admit the Book of Mormon to be the particular revelation upon which their church is built, yet it is safe to say that no Latter Day Saint can be found who will not freely admit that only for Joseph Smith's revelation of the Book of Mormon no such organization as the "Church of

Jesus Christ of Latter Day Saints" would now be in existence.

Technicalities aside, there can be no question that the revelation of the Book of Mormon is the real and only foundation of the Church of the Saints.

I shall now undertake to show that CHRIST, and not revelation, is the "rock" of Matt. 16: 18; and, therefore the foundation of the Christian superstructure.

If in this effort we shall be successful, it will require no argument to prove that the Church of the Saints is on the wrong foundation, and hence cannot be the Church of Christ. In Mormon theology there are but two churches. One is the Church of Christ, and the other is "the church of the devil," quoth the Book of Mormon.

"Behold, there is, save it be, *two churches:* the one is the Church of the Lamb of God, and the other is the Church of the Devil; wherefore, whoso belongeth not to the Church of the Lamb of God, belongeth to that great church, which is the mother of abominations, and she is the whore of all the earth." (B. of M., page 33).

This narrows the issue down to a very simple proposition, namely, "*Mormonism against the world.*"

But we shall permit neither the Book of Mormon nor the arbitrary dictum of Joseph Smith to decide a question fraught with so much importance. We appeal to "the law and the testimony," which the Saints profess to so firmly believe, and to the arbitrament of whose testimony we are willing to submit the issue.

"Upon this rock I will build my church." Upon what rock? Peter, revelation, Christ, are each, in their turn, pronounced in answer to this important question. It is perfectly clear that somebody must be wrong. If *Peter* is the "rock," then the papal church is right, and all Protestants, including the Saints, are decidedly wrong.

If, as they claim, "*revelation*" is the rock, then all others, both Catholic and Protestant, are in error, and Latter Day Saints only are right. But if CHRIST is the "rock"—the "Rock of Ages"—then both Catholics and Mormons are grossly in error, and neither can be the Church of Christ.

I feel quite sure that even Latter Day Saints will admit the above to be a fair statement of the case. That Christ was the Divine Rock upon which were founded the hopes of a fallen race will clearly appear as we proceed.

By a careful examination of the preceding part of the chapter from which the text is quoted, it will be seen that Christ was himself the absorbing topic of the conversation leading up to this remarkable declaration. Jesus inquires of the disciples: "Whom do *men* say that I the Son of Man am?" (V. 13).

To this significant inquiry various answers were reported. Then addressing himself to the apostles, he says: "But whom say *ye* that I am?" (V. 15).

Peter, always ready with an answer, replies: "Thou art *the Christ*, the Son of the living God." (V. 16).

Thus it appears that Jesus had drawn from Peter the exact reply which he sought. As compared to the question of his Sonship—his messianic mission—everything else sank into insignificance. This theme was paramount, and to which every other is subordinate and of secondary consideration.

Incidentally other topics were injected into the principal question—such as "thou art Peter;" "flesh and blood hath not revealed it unto thee;" "I will build my church," etc., but the Christ was the absorbing theme, the underlying quantity, the fundamental quality—the Alpha and Omega of the entire discourse. With this primal fact in view, let us now read, omitting the interlocutory form, and we have substantially the following:

"Some men say I am John the Baptist; some, Elias; and others, Jeremias, but *you* say *I am the Christ*, and upon *this rock* I will build my church."

Relieved from interlocution and redundancy of speech, this, and nothing more, is doubtless just what Jesus wished to impress upon the minds of his apostles, and is exactly what they afterwards declare, and hence, must have been just what they understood at the time

It is, therefore, simply impossible that either "revelation," or apostles and prophets can form any part of the foundation of the Church of Christ. If, indeed, either Peter, or revelation, or apostles and prophets had been regarded as the foundation of the spiritual house, it is quite reasonable to conclude that some of the divine writers would have mentioned the fact. If neither is referred to as the "rock" or the "foundation," then it is fair to presume that no such thing was ever understood by them.

What, then, saith the Scriptures? "To the law and to the testimony, for if they speak not according to this word, it is because there is no light in them."

Jesus understood Ps. 118: 22 to apply to himself. (See Matt. 21: 42; Mark 12: 10; Luke 20: 17). He was "the *stone* which the builders refused," but who, nevertheless, " became the head stone of the corner."

Referring to the establishment of the spiritual Zion—the Church of Christ—the prophet Isaiah says:

"Therefore thus saith the Lord God, Behold, I lay in Zion for a foundation a *stone*, a tried stone, a precious corner-stone, a *sure foundation*." (Isa. 28:16).

There can be no mistake as to either the character of the stone or the purpose for which it was to be employed. This "precious stone," which the prophet declares was to be laid in Zion, while it should become a "rock of offense," and a "stone of stumbling," it should also become a "sure foundation" to such as should receive the truth.

If we shall be able to determine who or what this "foundation" was, we shall then have determined the meaning of the term "this rock," in Matt. 16:18; for the "rock," whatever that may be, was to be the foundation of the church. Concerning this matter Paul testifies as follows:

"For they [Israel] stumbled at that stumblingstone; as it is written, Behold, I lay in Zion a stumblingstone and rock of offense: and whosoever believeth in him shall not be ashamed." (Rom. 9:32, 33).

Comment seems useless. Concerning the same matter Peter says:

"As newborn babes, desire the sincere milk of the word, that ye may grow thereby: if so be ye have tasted that the Lord is gracious. To whom coming, as unto a living stone, disallowed indeed of men, but chosen of God, and precious, ye also, as lively stones, are built up a *spiritual house*, an holy priesthood, to offer up spiritual sacrifices, acceptable to God by Jesus Christ.

"Wherefore also it is contained in the Scripture, Behold, I lay in Zion a chief corner-stone, elect, precious; and he that believeth on *him* shall not be confounded. Unto you therefore which believe he is precious, but unto them which be disobedient, the *stone* which the builders disallowed, the same is made the head of the corner, and a stone of stumbling, and a *rock* of offense." (1 Pet. 2: 2-8).

Here we have Peter's direct reference to Ps. 118:22, and Isa. 28:16, as having their fulfillment in Christ, and in this view Peter and Paul are in perfect accord. Peter arrogates not to himself the honor of being the rock upon which the Lord was to build his church, nor is there the slightest intimation by either of the apostles that "revelation" was the rock.

That God revealed to the apostles the fact that Jesus was the Christ, there can be no doubt; but that such *revelation* was the rock upon which his church should rest, the evidence certainly does not show.

I regard it as a truth not to be questioned that nowhere in the Bible—from Genesis to Revelation—is there an instance where the word "rock" can be substituted by the word "revelation" without doing violence to the obvious meaning of the passage. But the noun "Christ" may be used as synonymous with the word rock without such results, as may be seen by the following examples:

"Upon this Christ I will build my church." "To whom coming as unto the living Christ." "They all drank of that spiritual Christ," etc.

So while the word rock does sometimes mean Christ, *it never means revelation.*

CHAPTER XIII.

THE SPIRITUAL HOUSE.

The spiritual house—Christ the chief corner-stone—In types—Pillar of fire—The smitten rock—The question settled—No other foundation but Christ—Book of Mormon and the rock—Joseph Smith *vs.* Joseph Smith—Witnesses in the balances—Summary.

As we have already learned, Peter declares that Jesus was the "precious stone" of Isaiah, laid in divine wisdom, as the sure foundation of the "spiritual house" which God should build; and we find Paul in delightful harmony with this sentiment, as may be seen by the following:

"Now therefore are ye no more foreigners and strangers, but fellow-citizens with the saints, and are built upon the foundation of the apostles and prophets, Jesus Christ himself being the chief corner-stone; in whom all *the building* fitly framed together groweth into an holy temple in the Lord." (*Eph. 2: 19-21.)

Here the church is called "the building." This building was to grow into "an holy temple," whose "builder and maker is God." As to the foundation upon which this building—this "spiritual house"—was to rest, much depends. Upon what foundation, think you, would such a structure be likely to rest? Upon Peter? No. Upon "revelation?" Hardly.

---

* This is the text quoted by Apostle Smith to prove that apostles were the foundation of the church, and that revelation is the rock upon which both Christ and the apostles are built.

Upon what, then, does it rest? Let the apostle answer. Concerning these recently-baptized converts at Ephesus who had now become "fellow-citizens with the saints," Paul says:

"You are of the household of God, and are built upon *the foundation of the apostles and prophets*, Jesus Christ being the chief corner-stone."

Here the "chief corner-stone" of Isaiah becomes the "foundation" of this great spiritual house— God's "building"—and we are assured that CHRIST, and not "revelation," is the basis upon which it securely rests. The foundation upon which the "household of God" were directed to rest their hopes was common to both the apostles of the Christian age and the prophets of the Mosaic dispensation.

It becomes important, then, that we shall understand just who or what was the "foundation of the apostles and prophets." With this determined, every thing else is made clear

The journey of the Israelites from Egypt to Palestine was characterized by some of the most stupendous miracles of the ages, to say nothing of those wrought for their deliverance. They were instructed not only by the types and shadows of the law, but by the types of the grandest miracles the world ever knew.

Fleeing from the wrath of Pharaoh and the bondage of Egypt, the armies of Israel were protected from the assaults of a deadly enemy by the presence of "a pillar of cloud" by day and "a pillar of fire" by night. Later, when in the wilderness of Sinai they were famishing of thirst, the miracle of the smitten rock saved a nation. These were among the most significant incidents in the history of ancient Israel. They both unmistakably point to Christ.

With his rod Moses smote the great rock, and out gushed fountains of living water, from which Israel quenched his burning thirst. The smitten rock, the flowing fountain, the quenched thirst and the saved lives were all most strikingly typical of Christ.

In the midst of a perishing world—perishing for the water of life—Jesus was smitten by the rod of Roman power. Smitten as the rock in the great desert, there gushed forth a "fountain" in whose lavatory famishing souls may bathe, and at which they may freely drink and "never thirst again"—*the water of life*.

This was the second exhibition of divine power pointing to the Rock Christ. When first they started from the land of bondage to the land of promised liberty, and the hosts of Israel were pursued by a relentless foe determined to return them to a slavery more terrible than death to a proud-hearted, liberty-loving people, they were saved by the timely interposition of divine power. The Lord stood between the armies of Israel and the advancing hosts of Pharaoh, in a "pillar of cloud" by day and a "pillar of fire" by night. Christ was their vanguard and their rearward. This "pillar" was their shade and protection through the day, and their *light* and guide through the shadows of the night.

With reference to this marvelous event Paul has this to say:

"Moreover, brethren, I would not that ye should be ignorant, how that all our fathers were under the cloud, and all passed through the sea; and were all baptized unto Moses in the cloud and in the sea; and did all eat the same spiritual meat; and did all drink the same spiritual drink: for they drank of that spiritual Rock that followed them: and that Rock was—Peter."

"Hold, sir! you have not quoted that correctly," someone exclaims. Possibly. Let us try again. " And that rock was—revelation."

"Hold on, there! that is not right—that is the Mormon idea."

Certainly it is, but you must remember the "Mormon idea" is the very thing we are after; and they say "revelation" is the rock, and *it must read that way* if their view is to be sustained.

In order to make sure of the right let us now read again.

"And they drank of that spiritual Rock that followed them, *and that Rock was* CHRIST." (1 Cor. 10: 1-4.)

That settles it. No Peter, no "revelation" here. Christ, the "spiritual Rock," was the "foundation" and only hope of the children of Israel in every time of trouble. Confirmatory of this, Moses afterwards said unto them:

"The Lord thy God will raise up unto thee a Prophet from the midst of thee, of thy brethren, like unto me; unto him ye shall hearken." (Deut. 18: 15; See Acts 3: 22.)

Here again the great law-giver of Israel pointed them to *Christ* as being the Rock of their salvation.

Not only, then, was Jesus regarded as being the "foundation" of the prophets, of whom Moses was chief, but also of the entire kingdom of ancient Israel. Upon him depended their hopes of future happiness and perpetual peace.

He was likewise the Rock upon which spiritual Israel—the church—including the apostles and prophets, founded their hopes of eternal life. This fact is rendered indisputable from the following:

"For we are laborers together with God; ye are God's husbandry, *ye are God's* building."

If these Corinthians were God's building—God's house—it is pertinent to inquire, Upon what foundation were they built? That there may be no misunderstanding, no quibbling as to the conclusion, we shall let the apostle himself answer. He continues:

"According to the grace of God which is given unto me as a wise masterbuilder I have laid the *foundation*, and another buildeth thereon. But let every man take heed how he buildeth thereon. For other foundation can no man lay than that is laid, *which is Jesus Christ.*" (1 Cor. 3: 9-11.)

Is further evidence necessary? Can you reasonably demand any additional proof that Jesus, the Christ, is the Rock—*the foundation*—upon which the church of God is built?

Here we have the express declaration of a witness whom Latter Day Saints will not dare attempt to controvert, that Christ is not only the Rock, but that he is also the *foundation* upon which "God's building" was based, and against which the "gates of hell" should not prevail. Not only so, but, in order to preclude the least shadow of doubt, he declares in the most positive terms that, "*Other foundation can no man lay* [not even Joseph Smith] *than that is laid, which is Jesus Christ.*"

How are the Saints to defend Joseph Smith's inspired (?) dictum that "revelation" is the rock—the foundation—with such a declaration as this staring them in the face at every turn? They simply can not do it. They are unable to appeal to Joseph's

"Inspired Translation," for it is a word-for-word reproduction, of every passage quoted, from the King James translation. Neither dare they invoke the aid of the Book of Mormon, for that clearly contradicts the prophet Joseph's "thus saith the Lord" on the subject. Helaman, one of the chief judges of the people of Nephi, just before his death thus instructs his two sons:

"And now, my sons, remember, remember, that it is upon the *rock of our Redeemer*, which is *Christ*, the Son of God, that ye must build your foundation, that when the devil shall send forth his mighty winds, yea, his shafts in the whirlwind; yea, when all his hail and mighty storm shall beat upon you, it shall have no power over you to drag you down to the gulf of misery and endless woe, because of the ROCK *upon which ye are built*, which is a SURE FOUNDATION." (See Helaman 2: 12, Book of Mormon, page 418, Palmyra edition.)

Defenders of the "revelation" dogma cannot dodge this issue. The evidence is all against them and they must yield. As may be seen by the above, the Book of Mormon declares in language not to be misunderstood that the "rock" upon which the sons of Helaman were built—and Nephi was then its chief minister—was Christ, and that he was also the "sure foundation." The *rock*, then, was the *foundation*, and the foundation was *Christ*.

In this controversy we have the Book of Mormon, the Inspired Translation, and we may include the book of "Doctrine and Covenants," all to stand arrayed against the pet theory of the Saints concerning the "rock revelation," and present the troublesome and iconoclastic spectacle of

JOSEPH SMITH, THE PROPHET,
vs.
JOSEPH SMITH, THE PROPHET.

Briefly summing up the testimony of the witnesses, the evidence in the case stands thus:

FOR THE ROCK CHRIST.	FOR THE ROCK REVELATION.
Witnesses.	Witnesses.
1. The Bible.	1. Joseph Smith.
2. The Inspired Translation.	
3. Book of Mormon.	
4. Doctrine and Covenants.	

It may readily be seen that our Latter Day Saint friends have the long end of the teeter-board, which may be the funny end, but it is also the dangerous one. My good brother Mormon, how do you like the long end of the plank? Does the altitude make you dizzy? Don't you have some misgivings about ever being able to set your foot on solid earth again?

Come down from your giddy perch, even if, catlike, you have to climb backwards down the plank. Indulge no longer in theories of speculative theology. Never stop until you feel the solid earth beneath your feet, then dig down through all the superficial rubbish of modern revelation, and build your house upon the solid Rock, CHRIST. Built upon this Rock, the winds may blow and the storm beat upon your house, but it cannot fall, "for it is founded upon a rock"—the Rock of eternal ages.

Thus it seems to me that he who runs may see that the Mormon house is built upon the wrong foundation—a foundation alike unauthorized, unstable and extremely dangerous; a building receiving not the sanction of the "wise masterbuilders" of former times.

Finally: A church built upon the wrong foundation is not the Church of Christ.

The Mormon Church is built upon a wrong foundation.

Therefore, the Mormon Church *is not the Church of Christ.*

CHAPTER XIV.

PRIESTHOOD AND PREACHERS.

Priesthood and preachers—Ministers must be called by revelation—Joseph was like Moses—Joseph and Oliver ordained to the Aaronic priesthood by an angel—Ordained by Peter, James and John to the Melchizedek priesthood—Questioned by President Smith of the Reorganized Church—His view criticised—How priesthood is conferred—Angels do not officiate at ordinations—Who ordained Moses, Melchizedek, or Christ?—Christ the only Melchizedek priest.

"No MAN taketh this honour unto himself but he that is called of God as was Aaron." (Heb. 5: 4).

Strangely enough, all Latter Day Saints, it matters not to which of the various factions of the Mormon Church they may belong, quote the above text to prove that all ministers of the Church of Christ, and especially those called to the higher "offices *in* the priesthood," must be called by "revelation" *as was Aaron*.

As ministers of other churches make no such claim they are, without exception, denounced by the Saints as "false teachers," having a *form* of godliness, but "denying the power thereof." In other words, all ministers not called by a direct revelation from God through a prophet "like unto Moses," are utterly and absolutely without authority to minister in divine things.

Joseph was "like unto Moses," and could, therefore, call as many Aarons into the field as he choose. Revelations were in demand, and the prophet manufactured them by the gross. The fact is, these revelation-made Latter Day priests bear no more resemblance to Aaron, either in duty or dignity, than does their prophet to the great law-giver of ancient Israel. Every thread in the Mormon fabric, both in warp and woof, upon close inspection is found to be the merest shoddy.

The manner in which "the priesthood" was "conferred" upon Joseph and Oliver is enough to condemn the entire system, and brand it as a fraud. As already shown, an angel, John the Baptist (!) came down from heaven, and laying his hands upon them ordained them to the ministry:

"Upon you, my fellow-servants, in the name of Messiah, I confer upon you the priesthood of Aaron." (Smith's History, Vol. 1, page 34; also Tullidge's History, page 43).

PETER, JAMES AND JOHN—DID THEY ORDAIN JOSEPH AND OLIVER?

The messenger—John the Baptist—promised them that they should, in the near future, be ordained to the Melchizedek priesthood, without which they could not confirm the church by the laying on of hands. Accordingly, Peter, James and John—once apostles, but now angels, or "ministering spirits"—in due time appeared and ordained them to the higher, or Melchizedek priesthood, with which Mormon theology invests them.

This ordination was performed by the laying on of hands; at least this is the tradition in the church, as it has been handed down from the earliest days of Mormonism, and as it has ever been taught by the leading men among the Saints. As John the Baptist ordained Joseph and Oliver to the Aaronic priesthood, so Peter, James and John ordained them to the Melchizedek priesthood. For the first time in the history of the denomination this is now called in question by President Joseph Smith of the Reorganized Church. President Smith enters into a somewhat elaborate argument to show that said ordination should be regarded in the light of an "appointment," and the actual and *only* ordination ever performed by the laying on of hands was when Joseph and Oliver ordained each other, at the time the church was organized. Concerning this matter President Smith says:

"Some have concluded from the language found in Doctrine and Covenant, 26: 3, . . . that Peter, James and John literally laid their own hands on the heads of Joseph and Oliver. But this command was to the effect that they should ordain each other." (Smith's History, vol. 1, page 63).

Mr. Smith continues:

"Some have supposed that they received two ordinations; one under the hands of Peter, James and John, and one by each other; but . . . there is no historical evidence of such an event." (Ibid, page 64).

The historian continues his argument to show that no such ordination ever occurred, and urges that, "The words of the revelation, 'by whom I have ordained you,' do not furnish the proof." (Page 65).

The above declaration is based upon the assumption, that, if the ordination ever occurred it must have been at the time "when the instruction was given to ordain or when the ordination actually took place." (Page 65).

This by no means follows. It is not claimed, neither is it pertinent to the issue, that they should be ordained by the angel and by each other at the same time and at the same place. President Smith does not even question the fact that Joseph and Oliver "received two ordinations" to the Aaronic priesthood, one by the angel, and "one by each other;" and yet the ordinations took place *at two different times* and *places*. They were ordained by the angel while at prayer *in the woods*, and were then commanded to baptize each other.

"Accordingly," says Joseph, "we *went* and were baptized, . . . after which I laid my hands upon his head and ordained him to the Aaronic priesthood; afterwards he laid his hands on me and ordained me to the same priesthood—for so we were commanded." (Tullidge's History, page 43).

If the ordinations in this case were not simultaneous, why does President Smith insist that the "two ordinations" to the Melchizedek priesthood should be at the same time?

The "ordination" under the hands of Peter, James and John is understood to have occurred "in the wilderness, . . . on the Susquehanna River" (see Smith's History, page 65), while the ordination by each other occurred at the residence of "old Father Whitmer, in Fayette, Seneca Co., N. Y." (Ibid, page 65).

While President Smith assures us that "there is no historical evidence of such an event," yet on the same page with this declaration, we find the following:

"In regard to this event Oliver Cowdery is reported

by George Reynolds [a Mormon writer] in his 'Mith of the Manuscript Found,' page 80, . . . as saying: 'I was also present with Joseph when the higher or Melchizedek priesthood was conferred by the holy angel from on high. This priesthood was then conferred on each other by the will and commandment of God." (Ibid, page 64.)

Here we have *two ordinations*, one by an "angel from on high," the other by each other. How were these ordinations performed? Oliver says the Melchizedek priesthood was "conferred" first by the angel, then by each other. In Mormon parlance and practice, how is priesthood conferred? *By the laying on of hands*, and NEVER in any other way.

"Upon you, my fellow-servants, I *confer* the priesthood of Aaron," and Joseph says the angel had his hands upon their heads *at the time*. This being the manner, and the *only* manner, of conferring priesthood, then it follows as a logical necessity that when angels confer priesthood it is in *exactly* the same manner that men confer it, namely, *by the laying on of hands*. There is no possible means of escape from this conclusion.

The revelation to which President Smith refers us, 26: 3, declares that Peter, James and John were sent to Joseph and Oliver, and by whom they were ordained. Joseph said these three apostle-angels came to them, and that he heard their voices "in the wilderness on the Susquehanna River," in Pennsylvania; and Oliver declares the Melchizedek priesthood was *conferred*, and presumably at this meeting, as it is the only reference to a visit from Peter, James and John. The revelation in question reads thus:

"And also with Peter, and James, and John, whom

I have sent unto you, by whom I have ordained you and confirmed you," etc. (D. and C. 26: 3, page 113).

The point raised by President Smith is that which relates to the meaning of the word "ordain." He quotes Webster to show that to ordain does not necessarily mean to set apart a man to an office by the laying on of hands. This is undoubtedly correct; but the question is, Does the word as it is used in this revelation mean to ordain by the laying on of hands? or does it merely mean to appoint, to set in order, to regulate, etc.?

If the words " by whom I have ordained you " mean only to adjust, regulate, set in order, etc., having no reference to the imposition of hands, it must mean the same thing when it relates to John the Baptist. In the same revelation, at paragraph 2 (page 112) we find this language:

" Which John I have sent unto you, my servants, Joseph Smith, Jr. and Oliver Cowdery, *to ordain you* unto this first priesthood which you have received, that ye might be ordained even as Aaron."

As the language is exactly similar, John was sent to *ordain* them to the Aaronic priesthood, while Peter, James and John were sent to ordain them to the Melchizedek priesthood. If in the one case ordination is shown to have been performed by the laying on of hands, it will prove that the other must have been done in the same way. If to ordain here means simply and only to appoint, set in order, etc., then John the Baptist only *appointed* Joseph and Oliver to set things in order. In this case neither was ordained to the Aaronic priesthood by the laying on of hands, which would be to flatly contradict both Joseph and Oliver upon this point, and this will never do.

Concerning this ordination President Smith says:

"Friday, May 15, . . . the Aaronic priesthood was conferred upon them through the instrumentality of John the Baptist." (Smith's History, Vol. 1, page 34.)

He then quotes Joseph as saying that John the Baptist, "*having laid his hands upon us, he ordained us.*"

Here we have the fact established by the very *best* Mormon authority that to *confer* the priesthood is to *ordain* by the laying on of hands. Hence, when Peter, James and John "conferred" the Melchizedek priesthood upon Joseph and Oliver, they did so by the laying on of hands.

Briefly stated, the matter stands thus: If John the Baptist ordained Joseph Smith and Oliver Cowdery to the Aaronic priesthood by the laying on of hands, then Peter, James and John must have ordained them to the Melchizedek priesthood in precisely the same manner.

If Joseph and Oliver were not so ordained, then neither of them possessed the Melchizedek priesthood, and could not confer it upon each other, for the very palpable reason that they could not give or "confer" what they did not possess; and hence if they were not thus *ordained* by Peter, James and John, then the Melchizedek priesthood has never been restored, and the *entire Mormon Church is absolutely without* authority. This is the inevitable result of President Smith's logic.

And it is thus rendered reasonably clear that both Joseph and Oliver were not only favored with numerous visits by heavenly messengers, but that they were actually ordained to the Gospel ministry by the incomparable touch of angelic hands. O, for the depravity of fallen human nature and the depravity of the human heart! What presumption! What an unmitigated and heaven-daring fraud! What an unholy farce! How dare these men make such preposterous and unprecedented claims?

Where do we read of angels ordaining men to office by the laying on of hands? What angel ordained Melchizedek, the great high priest, to whom even Abraham, the friend of God, paid tithes?

What messenger left the courts of eternal glory, and wending his way to earth laid his hands upon Moses, the great law-giver of Israel, and ordained him to the priesthood of Melchizedek?

What angel left the shining courts of the Eternal, and, descending to earth on lightning wing, laid his hands upon the Lord, the "King of glory," to ordain him a priest after the order of Melchizedek? No patriarch, no prophet or sage, not even the Lord himself, ever felt the touch of angelic hands in ordination, and yet this daring pretender, this unblushing impostor, comes to an intelligent public with the incredible and unsupported story that God sent an angel to earth and ordained him and his accomplice, Oliver Cowdery, to be priests of the most high God!

In the very nature of things such an event is simply impossible. There has been but one priest after the order of Melchizedek, and he was not such by the laying on of hands of either angels or men; and I challenge the scholarship of the entire Mormon Church to give an instance of "conferring" the Melchizedek priest-hood upon either Christ or his apostles by the laying on of hands, or by any other means.

Let the advocates of this heretical dogma step to

the front and defend their position if they are intelligently honest in what they profess to believe; and we shall not limit them to the Bible for proof, as we might very properly do, but they may have access to the Book of Mormon, also, which, as the Saints claim, contains the "*fullness* of the Gospel."

Nowhere, and I speak advisedly, does the Book of Mormon hint, even remotely, that there were "two priesthoods" in the church among the Nephites, and the term "Melchizedek Priesthood" *is nowhere to be found in the book*. The only reference to Melchizedek is in Alma, tenth chapter, page 260, where the name occurs five times, but "the Melchizedek Priesthood," and "the Aaronic Priesthood," are terms nowhere to be found in the book.

Melchizedek is referred to as having "received the office of the High Priesthood," but there is not the slightest intimation that such office was "conferred" by the laying on of hands.

It is likewise true that the Book of Mormon contains no account of the ordination of the Nephite "twelve disciples" by the laying on of hands, either by Christ when he chose them, or by anybody else afterwards. The only record of the event says that he simply "Touched with his hand the disciples whom he had chosen, one by one, even till he had *touched them all*, and spake unto them as he touched them." (Book of Mormon, Nephi, chapter 10, page 493).

Thus it appears that the revelation which contains the *fullness* of the everlasting Gospel, is as silent as an Egyptian tomb on a question of paramount importance with the Saints, namely, ordination to the apostleship by the laying on of hands.

MELCHIZEDEK PRIESTS.

I have said that there has been but *one* Melchizedek Priest since the time of Salem's great king-priest, and that was Christ. I have likewise declared that it is simply impossible that Joseph Smith and Oliver Cowdery could have been Melchizedek priests, and I will state my reasons for this belief.

First. The Bible contains no allusion to the fact that Moses, or any other prophet, priest or king of Bible times was ever ordained a priest after the order of Melchizedek. If it were a common practice, as Mr. Kelley would have us believe, why was such prominence given to the fact that Christ was such an high priest? If Melchizedek high priests had come down in a regular line of descent from Moses to Christ, as Mr. Kelley tries to prove, and as Joseph's great "revelation on Priesthood" affirms, why should Paul lay such stress upon this particular fact in the case of Christ? Why should it be regarded as a significant and very important fact that Christ was a "priest forever after the order of Melchizedek?" (See Heb. 7: 1-16).

Second. The apostles of Christ were not—indeed they could not be—priests in any proper sense of that word, much less Melchizedek priests. The reasons which would preclude the apostles would also bar out Joseph Smith, or any other man.

Two things are especially necessary in order to constitute a Melchizedek priest:

First. The individual *must be a king*.

Second. Being a king, *he may become a priest*.

Hence, a priest of the Melchizedek order is at once a king and a priest—a king-priest.

For proof of this read:

"For this Melchizedek, *king of Salem*, priest of the most high God, who met Abraham returning from the slaughter of the kings, and blessed him; to whom also Abraham gave a tenth part of all; first being by interpretation *King of righteousness*, and after that also *king of Salem*, which is *King of peace.*" (Heb. 7: 1, 2).

Of no other earthly king in Biblical history can as much be said. All kings, whether of Israel or of the Gentile nations, were "men of war." But here, amid the tumult of war and strife—a strife for mastery and dominion—we have a King, the ruler of a single city, who is dominated, by way of unique distinction from all others, the "King of righteousness," the "King of peace," and his city was the city of peace, or Salem.

The patriarchal and prophetic ages abounded in incidents which clearly foreshadowed Christ, and of which this is perhaps the most striking. In every minute particular he conformed to his great antetype, Melchizedek.

Melchizedek was a king of righteousness, and so was Christ, and Jesus was in the pre-eminent sense of that term, the Prince of life—THE KING OF PEACE. Ordained of God, he gave himself as the great and last sacrificial offering under the law, for the redemption and salvation of the race. He was proclaimed by angelic voices to be Heaven's great King. He was and is King of kings and Lord of lords.

Hence, Paul's declaration that he was made "a priest *forever* after the order of Melchizedek."

When Latter Day Saints shall give us *proof*, not assertion, bare and unsupported, that any other Melchizedek priest was ever ordained, either under the law or under the Gospel, then, and not till then, will thinking people regard it as being necessary to examine the claims of modern apostles and prophets to such an honor. Give us *facts*, gentlemen, and let your fine-spun theories rest.

Were the apostles of Christ, or any other class of ministers of his church, ever referred to, or in any proper sense of that word regarded as kings? If so, then it was possible for them to become priests of the Melchizedek order; otherwise never. Not even a Mormon apostle will dare assume that the apostles were kings except in the sense that *all* God's people are, or may be, "kings and priests unto God."

If they were not kings in the proper sense of that word, they were not Melchizedek priests, and if they were not, and, indeed, could not become priests after the Melchizedek order on that account, then it is simply impossible that Joseph Smith and Oliver Cowdery could have been such priests, all their pretended visions and revelations to the contrary notwithstanding; and if they were not "ordained to the Melchizedek priesthood," then they were deceivers, and Mormonism is a fraud.

CHAPTER XV.

PRIESTHOOD—WHAT IS IT?

Priesthood—What is it?—Webster *vs.* Kelley—Mormon definition erroneous—Joseph's revelation on priesthood—Handed down from father to son—Isaiah lived in the days of Abraham—Moses ordained by his father-in-law, Jethro—Abraham ordained by Melchizedek—A table of dates and ordinations—Gad ordained Jeremy 1120 years before the prophet was born.

With Latter Day Saints of every class and name everything ecclesiastical depends upon the "priesthood." It is the touch-stone of all Mormon philosophy. Absolutely nothing can be accomplished without it. "No man can see God and live," quoth the prophet Joseph, without this priesthood.

The definition of this word as authorized by our standards is altogether too limited for a Mormon writer or speaker. If for any reason he has occasion to appeal to a dictionary, he usually appends his own definition, as in the following from Mr. Kelley:

"Priesthood—What is it? Webster defines it to be,

"'1. The office or character of a priest.'

"'2. The order of men set apart for sacred offices.'

"More fully defined, priesthood on earth [just as if there can be human priests in heaven] is the authority and *order of God committed to men*, by which they are duly empowered and commissioned to preach the Gospel and administer the ordinances thereof, namely, administer the Lord's Supper, ordain, and perform any and all other duties required in the administration of the government of his church and kingdom among men." (Presidency and Priesthood, page 1).

It is really too bad that Noah Webster could not have been permitted to live contemporaneously with this linguistic luminary, for had he been so fortunate, had the wisdom of the gods of fortune so ordained, he would no doubt have been able "more fully" and correctly to define this magical word "priesthood." Lexicographers of the present and future, however, will doubtless avail themselves of the opportunity which this apostolic flash affords, and under the light of its beneficent rays correct Mr. Webster's blunder.

Anybody can see that Mr. Kelley's definition does not define. It merely defines the duties of a priest as he understands them.

The Saints talk of "priesthood" as a thing to be carried about in your vest pocket, or donned or laid aside as a Sunday suit. You may "hold" a priesthood as a jug holds water, or as Douglass held Lincoln's hat.

The individual Mormon preacher does not belong to the priesthood—to that "order of men set apart for sacred offices"—but the priesthood belongs to him; it has been "conferred" upon him, having "received" it under the hand of Elder Jones or Apostle Smith.

To illustrate their manner of using the word, permit me to quote a few passages from Mr. Kelley's Presidency and Priesthood:

"The organization [of the church] took form in the offices of the priesthood." (Preface, page 8.)

"God has *committed* the priesthood as a means of authorizing men to minister." (Page 3.)

"The inspired records clearly reveal and provide

for the existence of *two priesthoods*." (Page 3.)

But Mr. Kelley fails to cite his readers to a single passage where this revelation is so *clearly* made, and he cannot do so for the reason that the inspired records make no such revelation. Instead of having two *orders* or grades of priesthood, the Saints have *two priesthoods*.

"These two priesthoods were *conferred upon men*, . . . as a means of authorizing them to administer acceptably in the government of God." (Page 4.)

"The Gospel is administered by the authority of the Melchizedek priesthood." (Page 5.)

But Mr. Kelley does not inform us where he finds authority for this remarkable statement.

"The priesthood was not limited to a given time and then to cease. . . . It was *transmitted* from Abel to Noah." (Page 6.)

"Melchizedek *held* the high priesthood at this time and *received it from his* predecessors." (Page 6.)

"Moses' father-in-law seems to have *held* the *true* priesthood." (Ibid.)

You may be curious to know where Mr. Kelley gets all these odd notions about priesthood. I will try to enlighten you. None of these ideas are original with Mr. Kelley. From an acquaintance of nearly thirty-five years with that gentleman, I regard him as a man of too much good sense to ever have entertained such absurd notions had he not, like myself, been taught them from his infancy. They originated in the fertile brain of Joseph Smith, with many others of like character, as may be seen by the following:

"REVELATION ON PRIESTHOOD."

"A revelation of Jesus Christ unto Joseph Smith,

Jr., and six elders. . . . And the sons of Moses, according to the holy priesthood which he *received under the hand of his father-in-law, Jethro;* and Jethro received it under the hand of Caleb; and Caleb received it under the hand of Elihu; and Elihu received it under the hand of Jeremy; and Jeremy received it under the hand of Gad; and Gad received it under the hand of Esaias; and Esaias received it *under the hand of God.* Esaias also lived in the days of Abraham and was blessed of him—which Abraham received the priesthood from Melchizedek, who received it through the *lineage of his fathers,* even till Noah; and from Noah till Enoch through the lineage of their fathers; and from Enoch to Abel, who was slain by the conspiracy of his brother, who received the priesthood by the commandment of God, by the hand of his father Adam, who was the first man—*which priesthood continueth in the church of God in all generations,* and is without beginning of days or end of years." (Doc. and Cov., pages 223, 224.)

This is a brief history of the Melchizedek priesthood as it came down from the days of Adam. The revelation then continues:

"And the Lord confirmed a priesthood also upon Aaron and his seed, throughout all their generations —which priesthood also continueth and abideth *forever* with the priesthood, which is after the holiest order of God: and this greater priesthood administereth the Gospel and holdeth the key of the mysteries of the kingdom, even the key of the knowledge of God; therefore, in the *ordinances thereof,* the power of godliness is manifest; and without the ordinances thereof, and the authority of the priesthood, the power of godliness is not manifest unto men in the flesh; for without this *no man can see the face of God*, even the Father, and live." (See Doc. and Cov., sec. 83, par. 3).

I wish now to call especial attention to a few points contained in the above. I have italicized in the quotation to avoid repetition.

First. If Moses received the Melchizedek priesthood under the hand of his father-in-law, Jethro, it is one of the remarkable things in history that no mention is made of the fact by any of the divine writers. That an event of so much vital importance should be passed over without mention is altogether incredible, and cannot be true.

Perhaps one of the most remarkable things about this "revelation on priesthood," is found in the fact that Esaias—or Isaiah—is made the contemporary of Abraham, who received the priesthood under the hand of Melchizedek. Yet Esaias was, by some unaccountable means, placed under the necessity of receiving it "under the hand of God." Why did not Esaias receive the priesthood under the hand of Abraham at the time he was "blessed of him?" or, what would have been still better, perhaps, under the hand of Melchizedek himself? Why should God leave his throne in heaven, come to earth and ordain Esaias by the laying on of hands, when two such great priests as Melchizedek and Abraham were accessible to him?

The idea is simply preposterous, and is but another exhibition of the wonderful power of imagination—the creative faculty—with which this remarkable man was so liberally endowed.

While Abraham lived B. C. 1913, Isaiah, or Esaias, did not appear upon the stage of action till 1153 years later, in the year B. C. 760. Joseph certainly neglected to consult his chronological tables while receiving this revelation.

But it may be urged that the Esaias referred to was not Isaiah the prophet, but another man of the same name, who lived in the days of Abraham. Well, if we admit the possibility of this explanation, which is highly improbable, as no other Esaias is mentioned in Scripture history except the prophet, even then the so-called revelation is proved to be a fabrication from the following considerations, namely:

1. While it is possible that Jethro might have been ordained under the hand of Caleb—both being contemporary with Moses—it is simply impossible that the latter could have been ordained by Elihu, as may be seen by a glance at the following table; and the same is true of all the persons named:

NAME.	WHEN LIVING, B. C.	DIFFERENCE IN TIME.	SCRIPTURAL REFERENCE.
1.			
Caleb.	1452.		Num 26:65.
Elihu.	1171.	281.	1 Sam. 1:1.
2.			
Elihu.	1171.		
Jeremy.	629.	442.	Jer. 31:15; Mat. 2:17.
3.			
Jeremy.	629.	1120.	
Gad.	1749.		Gen. 30:11.
4.			
Gad.	1749.		
Esaias.	760.	989.	Isa. 1:1; Acts 8:28.

Thus it appears that Elihu ordained Caleb 281 years before he was born; or, to reverse the conditions, Caleb had been dead 281 years when he was ordained by Elihu.

2. Elija had been dead 542 years when he was ordained by Jeremy.

3. Here we have Gad to have ordained Jeremy

1120 years before the prophet was born; and finally,

4. Esaias is represented to have ordained Gad to the "Melchizedek priesthood," 989 years after the latter's death.

I certainly see no means by which Latter Day Saints can extricate themselves from the embarrassing predicament in which these figures place them. But the most absurd thing about the whole affair, and which stamps fraud upon the very face of the pretended revelation, is found in the representation that God vacated his throne in heaven, descend to earth, laid his hand upon Esaias and ordained him to the office of a priest after the order of Melchizedek.

We might extend the list of Mormon absurdities relative to this question of priesthood, but enough has been said to show that the prophet gave free rein to his wildest fancies, and that his "revelations" are the merest vagaries of the human mind, and wholly unreliable as a means of obtaining either light or truth.

"Called of God as was Aaron," indeed! In the first place, the passage quoted has reference only to priests under the law, and does not, therefore, apply to the calling of Gospel ministers. Besides this, Aaronic priests, after the *first* revelation calling Aaron, and establishing the *rule* by which all subsequent priests were to be chosen, *were never called by revelation*. The law provided that the sons of Levi should, from that time, be set apart—consecrated to this service. No revelation after that was necessary to set apart an Aaronic priest.

The same rule applied to the calling of ministers of the Gospel obviates the necessity for any modern revelation in order to their acceptance with God.

CHAPTER XVI.

APOSTLES, THEN AND NOW—HOW CALLED?

Apostles, then and now—How called?—What is an apostle?—Called by Jesus personally—Not ordained by the laying on of hands—How were the apostles qualified?—Endued with power from on high—Mormon apostles—How called?—Chosen by Oliver Cowdery, David Whitmer and Martin Harris—Names of the twelve apostles.

WHAT is an apostle? Webster defines the word thus:

"A person deputied to execute some important business, but *appropriately* a disciple of Christ commissioned to preach the Gospel."

The twelve whom Christ ordained were persons "deputied to execute some important business," and that "important business" was to preach the Gospel and permanently establish the Church of Christ. They were in fact Christ's ambassadors.

Latter Day Saints claim not only that apostles must be in the church to-day *because they were then*, but they make the further claim that such apostles must be called to-day *exactly* as they were in the apostolic age.

If we are to have apostles in the church now, I freely admit, nay, urge, that they must be *called and qualified* exactly in the same manner as were the first apostles.

Any persons claiming to be apostles who are not so called and qualified cannot be apostles of Christ, and should be rejected as impostors. This leads us to inquire,

HOW WERE THE APOSTLES OF CHRIST CHOSEN?

To Bible readers I hardly need say the call was personal and direct. To Peter and Andrew, James and John, he simply said, "Follow me, and I will make you fishers of men." (Matt. 4: 18-22).

To Matthew, whom Jesus saw while "sitting at the receipt of customs, he said, Follow me. And he arose and followed him." (Matt. 9: 9).

John extends the list to include Philip and Nathanael, to whom, as on other occasions, Jesus said, "Follow me." (John 1: 43-46).

This is the unostentatious manner in which Jesus called his apostles. No formal ceremony of any kind. They were not even consecrated by the laying on of hands. From this we may very reasonably infer that apostles were not made, and indeed cannot be made, by the laying on of hands. Nay, I go further than this and declare that there is not an instance on record in the New Testament where any man ever laid his hands on another and ordained him to the office of an apostle. "Well," says the objector, "were not the twelve *ordained* by Jesus? Does he not say, 'I have chosen you and *ordained* you?'" (See John 15: 16).

Jesus certainly both chose and *ordained* his twelve disciples; but there is not the slightest hint that they were ordained by the laying on of hands. "ORDAIN: To appoint; to decree; to set; to establish; to institute; to set apart for an office."—*Webster.*

Thus it may be seen that the word "ordain" does not necessarily imply a consecration by the laying on of hands.

In a recently published Church History, written by President Joseph Smith and Apostle Heman C. Smith of the Reorganized Church, we find an elaborate argument to prove that Peter, James and John did not ordain Joseph Smith to the Melchizedek priesthood by the laying on of hands, a claim perhaps never before questioned by any Mormon writer.

After quoting Webster, the following comments are offered:

"Hence Peter, James and John could have been ordained by holding and exercising the power to direct, set in order, arrange, regulate, establish, appoint, decree, enact or institute, etc. In the absence of any evidence that Peter, James and John ordained in the sense of Webster's fourth definition [that is, "by the laying on of hands"] we are not justified as historians in saying that Joseph and Oliver were so ordained." (Smith's Church History, page 65.)

Neither the authority cited nor the argument of the above can be successfully questioned. Let us, therefore, apply the rule to the case in hand. We have said that Jesus did not ordain his apostles by the laying on of hands, and insist that the meaning of the word does not necessarily imply such an act. Hence Jesus could have ordained his disciples by exercising the power to "direct, set in order, arrange, regulate, establish, appoint, decree, enact or institute;" and "in the absence of any evidence" that Jesus did ordain "according to Webster's fourth definition we are not justified in saying" that the apostles were so ordained. That they were so ordained we most emphatically deny, and challenge the proof.

This brings us to consider,

HOW WERE THE APOSTLES QUALIFIED?

The story is brief and is thus related by the witnesses:

"And behold, I send the promise of my Father upon you: But tarry ye in the city of Jerusalem, until ye be endued with power from on high." (Luke 24:49.)

"Ye shall be baptized with the Holy Ghost not many days hence." (Acts 1:5.)

"And when the day of Pentecost was fully come, they were all with one accord in one place. And suddenly there came a sound from heaven as of a rushing mighty wind, and it filled the whole house where they were sitting. And there appeared unto them cloven tongues like as of fire, and it sat upon each of them. And they were all filled with the Holy Spirit, and began to speak with other tongues, as the Spirit gave them utterance." (Acts 2: 1-4.)

Who were present at this wonderful enduement meeting?

"Now when this was noised abroad, the *multitude* came together, and were confounded, because that every man heard them speak in his own language." (Verse 6. See also verses 7-11.)

What was the result of this marvelous exhibition of divine power?

"Then they that gladly received his word were baptized: and *the same day* there were added unto them about *three thousand souls*." (Acts 2: 41.)

These disciples were now qualified to "go into all the world and preach the Gospel to every creature," it mattered not what his nationality or what his tongue.

Bearing in mind the fact that, if apostles exist in this age, they must be *called* and *qualified exactly* as they were anciently, let us now determine—and from Mormon sources—just how the latter day apostles were called and qualified, and compare them with Christ's apostles.

MODERN APOSTLES—HOW CALLED?

The twelve apostles of Joseph Smith were called at a meeting appointed by Joseph himself for that purpose, at Kirtland, Ohio, Feb. 14, 1835. President Smith, in stating the object of the meeting, said " it was made known to him by vision and by the Holy Spirit" that the meeting should be called.

"President Joseph Smith, Jr., after making many remarks on the subject of choosing the Twelve, wanted an expression from the brethren, if they would be satisfied to have the Spirit of the Lord dictate in the choice of the elders to be apostles; whereupon all the elders present expressed their anxious desire to have it so.

"President Joseph Smith, Jr., said that the first business of the meeting was, for *the three witnesses* of the Book of Mormon, to pray, each one, and then proceed *to choose twelve men from the church, as apostles*, to go to all nations, kindreds, tongues and people.

" The three witnesses; viz., Oliver Cowdery, David Whitmer, and Martin Harris, united in prayer.

"These three witnesses were then blessed by the laying on of the hands of the Presidency.

" *The witnesses then*, according to a former commandment, *proceeded to make choice of the Twelve.* Their names are as follows:

1. Lyman E. Johnson.
2. Brigham Young.
3. Heber C. Kemball.
4. Orson Hyde.
5. David W. Patten.
6. Luke Johnson.
7. William E. McLellin.
8. John F. Boynton.
9. Orson Pratt.
10. William Smith.
11. Thomas B. Marsh.
12. Parley P. Pratt.

"Lyman E. Johnson, Brigham Young and Heber C. Kimball came forward; and the three witnesses laid their hands upon each one's head and prayed separately." (Smith's Church History, pages 540 and 541. Also page 538.)

At subsequent meetings the other nine were in like manner ordained. (See page 542.)

And thus were chosen the first twelve apostles of Mormonism. Reader, do you observe one single mark of similarity between the methods employed in calling the apostles of Jesus Christ, and those adopted by Joseph Smith in calling his twelve? Not the slightest. In the former case the disciples were not even known personally to the Saviour, much less to be his followers. (See John 1: 46.)

Not so with Joseph Smith. His twelve were chosen from his tried followers,—most of them members of "Zion's Camp," a company over 200 strong, who followed Joseph to Missouri, in 1834, to "redeem Zion," but who were so disastrously defeated in their purpose. (See list of names on pages 462–464, Smith's History.)

To his twelve Jesus simply said, "Follow me." But Joseph said: "The first business of the meeting was for the three witnesses to choose the twelve apostles," and they chose them.

The apostles of Christ were chosen by Jesus himself, while those of Joseph were chosen by Oliver Cowdery, David Whitmer and Martin Harris.

Jesus said, "I will make you fishers of men." But Joseph said, "Are you satisfied to have the Spirit of the Lord dictate [to the three witnesses] in the choice of the elders to be apostles?"

The apostles of Christ were chosen *before* the establishment of the church, while the apostles of Joseph were an after-thought, and were called five years *after* the establishment of his church.

The apostles of Jesus were steadfast to the end; while many of Joseph's, and even the three witnesses who chose them, denounced Joseph and withdrew from the church, some three years after their ordination. (See Smith's History pp. 651, 652, 657.)

See also page 49, for an account of, and apology for, the disaffection of not only the *three* witnesses, but also that of the "eight witnesses."

CHAPTER XVII.

JOSEPH'S APOSTLES—HOW QUALIFIED—AN IMITATION.

Joseph's apostles—How qualified—Tarry at Kirtland—Dedication of the Kirtland temple—House filled with angels—Questions and answers—Jesus did not appear—The Reorganized Church—When organized, and by whom—Of whom composed—Seven apostles chosen—Their names—Chosen by a committee of three—The lesser ordains the greater—Can a stream rise above its fountain?—Apostasy of Apostle Briggs—Repudiates his own revelation—Three of the seven apostles reduced to the ranks—Ells and Derry chosen by a committee of three—Apostle Derry resigns—Summed up.

In delivering the charge to the new apostles, President Oliver Cowdery said:

"Have you desired this ministry with all your hearts? If you have desired it you are called of God, not man, to go into all the world." (Tullidge's History, page 154).

Further along in his address he charges them to,

"Tarry at Kirtland until you are endowed with power from on high." (Page 157). An imitation.

In December following (1835), when addressing the twelve concerning the promised "endowment," Joseph said to them:

"I feel disposed to speak a few words more to you, my brethren, concerning the endowment. All who are prepared, and are sufficiently pure to abide the presence of the Lord, will see him in the solemn assembly." (Smith's History, page 603).

At this time the Kirtland temple was nearing completion, and within its sacred walls the elders expected to receive their endowment. Finished at last, Sunday, March 27, 1836, was the time appointed for its dedication.

"The dedication was looked forward to with intense interest, and when the day arrived a dense multitude assembled. . . . At the hour appointed the assembly was seated, and President Rigdon began the services of the day. . . .

"After singing by the congregation, Joseph offered the following dedicatory prayer. . . .

"After the close of the above prayer and singing by the choir, the Lord's Supper was administered, 'After which,' says Joseph, 'I bore record of my mission and the ministration of angels. . . . President F. G. Williams arose, and testified that while President Rigdon was making his first prayer, an angel entered the window and took his seat between Father Smith and himself, and remained there during his prayer. President David Whitmer also saw angels in the house.'

"'At the evening meeting of the same day,' says Joseph, 'Brother George A. Smith arose and began to prophesy, when a noise was heard like the sound of a rushing mighty wind, which filled the temple, and all the congregation simultaneously arose, being moved upon by an invisible power. Many began to speak in tongues and prophesy; others saw glorious visions; and I beheld the temple was filled with angels, which fact I declared to the congregation. The people of the neighborhood came running together, (hearing an unusual sound within, and seeing a bright light like a pillar of fire resting upon the temple) and were astonished at what was transpiring." (Tullidge's History, pages 189, 190, 191, 199, 200).

Without a word of comment we might let the matter rest here, asking the reader to make his own comparison of this so-called endowment with that of the apostles, yet I cannot forbear a few suggestions:

1. Who were present at the Kirtland endowment? Latter Day Saints only, so far as the history informs us.

2. Who undertood the "tongues" in which *not one of the apostles is declared to have spoken?* Not a soul, for they were all English-speaking people.

3. How many were converted by the presence of the houseful of angels? *Not a soul*, for no one saw them except Joseph and his "counselor," F. G. Williams, while at Pentecost *three thousand* were added to the church in a single day. Jesus did not appear at the endowment as Joseph said he would do —nothing but angels.

4. How many of the apostles of Christ denied the faith, and turned away from the Master *after their endowment?* Not one of them. And yet Presidents Oliver Cowdery, David Whitmer, Frederick G. Williams; and Apostles Thomas B. Marsh, Wm. E. McLellin and John F. Boynton; witness Martin Harris, and many others, all denounced the prophet and left the church after their "endowment."

If they witnessed what is said to have transpired, it seems incredible that they should ever have thus fallen away. The reader must decide for himself whether the evidence is competent to prove what is alleged. One thing, however, is perfectly clear, and that is, not a point of similarity is to be found between the two events.

Passing now from the original Mormon Church and its apostles, let us take a brief view of the

APOSTLES OF THE REORGANIZED CHURCH.

At the death of Joseph and Hyrum Smith in 1844, the church was divided into various factions upon the question of leadership. The great body of the church followed Brigham Young and "the twelve" to Utah. William B. Smith, brother of the prophet, had quite a following, but soon went to pieces on the rock of polygamy. James J. Strang, then of Wisconsin, but later of Beaver Island, Mich., had quite a following, while a "company" followed Lyman Wright, one of Joseph's apostles, to the wilds of western Texas.

The Reorganized Church is the youngest of the Mormon brood, and had its inception in Beloit, Wis., June 1st, 1852, and was finally organized April 6th, 1853.

This organization was composed, in the beginning, of defections from Strang's church and that of Wm. B. Smith, principally on account of polygamy. (See Tullidge's History, page 594).

"In obedience to the above instruction an article was written *against polygamy* by J. W. Briggs." (Ibid, page, 594).

At the Conference of April 6, 1853, a committee of *three*—not the "three witnesses," however—was appointed "to *select seven men* to be ordained into the quorum of apostles."

"The committee of three . . . chose Zenas H. Gurley, Henry H. Deam, Jason W. Briggs, Daniel B. Razey, John Cunningham, George White and Reuben

Newkirk, who were accordingly ordained." (Tullidge's History, page 600).

Thus *three men*, not Christ, chose the first apostles of the Reorganized Church, in accordance with the pattern set by Joseph in the beginning of Mormonism; and what constitutes the most remarkable feature of the entire transaction is there was not a man in the conference, or in the church at the time, who held an office above that of "high priest," which, as you doubtless are aware, is lower in rank than that of an apostle.

Query.—How can the lesser ordain the greater? Can the stream rise above its fountain? If not, then these high priests could not ordain apostles; and this being true, *these seven men were not apostles*, in any sense of that word.

The "revelation"—yes, they had a revelation to "*organize*"—and this revelation was received through Jason W. Briggs, Nov. 18, 1851, and may be found in Tullidge's History, page 578. He became the President of the quorum of "twelve," and later, Historian of the church. But alas! how the mighty are fallen! Jason became dissatisfied with his own work; and by his actions, at least, renouncing his own "revelation" and the work built upon it, he resigned his apostolic office and withdrew from the church at a conference held at Independence, Mo.

Of the remaining portion of these *seven men*, three of them were afterwards *removed from office* by resolution of a General Conference, held at Plano, Ill., April 6, 1865, Joseph Smith presiding.

Their names were Daniel B. Razy, David Newkirk, and George White. (Tullidge's History, page 667).

At the same conference another committee of *three*

was appointed to select men for the apostleship. This committee,

"Nominated Josiah Ells and Charles Derry to fill the places of D. B. Razy and David Newkirk in the Quorum of Twelve, which passed into a resolution, and they were ordained apostles under the hands of Joseph Smith, [son and successor to the original Joseph] James Blakeslee and Z. H. Gurley." (Ibid, page 667).

Elder Charles Derry did not long remain in the "Quorum of Twelve." He resigned his apostleship soon after his return from the English Mission, for the reason, as he told the writer shortly afterwards, that he had no evidence that God had ever called him to be an apostle. He was too honest to retain a place of honor to which he felt assured God had never called him. He called on me a few days ago, and on departing left his benediction. He baptized me into the Reorganized Church nearly thirty-six years ago. I would that all men were like him in honor and integrity, and may his soul find rest and peace in the paradise of God.

But other apostles have been called more recently, and by a different method. By means of a "revelation" to the present Joseph Smith, given March 1, 1873, *seven other men* were chosen to be apostles, and duly ordained by the laying on of hands. (See Tullidge's History, page 715).

Of these all remained with the church except one, Zenas H. Gurley, who withdrew when Apostle J. W. Briggs stepped down and out.

I have been thus particular to give the history of apostolic callings simply to show that no comparison can be made between the apostles of Christ and the apostles of *men*, either as to their calling or their enduement or qualification.

While the apostles of the Reorganized Church, like all others, claim miraculous powers, they do not pretend to have been "endued with power from on high," as were the apostles of old. In the foregoing we have shown:

1. That Joseph Smith's apostles are not apostles of Christ, because *not one of them* has ever professed to have seen Christ, which is one of the first qualifications of an apostle.

2. That they were not called as Christ's apostles were, namely, *by Jesus himself*, but by *three men*—an earthly committee appointed by human means.

3. That the "endowment" they profess to have received was in no respect whatever like that of the great Pentecost.

4. That while the apostles of Christ were steadfast unto death, the man-made Mormon apostles were ever vacillating or denying the faith.

5. That the powers possessed by the apostles of Christ were of a character not to be questioned by even the most skeptical, while the gauzy imitations of Joseph Smith were such as to fill honest men with shame and disgust, and to render skeptical many of the most faithful and believing.

For these cogent reasons, together with those previously given, any man of intelligence will be compelled to regard all pretenses to miraculous powers as fraudulent, and denounce all lattter-day pretenders to apostolic honors as pseudo-apostles.

Wrong in doctrine, wrong in organization, with man-made and false apostles, the Mormon Church cannot be the Church of Christ, all her boastful claims to the contrary nothwithstanding.

CHAPTER XVIII.

THE BOOK OF MORMON—WHAT IS IT?

The Book of Mormon—What is it?—History of a Jewish colony—Written on metallic plates—Plates discovered near Palmyra, New York—Joseph's account of the discovery—New revelation—Orson Pratt's view—All authority lost in the great apostasy—Restored by an angel—Joseph's key to the Revelation of St. John—The man-child is the priesthood—Mr. Pratt answered—A monstrous claim.

THE Book of Mormon is confidently believed by Latter Day Saints of every name and class to be a divinely-inspired record of a people who came from Jerusalem some six hundred years before Christ, who, although few in number at the beginning (about twenty persons all told), grew into a "multitude of nations in the midst of the earth." (See Gen. 48: 15-19).

This little colony, the book relates, were directed in their journey to the promised land by divine power. Although the Book of Mormon itself does not give a hint as to the direction their ship sailed, or the distance traversed, yet it is maintained by its interpreters and defenders that the little colony of *Jews* landed on the west coast of South America, just south of the Isthmus of Panama; but the source from which this information is derived you are left to imagine, for the narrative is as silent as the tomb as to the point from which they sailed or the place where they landed.

No attempt is made to describe the "promised

land" either at the place of landing or at any point in the interior.

Of course if the Book of Mormon be accepted as true, all these difficulties at once disappear; for the "record" describes the terrible wars which led to the final extinction of the white or Nephite race by their copper-colored brethren, the Lamanites or American Indians, and gives an account of the last days of Moroni, who, (after all but himself had been slain in the decisive battle at Camorah—Indian Hill, New York—and where over "two million" Nephites fell, with nearly as many Lamanites) "hid up unto the Lord" the plates from which the Book of Mormon is said to have been translated. Following is the account of their discovery by Joseph Smith:

"Convenient to the village of Manchester, Ontario County, New York, stands a hill of considerable size, and the most elevated in the neighborhood. On the west side of this hill, not far from the top, under a stone of considerable size, lay the plates deposited in a stone box." (Smith's History, Vol. 1, page 16.)

If the above statement concerning the discovery of the gold plates in "Indian Hill," as the Manchester people call it, but known in Mormon parlance as "Camorah," be accepted as correct, it does not only locate the Nephite colony upon this continent, but it proves the entire theory upon which Mormonism is based to be true. But the veracity of this remarkable claim is the very point in dispute, and the question as to whether ancient America was peopled by a colony of Hebrews from Jerusalem remains an open question.

I shall now proceed to a direct examination of the "evidences" adduced in support of this very fine theory. The Saints confidently assert that the Book of Mormon "came forth" in exact fulfillment of many direct prophecies of the Bible; and this view is presented with so much plausibility that many are led to accept it.

To pave the way for the more direct evidences in support of the Book of Mormon, the advocates of "the latter-day work," as the Saints call it, claim that, owing to a total apostasy of the primitive Christians from the original doctrines and practices of the church and the abrogation of all authority to minister in Gospel ordinances, a new revelation from God is *indispensably necessary*.

Apostle Orson Pratt, universally conceded to be the ablest writer the Mormon Church ever produced, in a pamphlet entitled, "More Revelation is Indispensably Necessary," undertakes to establish this pet dogma of Mormonism. Following is one of his strongest arguments:

"The Church of Christ cannot exist on the earth without an authorized ministry. This ministry can not be called and authorized *without new revelation*. . . . Without new revelation every office in the church would necessarily become vacant. . . . If revelation ceased at the close of the first century, it is not at all likely that any of the officers then holding authority would be alive a century afterwards; and as they would have no authority to ordain others without new revelation, when they died the authority upon the earth *would necessarily become extinct*. . . . Hence, without continued revelation the church could no more continue its existence on the earth than a body could live without the spirit." (Pratt's works, More Revelation Necessary, page 18.)

Thus all authority, and even the church itself, ceased to exist when new revelations were no longer received, and revelation ceased *because of a general apostasy.*

While the Latter Day Saints admit that Christ set up his kingdom, or established his church, and authorized his apostles and others to preach the Gospel and administer its ordinances, yet they claim, as the above extract clearly shows, that through apostasy all authority was taken from the earth, and the Church of Christ actually ceased to exist. "The priesthood"—by which they mean *authority*—they tell us, "was taken from the earth," and cite certain Scriptures to prove it, and among them the following:

"And there appeared a great wonder in heaven; a woman clothed with the sun, and the moon under her feet, and upon her head a crown of twelve stars: and she brought forth a man-child, who was to rule all nations with a rod of iron: and her child was caught up to God and to his throne." (Rev. 12: 1, 5.)

The woman, they very correctly hold, is the church, and the man-child, they erroneously maintain is "the priesthood." Concerning this Mr. Kelley says:

"An angel of glory,—sent by Jesus . . . wends his way to earth, and conferred with his own pure hand and divinely uttered words the priesthood,—long since lost, *taken to heaven,* as represented by the man-child of Rev. 12, and thus authorize men once more, to preach the Gospel." (Presidency and Priesthood, page 224.)

In his "Key to the Revelation of St. John," Joseph Smith says:

Q. "What are we to understand by the man-child,

in the 12th chapter of Revelation, and 5th verse?

A. "We are to understand that the man-child is the priesthood."

The above question and answer are quoted from memory, and are substantially, if not verbally, correct.

The man-child was the priesthood; the priesthood was "caught up to God and to his throne," therefore, all authority to minister in divine things *was taken from the earth*. In harmony with this view, Apostle Orson Pratt says:

"Since the church with its *authority* and *power* has been *caught away from the earth*, the great 'mother of harlots,' with all her descendants, has blasphemously assumed authority of administering *some* of the sacred ordinances of the Gospel." ("Revelation Necessary," as before quoted, page 18.)

According to all Mormon lexicography Priesthood means,—

"The authority of God committed to men, . . . to preach the Gospel and administer the ordinances thereof." (Kelley.)

The priesthood having been "caught up to heaven," *no man on earth has authority to minister in Gospel ordinances*, and hence the necessity for a new revelation

That there was, after the death of the apostles, a departure, in some measure, at least, from the simplicity of primitive methods, few Protestants care to deny; but that such departure involved the abrogation of all authority, they do not admit. The proposition is one affirmed by the Latter Day Saints, and which they have utterly failed to establish by competent testimony.

Mr. Pratt sums up the whole case in a few words,— and no writer among the Saints has ever produced stronger reasoning,—when he says that "the Church of Christ cannot exist without an authorized ministry," and that "this ministry cannot be authorized without *new revelation*," that is to say, every man called to the ministry must be called by a direct revelation from God. But is this true? Is it a fact that God has obligated himself to point out, by direct revelation, every man who officiates in his church. If so, where may we find such a declaration?

That some individuals were miraculously called, as Paul, for example, nobody doubts; but that all men must be so called does not appear, and neither can it be proved.

If Mr. Pratt's logic is good, and his premise be not at fault, then what becomes of the very first apostles chosen, himself among the rest, who were called, not by Christ, not by a revelation from God, *but by three men*, Oliver Cowdery, David Whitmer and Martin Harris?

If, indeed, ministers can only be chosen by direct revelation, how about the *seven men*, the first apostles of the Reorganized Church, who were also chosen by *three men selected for that purpose*, and not by revelation?

If ministers can be called only by divine revelation, through what particular channel must such revelation come? "O," says one, "it must come through the prophet, the President of the church." Very well, but through which one of all the dozen or more presidents of as many different Mormon churches, must this revelation come? When some advocate of the Mormon heresy answers the above impertinent questions to the satisfaction of reasonable people, then, and not till then, need they expect to mislead thinking people by such modes of reasoning.

The monstrous claim that no man, since the beginning of the third century, has been authorized to preach the Gospel till Joseph Smith and Oliver Cowdery, by the hand of an angel, were so authorized, is simply blasphemous, almost heaven-daring. And all this is founded upon the assumption that the "priesthood" was taken up to heaven, and all authority annulled because of apostasy.

CHAPTER XIX.

IS A NEW REVELATION NECESSARY?

Is a new revelation necessary?—The great apostasy—Did it annul all existing authority?—The great Jewish apostasy—Authority not destroyed—Devout Zacharias—John the Baptist—The old kingdom and the new—Authority transferred—The latter day apostasy—How does it affect the Mormon Church?—Joseph's church apostatized—Church rejected of God—The Reorganized Church the result of apostasy—The Church of Christ transmitted from the times of the apostles.

The proposition to which I shall now address myself is this:

Did the apostasy, which followed the death of the apostles, render a new revelation indispensably necessary?

If the above question be answered affirmatively, then it logically follows that wherever there occurs an apostasy, general in its character, then all existing authority is thereby abrogated, and the necessity for a new revelation to restore it becomes absolutely imperative. Either this is true or it is a fact that apostasy does not annul existing authority. Please bear this in mind.

In order to determine the facts relative to the matter under consideration, it becomes necessary to examine a little history, both ancient and modern. That the Jewish people were in a lamentable state of apostasy at the time Christ came to minister among men, may not be seriously questioned by any well-informed Bible reader. The condition in which he found the Israelites may be seen from such passages as the following:

"O, Jerusalem, Jerusalem, thou that killest the prophets, and stonest them which are sent unto thee, how often would I have gathered thy children together, even as a hen gathereth her chickens under her wings, and ye would not." (Matt. 23: 37).

"Woe unto you, Scribes and Pharisees, hypocrites! . . . Ye serpents, ye generation of vipers, how can ye escape the damnation of hell?" (Vs. 29, 33).

"That upon you may come all the righteous blood shed upon the earth, from the blood of righteous Abel unto the blood of Zacharias son of Barachias, whom ye slew between the temple and the altar." (V. 35).

"Behold, your house shall be left unto you desolate." (V. 38).

"He came to his own and his own received him not." (John 1: 11).

"Why do ye also transgress the commandment of God by your traditions?" (Matt. 15: 3).

"It is written, My house shall be called the house of prayer; but ye have made it a den of thieves." (Matt. 21: 13).

So wicked had become God's chosen people; so far lost were they in the mazy depths of apostasy, that their beloved city was laid waste, the temple destroyed and its altars desecrated, and the nation itself carried away into captivity among the Gentile nations of the earth, thus becoming "a hiss and a by-word" among the people.

Not in the annals of the past can be found an apostasy so entire, so complete as that which befell the Jewish people, and yet the authority to minister at the altar of God's house was not wanting. The apostasy, great, and so well-nigh universal though it was, did not, and, indeed, could not, abrogate the authority of the faithful. Some there were, standing erect amid the wreck and ruin of a great nation, like the high rock in a great desert, who refused to bow the knee to Baal, and whose authority God was pleased to recognize. Such was the faithful, devout, Zacharias, to whom, indeed, an angel of God appeared, not to restore the authority lost through a general apostasy, but rather to assure this faithful servant that both his authority and his offerings were still recognized in the sight of heaven, and were acceptable.

This divine messenger, instead of laying his hands on Zacharias to ordain him to the Aaronic priesthood, simply recognized *existing authority* by announcing the birth of John the Forerunner, a prophet who should go before the Lord and make straight the paths which had been made crooked through apostasy and disbelief. John came in the *spirit* of Elias —that is to say, he came as a means of restoring righteousness—*not priesthood*.

The foregoing historical facts prove,

1. That the apostasy of the masses does not, *cannot*, abrogate existing authority.

2. That authority once delegated can only be annulled by individual transgression.

3. That so long as there remains a righteous man on the earth, just so long does the authority remain to minister in divine things; and

4. That any man holding authority to minister before God, may confer that authority upon others.

Apostle Wm. H. Kelley, in his zeal to prove that

both the "Melchizedek and Aaronic priesthoods" were *transferred* from the old dispensation to the new, admits that authority to minister under the law was not disturbed by the great Jewish apostasy. He says:

"John the Baptist held the Aaronic priesthood. . . . He was a Nazarite from his birth (Luke 1: 15), and doubtless consecrated to the priesthood as he was to the service of the Lord, being a Nazarite." (Presidency and Priesthood, page 18.)

"In the persons of Jesus and John, therefore, there were represented upon the shores of Jordan, . . . the Melchizedek and the Aaronic priesthoods, by which the Gospel was preached and administered." (Ibid, page 20.)

If, as Mr. Kelley affirms, there were "two priesthoods in the church," how did they get there? Following is the explanation which he offers:

"A new nation was to be born; a new kingdom set up. All the *authority* and excellencies attaching to the old Levitical 'kingdom of priests' were to be *transferred to the new kingdom*." (Ibid, page 33.)

"*The priesthood was transferred.*" (Ibid, page 36.) (Italics are mine.)

Thus Mr. Kelley shows most conclusively that the fearful apostate condition in which Jesus found the "old levitical 'kingdom of priests,'" the priesthood, or "the *authority* and order of God committed unto men," as he defines "priesthood," remained intact, and was "transferred" to the kingdom of Christ.

Mr. Kelley, being an apostle, and therefore entitled to all the powers pertaining to that office, ought to know whereof he affirms; and if he is right, then *apostasy cannot annul existing authority.*

Let Latter Day Saints remember this. While this view is contrary to all Mormon theology, it is at the same time a position which Latter Day Saints dare not question; for the moment they do so, that moment they prove the Mormon Church and priesthood to be entirely destitute of authority.

But the question may be asked, and doubtless will be by some,—"Was not the authority to preach the Gospel and baptize believers into the church lost in the great apostasy after the death of the apostles? And was not this authority *restored* through Joseph Smith? If so, then, will it not *remain*, there still being persons living who received it under the hands of Joseph and Oliver?"

Well, let us see about that. In the first place we have shown by the *facts* of history and good Mormon authority—that of an inspired apostle—that authority cannot be destroyed, or cancelled, by a general apostasy—it must be absolutely universal, not a faithful, pure man left—and hence Joseph's claim to have "restored" that which has not been shown to be lost is a glaring absurdity, to say the very least. All this talk about the loss of authority through apostasy is but an idle fancy based upon the wildest speculation, having no foundation in fact.

But, for the sake of the argument, suppose we admit this groundless claim, what will be the result? If Joseph and Oliver received authority direct from heaven, and if others are now living who received it from them, then, according to this theory, the only way such authority can be retained is to avoid the fateful rock of "apostasy," upon which it is claimed the original Church of Christ and the apostles were hopelessly wrecked. I think no sane, fair-minded man will dispute the logic of this position. "The same cause under like circumstances will invariably produce the same effect," is a fundamental truth not to be questioned.

The one question now to be determined is this: Has there been an apostasy from the original doctrines of Mormonism? Has the church organized by Joseph Smith and Oliver Cowdery been perpetuated? or has there been a falling away from the original faith and doctrines of the church?

To determine these questions will be to determine the *facts* as to Mormon authority.

If there has been no departure from the faith, if there have been no sinful innovations from any quarter, then whatever of authority Joseph and Oliver could confer still remains; but if there have been hurtful and destroying doctrines introduced into the church by its leaders, then by this act of apostasy *all authority has been abrogated*.

If the Saints have "kept the faith," if there has been no departure from original Mormonism, then polygamy, "blood atonement," the Adam-God doctrine, Danites, or "destroying angels," and a thousand other abominable and soul-destroying doctrines were among the original tenets of the Mormon Church; for that all these things were practiced and taught by the church in Utah none will pretend to deny. If these things were not a part of original Mormonism, then who can deny the fact that there has been a terrible, a most wicked apostasy from the original doctrines of the church?

Reasoning from the premise furnished by the cardinal facts of Mormon theology as urged by both founders and defenders of the Mormon Church as an apology for its existence, all the authority that ever resided in the church *has been forfeited because of apostasy*.

The Reorganized Church owes its existence to the apostasy of the original church. Had there been no departure from the faith, and had not this departure been of such a character as to cause what is known among the Saints as the "rejection of the church," the Reorganized Church could never have had existence.

In one of Joseph's revelations, that of January 19, 1841, the matter is referred to as follows:

"But I command you, *all ye my saints*, to build a house unto me; and I grant unto you a *sufficient time* to build an house unto me, and *during this time* your baptisms [in the Mississippi river] shall be acceptable unto me. But behold, at the end of this appointment your baptisms for your dead shall not be acceptable unto me; and if ye do not these things, at the end of the appointment *ye shall be rejected* AS A CHURCH *with your dead*, saith the Lord your God." (Doctrine and Covenants, page 304.)

This was a commandment to build the temple and Nauvoo House—"the Lord's boarding house." As an historical fact, the temple was never finished, which was admitted by even Brigham Young himself, as the following shows:

"Have you ever seen a temple *finished* since the church was commenced? No, you have not." (Rejection of the Church, page 2. See also Journal of Discourses, published in Salt Lake City, Vol. 1, page 277.)

In a tract published by the Reorganized Church we find the following:

"Now it is a well known fact that the Nauvoo House was built only part on the second story, and that the temple was *never finished.*" (Page 1.)

"We now see that the temple was never built as commanded of God, and we are bound, therefore, to conclude that the church as organized, as also their baptisms for their dead, *were rejected of God.*" (Ibid, page 2.)

A pamphlet entitled, "A Word of Consolation," by Jason W. Briggs, president of the Twelve Apostles of the Reorganized Church, contains the following:

"But let us return to the *rejection of the church at Nauvoo.* . . . This event [the death of Joseph and Hyrum Smith] produced all the phenomena characteristic of such a calamity. . . . Pretenders began to arise to allure the unwary into their fatal meshes, *the devices of Satan,* to which the Saints had subjected themselves *by turning from the law of God.*" (Page 8.)

Thus it is made clear that the validity of the claim of the Reorganized Church to be the Church of Christ depends *entirely* upon the rejection of the original Mormon Church on account of apostasy.

If the original Mormon Church was not rejected, then the Reorganized Church is not the Church of Christ. But if it was rejected, the rejection was due to a general apostasy, general and sinful disobedience; and as such apostasy works the abrogation of all existing authority, the entire Mormon Church, reorganization and all, being deprived of authority and *rejected of God,* cannot be the Church of Christ.

But the warmest advocate of the "rejection" dogma will hardly be willing to accept the inevitable conclusion to which his reasoning leads. He will probably argue that although the church became so corrupt that God would no longer acknowledge it as his, yet there were righteous individuals whose authority was not revoked, and who therefore were still authorized to officiate and confer authority upon others.

Very well, if this view be accepted as the correct one—and to which we shall not object—the rule, when applied to the case of the first Christians, will prove beyond question or doubt that the authority to administer the ordinances of the Gospel *remained with the church*, and remaining, its ordinances could be administered and the church perpetuated.

That Christianity has been transmitted to us from the times of the apostles is historically true. That it has been more or less corrupted cannot be denied; nor is this a matter of astonishment. A stream whose waters are sparkling and pure at the fountain-head may be tinged or discolored more or less because of the loose character of the soil through which it may flow on its journey to the sea; but as it continues to flow it is purified, and again becomes as clear and pure as when first it gushed from its rocky source. So with the Church of Christ.

How is it to-day? Perhaps at no period of her history has the Church of Christ been characterized by such unquestionable deeds of charity and undoubted personal purity as at the present time.

The claim, then, that all authority conferred by Christ and the apostles was lost, and that no man possessed it until Joseph Smith received it back from heaven, is too absurd to be seriously considered for a single moment.

The idea that Christ built his church upon a "sure

foundation" and promised that "the gates of hell should not prevail against it," and yet leave it without the means of self-perpetuation and self-purification is altogether unbecoming the character and dignity and wisdom of the great Architect and Master-builder.

No new revelation is necessary, then, in order to minister in Gospel ordinances. A REFORMATION, not a *restoration* by means of a new revelation, is what the church needed, and the reformation came, and came to stay.

This boastful, arrogant claim is thus shown to have not the shadow of support in either the facts of Scripture, history or reason, and cannot, therefore, be true.

CHAPTER XX.

"A MARVELOUS WORK AND A WONDER."

A marvelous work and a wonder—An untenable claim—From President Blair—His comments on Isaiah 29—Mr. Kelley's points of identity—Ariel—Old and new—Book to be taken out of the ground.

HAVING shown that there exists no necessity for a new revelation to restore authority which had never been lost, and that the entire claim urged by Latter Day Saints as an apology for the appearance of the Book of Mormon is based upon an assumed promise, we might here dismiss the entire question; but as the scriptural arguments advanced by the Saints to prove the Book of Mormon a divine revelation are wholly untenable, I shall now proceed to show the utter fallacy of the positions assumed.

In pursuance of this pleasant task I shall, as heretofore, let good Mormon authorities state the premises upon which they predicate their arguments.

In a published sermon by President W. W. Blair, delivered at Laomi, Iowa, Nov. 27, 1892, on the Book of Mormon, from the text, "A Marvelous Work and a Wonder," he presents the view uniformly entertained by Latter Day Saints respecting the "coming forth of the Book of Mormon," as the favorite phrase runs with them, and endeavors to show how perfectly the 29th chapter of Isaiah sustains their contention. Elder Blair was considered one of the most scholarly and eloquent men in the church, and this, it may be remarked, was one of his favorite topics.

Although lengthy quotations are not considered just the proper thing, and are sometimes tedious, yet on occasions like this we regard it as quite necessary, in order that no dispute may arise respecting the premise upon the correctness of which the entire argument depends. I wish to call the reader's attention to the ingenious manner in which Elder Blair sandwiches in his own ideas (in brackets), in order to give the proper tone and coloring to the passage necessary to the maintenance of his peculiar views. He begins by saying:

"I will read a portion of Holy Writ that is a promise and a prophecy concerning an extraordinary work—a work that God decreed to establish and carry forward *in these latter days.*

"I do not expect to exhaust the subject that stands revealed in the chapter, but to simply present some of its salient points and bring from other portions of Scripture, as also from history, evidences that the work which is here described has been begun, and that it is being carried forward, all in fulfillment of this word of prophecy. I commence at the ninth verse of the twenty-ninth chapter of Isaiah:

"'Say yourselves and wonder; cry ye out, and cry: they are drunken, but not with wine; they stagger, but not with strong drink. [They have partaken of the cup of Mystery Babylon]. For the Lord hath poured out upon you the spirit of deep sleep, and hath closed your eyes: the prophets and your rulers, the seers hath he covered.'

"You will notice that it is a peculiar work that is in contemplation. . . .

"'And the vision of all [that is, of these seers and rulers, and prophets] is become unto you as the words of a book that is sealed, which men delivered to one that is learned, saying, Read this, I pray thee; and he saith, I cannot; for it is sealed: and the book is delivered to him that is not learned, saying, Read this, I pray thee; and he saith, I am not learned. Wherefore the Lord said [here comes the promise], Forasmuch as this people draw near me with their mouth, and with their lips do honor me, but have removed their hearts far from me, and their fear towards me is taught by the precepts of men: therefore, behold, I will proceed to do a marvelous work among this people, even a marvelous work and a wonder: for the wisdom of their wise men shall perish, and the understanding of their prudent men shall be hid. [Mark you; this relates to matters of religion; that is, it pertains to the government of God. These wise and prudent are the professedly wise teachers of religion]. Woe to them that seek deep to hide their counsel from the Lord, and their works are in the dark, and they say, Who seeth us? and who knoweth us? Surely your turning of things upside down shall be esteemed as the potter's clay [you see by this that religious matters are then wrong side up; are in a confused state]: for shall the work say of him that made it, He maketh me not? or shall the thing framed say of him that framed it, He hath no understanding? Is it not yet a very little while [that is, a little while after God commences this marvelous work and a wonder], and Lebanon [Palestine] shall be turned into a fruitful field, and the fruitful field shall be esteemed as a forest? And in that day [when God turns Lebanon into a fruitful field] shall the deaf hear the words of the book, and the eyes of the blind shall see out of obscurity and out of darkness. The weak also shall *increase* their joy in the Lord [and why? Manifestly for the reason that God just then set his hand to do this marvelous work and a wonder], and the poor among men shall rejoice in the Holy One of Israel. [They rejoice because they receive the 'marvelous work and a wonder' that the Holy One of Israel hath established]. . . . They also that erred in spirit shall come to understanding, and they that murmured shall learn doctrine.'

"I have read this chapter and made these explanations that you may see the scope, at least in the outlining, of what we propose by the blessing of God to present to you in our endeavor to prove that the Church of Jesus Christ of Latter Day Saints is not a man-made church, but that it was founded in the wisdom of God." (Pages 1, 2).

After referring to Joseph Smith's vision, finding the plates, and translating the Book of Mormon, Elder Blair asks:

"Is not this the book described in the 29th chapter of Isaiah, the words of which were delivered to one that is learned for him to read, but he could not?"

Commenting on the same chapter, Mr. Kelley makes the following argument:

"The points of identity between the predictions as found in the twenty-ninth chapter of Isaiah and their fulfillment in the revelation of the Book of Mormon, as the 'book that is sealed' of verse eleven, . . . are many and most wonderfully striking."

He then proceeds to give them as follows:

"(1) A certain people was to be unto the Lord 'as Ariel.' . . . Accepting that 'Ariel' proper was the city or people where David dwelt, Jerusalem, then the people who were to be unto the Lord ' AS Ariel' were to dwell elsewhere, become great, and constitute a new 'lion of God,' or dwell as around 'the hearth of God.' . . . The Margin reads, 'Woe to Ariel, to Ariel of the city where David dwelt.' So we have presented in these texts what may be termed an old and a new 'Ariel.' A comparison between two. The reading is, 'It shall be unto me *as* Ariel.

"(2) This new 'Ariel' after becoming great was to be 'camped against,' besieged, and 'forts' raised against it. It was to be 'brought down,' and 'speak out of the ground.' 'Thy speech shall be low out of the dust,' as one that has a familiar spirit 'out of the ground.' 'Thy speech shall whisper out of the dust.' (V. 4.)

"By reason of the great destruction which would eventually be sent upon this people, it is said their 'strangers' and 'terrible ones' would be like 'small dust' and as 'chaff that passeth away.' (v. 5.) Dissension, conflict, war, 'thunder,' 'storm,' 'earthquake,' 'tempest,' and the 'flame of devouring fire,' were to unite as the wrath of God to bring about their utter destruction. (V. 6.)

"Now, the only way that a people could 'speak out of the ground,' or 'whisper out of the dust' to intelligent mortals, in fulfillment of this prediction, would be that their history should be written at some period in the day of their power and prosperity, and it become lost, rest in mute silence among their former habitations or desolations, since their 'terrible ones' became as the 'chaff that passeth away,' and be discovered and brought to light by some means or other 'out of the ground,' to be read by an intelligent world that knew not of them. Such a history is *clearly indicated* in verse 11, as the 'vision of all' which was to become as the 'words of a book that is sealed,' and to be of special notice and importance at the time of its revealment.' Such are the claims set forth in the Sealed Book, or Book of Mormon." (Presidency and Priesthood, pages 197, 198, 199.)

Thus it will be seen that the advocates of Mormon hierarchy regard the 29th chapter of Isaiah as being a prophecy whose direct accomplishment is found in the "coming forth of the Book of Mormon," and the establishment of the " marvelous work and a wonder"—Mormonism.

The reader cannot have failed to notice the ingenuity of these giants of Mormon theology in the presentation of their case. President Blair is careful to create the impression that the "book" of Isaiah's prophecy came forth at the exact period predicted, that is, when the religious world was all "wrong side up"—in a "state of confusion" and "hopeless division." In fact the whole chapter "relates to matters of religion," and "these wise and prudent are the professedly wise teachers of religion," in our own times. Then after referring to the "book" which Isaiah is supposed to declare shall be taken "out of the ground," Elder Blair, in a tone of exultant triumph, asks:

"Is not this the book described in the 29th chapter of Isaiah?"

In my analysis of this chapter, I shall be able to show most conclusively that Isaiah has no reference, whatever, to any book which should be taken "out of the ground," or anywhere else; not even from Joseph

Smith's fertile brain, whence the Book of Mormon unquestionably had its origin.

Mr. Kelley points out several "points of identity" between the "predictions of Isaiah," and their fulfillment in the "revelation of the Book of Mormon," which have no existence save only in the mind of one imbued with the spirit of Mormon theology.

CHAPTER XXI.

"THE LAND SHADOWING WITH WINGS"—IS IT NORTH AND SOUTH AMERICA?

The land shadowing with wings—Is it North and South America?—Common ground—Ariel is Jerusalem—It shall be as Ariel—The Ariel of the West—A race exterminated—Their History—The land shadowing with wings is Egypt, not America—Views of Ira Maurice Price, Ph. D.

THE 29th chapter of Isaiah, which is believed by the Saints to contain a prediction concerning the Book of Mormon, begins by pronouncing a "woe" upon Jerusalem, thus: "Woe to Ariel, to Ariel, the city where David dwelt." (V. 1.)

In harmony with all scholars of eminence, Mr. Kelley, as we have seen, takes the ground, as do all the leading minds among the Saints, that Ariel here means Jerusalem, as shown from the fact that it was "the city where David dwelt,"—was the capital city of the people of Israel. (See 2 Sam. 5: 5-7.)

To begin with, then, we stand upon common ground respecting the application of the word Ariel—*Ariel is Jerusalem*. This furnishes the key by which we may unlock the door that shall lead out into the open sunlight of truth.

"Woe to Ariel, to Ariel, the city where David dwelt; add ye year to year; let them kill sacrifices. Yet I will distress Ariel, and there shall be heaviness and sorrow. And *it* shall be unto me *as* Ariel." (Verses 1 and 2.)

According to this reading a comparison is here introduced between Ariel, or Jerusalem, and some other land or people, who should become unto the Lord AS Ariel. Where is this land? Who are the people here described? These are very important questions in Mormon theology, and so Mr. Kelley concludes that, "We have presented in these texts what may be termed an old and a new Ariel."

As it was with the "old Ariel," so shall it be with the new. To locate the land of this new Ariel—this new Jerusalem—is a labor of love very dear to the hearts of all Latter Day Saints, for the reason that everything Mormon depends upon it.

"Woe to the land shadowing with wings, which is beyond the rivers of Ethiopia." (Isa. 18:1.)

This prophecy, according to Mormon exegesis, relates to North and South America, which lie between the world's two great oceans, expanded like the "shadowing wings" of some great tropic-bird.

Even the character of the government which should finally prevail in "the land shadowing with wings" is supposed to be indicated. The great American eagle, whose wide-spread, "shadowing wings" in our coat-of-arms, representing the escutcheon of American liberty, is supposed to have been foreseen by the prophet.

Upon the land "shadowing with wings," or America, the "New Ariel" of Mr. Kelley's imagination is located.

The Ariel of the West, according to this view, must share the fate of the Ariel of the East, that is, it must be "brought down" by a powerful foe, and should, like a familiar spirit, "speak out of the ground." This can only be accomplished, we are told, by means of a *written history*, concealed for ages, but at last brought to light by miraculous power.

The Book of Mormon, it must be borne in mind, professes to contain the "written history" of this new Ariel. The "Nephites" were a people "terrible from their beginning hitherto" (Isa. 18: 2), but were exterminated by their more wicked brethren, the "Lamanites," about A. D. 420.

The account of this war of extermination, together with their forms of religion, was written on metallic plates, brass and gold, and were concealed by Moroni, one of the Nephite prophets, and *the only survivor of his race*, and were finally discovered and translated by Joseph Smith, in fulfillment of the 29th chapter of Isaiah.

This theory, it must be confessed, is indeed fine; and if the theory is sustained by the *facts*, it amounts to a very strong presumption in favor of Mormonism. But if the facts are *opposed* to the theory, then the whole argument breaks down, and Joseph Smith stands revealed an impostor and the Book of Mormon a fraud.

Will the theory bear the test of truth? We shall see.

If the country described in Isaiah 18: 1, as "the land shadowing with wings," be America, and if the 29th chapter relates to events that were to transpire on this continent, and which, as a matter of fact, did take place as predicted, then all candid people will readily concede the fact that the Book of Mormon is probably true.

But if the "land shadowing with wings" is shown to be *not* the land of America, but some other land,

and if it shall transpire that the events described in the 29th chapter of Isaiah relate *not* to the people of ancient America, but to the people of Israel, then the Book of Mormon cannot be true, and Latter Day Saints should frankly admit the fact, confess their error, and openly renounce the heresy.

Is America the land shadowing with wings? Let us see.

"Woe to the land shadowing with wings which is *beyond the rivers of Ethiopia.*"

The land here described lies *beyond* the rivers of Ethiopia from Palestine, where the prophet resided. What direction is Ethiopia from Jerusalem? *Directly south*, as may be seen by any good map of Africa. The "rivers of Ethiopia" are the rivers of Africa, the Nile and its tributaries. Hence, the land described is Egypt, not America. In further proof of this we read:

"And it shall come to pass in that day, that the Lord shall hiss for the fly that is in the uttermost part of the *rivers of Egypt*, and for the bee that is in the land of Assyria." (Isa. 7: 18.)

Perhaps a more accurate rendering of the passage in question would be: "Woe to the land of the rustling of wings." Concerning this, and in answer to questions relative to this and other Scriptures, Ira Maurice Price, Ph. D., Associate Professor of Semitic Languages and Literatures in the University of Chicago, says:

"'The land of the rustling of wings' is Egypt, full of buzzing flies, gnats, etc., and the last passage [Isa. 7: 18, quoted above,] compared with hosts of warriors of Egypt and Ethiopia. 'Beyond the rivers of Ethiopia,' *i. e.*, extending southward even through and beyond Ethiopia to remotest lands."

Confirmatory of this view, the character of the "woe" pronounced in the 18th chapter is thus described:

"Like as my servant Isaiah hath walked naked and barefoot three years for a sign and wonder upon Egypt and upon Ethiopia; so shall the king of Assyria *lead away the Egyptians prisoners, and the Ethiopians captives*, young and old, naked and barefoot." (Isa. 20: 3, 4.)

It is thus shown to be simply impossible that America can be "the land shadowing with wings," for the very cogent reason that the land thus described lies SOUTH of Palestine, while America, as every schoolboy knows, is directly west.

No amount of sophistry or special pleading can change the *facts of geography* involved in this question, and so all this fine-spun theory, together with the fabric reared upon it, falls to the ground a hopeless mass of ruin, never again to be reconstructed.

CHAPTER XXII.

THE BOOK THAT IS SEALED.

The book that is sealed—Isaiah, chapter twenty-nine—The words of a book—Presented to Prof. Charles Anthon—A woe pronounced against Jerusalem—The city where David dwelt—Inspired translation—Different rendering of Isaiah twenty-nine—Quotation from—Comments—A safe rule—Isaiah twenty-nine relates to the destruction of Jerusalem—Ten propositions—No prophecy concerning a book—A question of exegesis and history—The prophecy of Isaiah concerning the destruction of Jerusalem literally fulfilled—Revolt of the ten tribes—Israel and Judah—The Assyrian captivity—A strange work.

"And the vision is all become unto you as the words of a book that is sealed." (Isaiah 29: 11.)

Having disposed of that part of the argument which is based upon the eighteenth chapter of Isaiah, let us now return to a consideration of the twenty-ninth chapter.

As already shown, the Saints believe that the "book that is sealed," mentioned at the eleventh verse of this chapter, has direct reference to the Book of Mormon.

When Joseph Smith had transcribed some of the "caractors" said to be found on the plates, he translated a *part* of them and gave them to Martin Harris, a farmer of limited attainments, with instructions to call upon Professor Charles Anthon, of New York, and see if he could read them. "Harris carried out his instructions." Handing the transcript to the Professor, with a request to read it, he is represented as saying he could not translate them, but if he had the plates he might be able to do so. Upon being informed that "a part of the plates were sealed," the Professor replied, "I cannot read a sealed book."

How beautifully this story seems to fit the case. Isaiah says the "*words* of a book," not the book, were "delivered to one that is learned," but he could not read them; while the "book" was "delivered to him that is not learned," who should be able to read it.

The most distinguished Professor of Semitic Languages of that day could not decipher the "words" of the book, but the entire book was read—translated by a man so lamentably ignorant of even his mother tongue that he could not correctly spell the simply word character.ˑ How supremely ridiculous and absurd!

Perhaps it is unfortunate that I should have referred to this fact, for the proverbial illiteracy of the boy prophet is one of the stock arguments employed to prove the "marvelous work and a wonder" to be of God. But we shall see about this later.

If these "plates" were written in Egyptian, Arabic, Assyrian and Aramaic, and were translated by a man wholly ignorant of these languages, it would amount to an argument absolutely unanswerable; and this is exactly what it is claimed has been done.

Upon the truthfulness of this claim depend the veracity of the Book of Mormon and the prophetic character of Joseph Smith, its pretended translator.

If these signs or letters are not "the true characters," if they shall prove to be but a clumsy effort to deceive, then we have in this act exhibited an amount of that modern commodity known as "cheek" which stands without a parallel in the annals of all time.

The fact is, the twenty-ninth chapter of Isaiah bears no more relation to the Book of Mormon or the inhabitants of pre-historic America than does Homer's Iliad to the aboriginal inhabitants of Australia or the nomadic tribes of Asia.

If the prophecy of this chapter does not apply to America and its former inhabitants, to what or to whom does it have reference? It related to Jerusalem and the children of Israel, as we shall show most conclusively.

That the "woe," or calamity, predicted of Ariel relates to Jerusalem, perhaps all are agreed; but in order that no possible disagreement may arise respecting this primal question, the following is introduced in its support:

"In Hebron he reigned over Judah seven years and six months; and in *Jerusalem* he reigned thirty and three years over all Israel and Judah." (2 Sam. 5: 5.)

David took the city from the Jebusites about the year 1043 B. C. After this it was called Zion, or "the city of David" (verse 7), and here the warrior-king continued to dwell till the day of his death. This removes all doubt as to the fact that "Ariel" is *Jerusalem*, "the city where David dwelt."

Joseph Smith's "Inspired Translation" makes this point stronger, if possible, than does the Common Version. In this translation of the Bible it is no unusual thing to find verses added, and in many instances entire chapters are manufactured out of whole cloth and added to the word of God. But as we design devoting a chapter to this subject we dismiss it for the present with a mere reference to the fact that in both the Old and New Testaments the authorized texts are changed to suit the fancy of the "translator!"

That Joseph's translation confines this prophecy to Jerusalem and her people will clearly appear as we proceed. Had Mr. Kelley consulted Joseph's "Inspired Translation" and governed his remarks accordingly, he could not have given expression to his theory concerning the "old and the new Ariel," for Joseph's rendering utterly demolishes the very foundation upon which his theory is founded.

Instead of making a comparison between Ariel and some people who should become unto the Lord *as* Ariel, *i. e.*, the extinct races of America, the "new translation" lays the whole scene of the prophecy at Jerusalem.

In order to a correct understanding of the purport of this so-called translation, let us substitute Jerusalem for Ariel, as, meaning the same, they may be used interchangeably, and it will read thus:

"Woe to Jerusalem, to Jerusalem, the city where David dwelt? Add ye year to year, let them kill sacrifices. Yet I will distress Jerusalem, and there shall be heaviness and sorrow; for thus hath the Lord said unto me, *It shall be unto Jerusalem;* that I the Lord will camp against her round about, and will lay siege against her with a mount, and I will raise forts against her.

"And she shall be brought down, and shall speak out of the ground, and her speech shall be low out of the dust; and her voice shall be as of one that hath a familiar spirit, out of the ground, and her speech shall whisper out of the dust." (I. T., Isa. 29: 1-4).

Thus it may be seen that the "woe" relates to Jerusalem, and to Jerusalem *only*.

If the argument be made that the "speaking out of the ground," and "whispering out of the dust," refer to the "written history" of the people upon whom the predicted calamity should fall; and if this "book," mentioned in verse 11, is to be taken "out of the ground," then the book containing such written history must be discovered in the region where the calamity occurred. As this particular "woe" relates to Jerusalem and her people, the Book of Mormon cannot be the "book" described.

The Saints believe that the "coming forth of the Book of Mormon," as they term it, completely and most perfectly fulfills this prophecy in every minute particular. If it does, then the Saints are right, and the Book of Mormon is true; but if they are wrong in their exegesis, the book cannot be a revelation from God.

The advocates of Mormonism are persistent in urging that "no prophecy of the Scripture is of any *private interpretation.*" (2 Pet. 1: 20).

The rule is a good one and perfectly safe. Keeping this rule in view let us inquire: Does the Book of Mormon contain an account of the land and people upon whom this calamity is pronounced? If so, then it must give an account of the overthrow and desolation of Jerusalem, and the captivity of the people of Israel. This conclusion is inevitable, for the reason that *no other people are described* in Isaiah's prophecy.

But if the book does not describe the desolation of Jerusalem, but a people quite distinct from the Jews and upon the American continent, then it is perfectly clear that there can be no connection between this prophecy and the events described in the Book of Mormon.

The "Inspired Translation" being the witness, every prediction made, and every event which transpired, had direct reference to Jerusalem and her disobedient people, together with the "multitude of all the nations" that should "fight against Mount Zion," and could, therefore, have no possible reference to an extinct race of men upon this or any other continent. There can be no reasonable excuse offered, nor any intelligent reason given, for the transfer of the scene of this prophecy from Palestine, where it clearly belongs, to America, where it as certainly was never intended to apply. In order to emphasize this point and render it plain beyond a doubt, let us itemize the events predicted in the order in which they occur, as follows:

1. A "woe" is pronounced against *Jerusalem*, "the city where David dwelt."
2. This woe was to be the direct result of a besieging army: "I will camp against thee round about, and will raise forts against thee."
3. Jerusalem shall be "brought down," and utterly destroyed.
4. Jerusalem, after she is "brought down," shall "speak out of the ground," and shall "whisper out of the dust" (verse 4).
5. The "multitude of her strangers" shall be very numerous—"like small dust," the particles of which cannot be numbered (verse 5).
6. These "terrible ones" shall come upon them "at an instant suddenly" (verse 5).
7. Jerusalem should be visited with other great

calamities, culminating in "flames of devouring fire" (verse 6).

8. "The multitude of all the nations that fight against Jerusalem" should finally pass away, and become "as the dream of a night vision" (verses 7, 8).

9. The condition of the Jewish people is then described as "drunken," and in a state of "deep sleep," their "prophets," their "rulers and their seers" all being "covered" (verses 9, 10).

10. "The vision of *all*"—the prophets, the rulers, the seers and the people alike—had become clouded, and their spiritual perceptions so blunted that they could no more "read" he handwriting of God concerning their future than they could read the words of "a book that is sealed." (V. 11.)

Thus, by ten consecutive steps—ten material and important points in this remarkable prophecy—we have reached what the Saints consider the vital and most important point in the whole chapter, namely, "*a book that is sealed.*"

They treat this as a prophecy setting forth a real, genuine *book* that should actually and really be taken out of the ground. Now, I am about to make a statement that may astonish them, but which is nevertheless true, and that statement is simply this:

I affirm, and do so without the least fear of successful contradiction, that the twenty-ninth chapter of Isaiah contains *no prophecy whatever concerning a* "*book*," much less that a "*sealed book*" should, at any time, or by any person or persons, be taken "out of the ground."

This proposition is easily understood, containing no ambiguity; and if it is erroneous, let the error be shown. Point to chapter and verse containing a prophecy concerning a "book" to "come forth" at any time or in any place, and thus silence, once for all, every opposition.

But aside from this, suppose we proceed to examine the question on the hypothesis that a "book" —a real book—was actually to "come forth" *out of the ground*, and see how much it supports the claim made for the Book of Mormon. If this supposed book is to be understood as containing the written history of the people described in the prophecy, and was to be taken out of the ground in the locality where the events predicted were to transpire, then we cannot escape the conclusion that the "book" must make its appearance *at Jerusalem*, that being the place designated, *and not in America*. If the "three witness" were, according to the "Inspired Translation," to add their testimony to the genuineness of the book, then, they, too, must have been residents of Jerusalem, where the "book" was to make its appearance.

But instead of this the plates from which it is claimed Joseph Smith translated the Book of Mormon are said to have been discovered near Palmyra, N. Y., the home of Martin Harris, one of the "three witnesses."

If the Book of Mormon contains a history of the destruction of "Ariel," the city where David dwelt, in Palestine, how came that history to be deposited in "Indian Hill," New York? Will you please explain? "But," you reply, "we do not claim that the Book of Mormon gives an account of the destruction of Jerusalem, but of another people, who were to be unto the Lord as Ariel." Very well, then, accepting your explanation, the Book of Mormon cannot be the sealed book of the twenty-ninth chapter of Isaiah, the words of which were to be given to " him that is learned," for the very cogent reason that the "Inspired Translation," as already shown, locates the entire scene of this prophecy at Jerusalem.

To briefly summarize, the "Inspired Translation" describes the destruction of Jerusalem and the desolation of Palestine, while the Book of Mormon describes a series of wars between two peoples, the desolation of the entire land "northward and southward," and the final extinction of the more civilized of the two contending races. It is impossible, then, that the Book of Mormon could have "come forth" in fulfillment of a prophecy made in reference to a different place, and a different people, from the place and people described by the Book of Mormon. It seems to me simply impossible that the Saints can extricate themselves from the difficulty in which these undeniable facts inevitably place them.

If Isaiah's prophecy had its fulfillment in what they are pleased to call "the coming forth of the Book of Mormon," then the extraordinary claims they make for the book are seemingly valid, and should be allowed. But, on the other hand, if the *facts* do not justify the conclusions, then surely the Saints ought to abandon their claim for the divine origin of the book, and account for its existence in some other way. This whole matter, then, is thus narrowed down to a question of exegesis and history.

From the foregoing summary of the principal points of this prophecy, it is shown most conclusively that the prediction of *every event* is made of Jerusalem and her people, otherwise the "Inspired Translation" is a *failure and a fraud*. As lovers of truth, and as fair and unbiased students of prophecy and

Biblical history, we are forced to the undeniable conclusion that every line of this wonderful prophecy had its complete accomplishment in the subsequent history of the Israelitish people in the utter destruction of their beloved city by Nebuchadnezzar, king of Babylon, some 588 years before our era, and 124 years *after* the prediction was made.

That these are facts, not mere assertions, we shall now endeavor to prove.

Latter Day Saints are very fond of quoting, when testing the doctrines and faith of others, the following words of Isaiah: "To the law and the testimony, for if they speak not according to this word, it is because there is no light in them." (Isa. 8: 20.) And I am quite sure they cannot object if we apply this test to their interpretation of the passage under consideration.

Holding the advocates of this view to the rule they prescribe for others, let us now proceed to a very careful consideration of the facts relative to the accomplishment of this remarkable prophecy. In order to a correct understanding of the prediction, it will be necessary that we understand the condition of both Judah and Israel at the time the prophet wrote. According to the most authentic chronological data, Isaiah began his prophetic career in the last year of Uzziah's reign, about 758 years B. C., and "prophesied during the space of about forty-five years." (Sacred Biography and History, by Tiffany, page 188.)

At this time "two tribes," or the Jews, dwelt in Judah, with headquarters at Jerusalem, while the ten tribes, or the house of Israel, occupied the land of Israel, with Samaria as their capital city. This division among the descendants of Abraham occurred at the time of the revolt in the days of Rehoboam, in the year 976, B. C., or two hundred and eighteen years before Isaiah began to prophesy.

Let us now take our stand along with this great prophet at Jerusalem, the place of his residence, and follow his prediction closely. The first thing of importance to claim our attention will be the question, Of *whom* does the prophet speak, and against whom is his "woe" directed? In order to avoid the possibility of any disagreement upon this point, suppose we let the prophet answer the question in his own language:

"The vision of Isaiah the son of Amos, which he saw *concerning Judah and Jerusalem*." (Isa. 1: 1.)

His first complaint seems to be of the rebellious and disobedient spirit of the Israelites dwelling at Samaria. Of them he says: "I have nourished and brought up children, and they have rebelled against me." V. 2. After enumerating their many sins and greater iniquities, the prophet then makes the following specific declaration concerning them:

"Your country is desolate, *your cities are burned with fire:* your land, strangers devour it in your presence, and it is *desolate*, as overthrown by strangers." (Verse 7.) And so with alternate warnings and exhortations to repentance, he continues, to the close of the chapter, to plead with the rebellious house of Israel.

Substantially the same prediction is made by Hosea, who was contemporaneous with Isaiah, in the following language: "Samaria shall become desolate; for she hath rebelled against her God: they shall fall by the sword." (Hosea 13: 16.)

Were these predictions by both Isaiah and Hosea,

concerning the people of Samaria, literally and circumstantially fulfilled? If they were, then we may reasonably expect those made concerning Judah and Jerusalem to have a like accomplishment. That they were fulfilled in a very striking and literal manner, every student of Biblical history is fully aware. From the time this prophecy was made, let us pass over a period of some thirty-seven years and see what then transpired. In the year 721 B. C., which was in the time of Hoshea's reign over Israel at Samaria, Shalmaneser, king of Assyria, came up against Samaria and "besieged it three years," and, "In the ninth year of Hoshea, the king of Assyria took Samaria, and carried Israel away into Assyria, and placed them in Halah and Habor by the river of Gazam, and in the cities of the Medes." (2 Kings 17: 3-6.)

So important is this fact of history, that the historian, in chapter eighteen, verses 9 to 11, repeats it with emphasis. By the armies of this invading king their land was literally "devoured by strangers," their cities made desolate, and the once powerful armies of Israel led away captive into Assyria.

Can anything be plainer? Can any fact be susceptible of stronger proof, than that that part of the prophecy of Isaiah which relates to Samaria has been completely and literally fulfilled in the historic events just related? It seems impossible that anyone who believes this—and who can doubt it?—can for one moment doubt that the prophecies relating to "Judah and Jerusalem," as recorded in the twenty-ninth chapter of Isaiah, must be fulfilled in the same striking and literal manner. And that such is the case, I shall now proceed to prove beyond question or doubt.

Having disposed of that part of the prophecy

which relates to Israel and Samaria, let us now turn our attention to that portion which describes Judah and Jerusalem.

In order that he may not be misunderstood, and so misrepresented, the prophet again assures us in chapter two, verse one, that his prediction is "concerning Judah and Jerusalem." Again in the twenty-eighth chapter we have the still further assurance that he speaks of the Jewish people and of Jerusalem in particular, as recorded in the following language:

"Wherefore hear the word of the Lord, ye scornful men, that rule Jerusalem. For the Lord shall rise up as in mount Perazim, he shall be wroth as in the valley of Gibeon, that he may do his work, his strange work; and bring to pass his act, his strange act." (Isa. 28: 14, 21.)

That Jerusalem is the subject of the prophecy is now placed beyond doubt, and that the "strange work" was to be wrought in her midst, and the "strange act" was to be directed against these "scornful men that rule Jerusalem," and incidentally against the whole people, is rendered equally apparent. While this, to my mind, is perfectly clear, I am quite aware that Latter Day Saints view it very differently. The Reorganized Church maintains, as also do all of the various factions which have grown up out of the ruins of the original Mormon Church, that this "strange work," and this "strange act," have been accomplished in the revelation of the Book of Mormon, through Joseph Smith, and the "restoration" of the Apostolic church and doctrine, all of which is predicted in the 29th chapter of Isaiah.

Let us now proceed to examine this matter in a straightforward, honest way, and see who is right.

CHAPTER XXIII.

The Babylonian Captivity—Nebuchadnezzar—Siege of Jerusalem—Raised forts against the city—Terms of Isaiah's prophecy—Jeremiah records its fulfillment—The nations that fight against Mount Zion—Become as the dream of a night vision—Have all passed away—Wise and prudent men—The blindness of all Israel—The Chaldean army besieges Jerusalem—Josephus describes it—Downfall of the Jewish kingdom—A marvelous work and a wonder.

It will be quite unnecessary for me to enter into details as to the subject matter of this prophecy, as this has already been done. It will, therefore, be regarded as quite sufficient to inquire as to whether the prediction of Isaiah has or has not had its accomplishment in the subsequent history of Jerusalem and her people.

The *place* described as the scene of this prophecy is *Jerusalem*, "the city where David dwelt." At the *time* the "woe" was pronounced Jotham was probably king of Judah. The city was to be in a state of "distress" because of the "multitude of strangers" that should "camp against her round about," and should "raise forts against her." This means that a great army, irresistible in force and numbers, was to "lay siege" against this stronghold of Judah, and as the result of this persistent attack Jerusalem was to be "brought down" and should be made tò "speak out of the ground." Says the prophet concerning Jerusalem:

"Thy speech shall be low out of the dust, and thy voice shall be *as* of one that hath a familiar spirit, out of the ground, and thy speech shall whisper out of the dust" (verse 4.) "Thou shalt be visited of the Lord of hosts with thunder, and with earthquake, and with great noise, with storm and tempest, and the *flame of devouring fire*" (verse 6.) With the "woe" thus briefly outlined, let us now carefully examine subsequent history for evidences of its accomplishment.

Some eight years after Samaria had been taken by Shalmanesser, king of Assyria, Sennacherib, his successor to the throne of the Assyrian Empire, "came up against all the fenced cities of Judah and took them," and placed Hezekiah, king of Judah, under heavy tribute, but failed to subjugate the city of Jerusalem. (See 2 Kings 18: 13-16.) His army defeated by the display of miraculous power, Sennacherib returned to Nineveh, where he was shortly afterwards assassinated by one of his sons.

The good king Hezekiah died about the year 710 B. C., and his wicked son Manasseh succeeded him, and reigned in his stead. Under his rule the people became very wicked, so much so that the Lord said concerning them: "Behold, I am bringing such an evil upon Jerusalem and Judah that whosoever heareth of it both of his ears shall tingle." (2 Kings 21: 12.)

In passing briefly over this period of Jewish history it is not in the least difficult to discover that the people became more and more corrupt until they were finally ripe for destruction. Their career of sin and wickedness was "suddenly" brought to an end by the invasion of Nebuchadnezzar, king of Babylon, during the reign of Zedekiah, king of Judah. A graphic description of the terrible calamity which befell the city may be found in the twenty-fifth chapter of 2 Kings, as follows:

"And it came to pass in the ninth year of his reign, in the tenth month, in the tenth day of the month, that Nebuchadnezzar king of Babylon came, he and all his host, against Jerusalem and pitched against it; and they *built forts against it round about*. And the city was *besieged* unto the eleventh year of king Zedekiah. And on the ninth day of the fourth month the famine prevailed in the city, and there was no bread for the people of the land. And the city was broken up, and all the men of war fled by night by the way of the gate between the walls, which is by the king's garden, . . . and the king went the way toward the plain.

"And in the fifth month, on the seventh day of the month, which is the nineteenth year of king Nebuchadnezzar, king of Babylon, came Nebuzar-adan, captain of the guard, a servant of the king of Babylon, unto Jerusalem: and he *burnt the house of the Lord*, and the king's house, and all the houses of Jerusalem, and every great man's house *burnt he with fire*. And all the army of the Chaldees that were with the captain of the guard brake down the walls of Jerusalem round about.

"Now the rest of the people that were left in the city, and the fugitives that fell away to the king of Babylon, with the remnant of the multitude, did Nebuzar-adan the captain of the guard carry away. *So Judah was carried away out of the land.*" (2 Kings 25: 1-4, 8-11, 21.)

To the above Jeremiah adds his testimony in the following language:

"In the ninth year of Zedekiah, king of Judah, in

the tenth month, came Nebuchadnezzar king of Babylon and all his army against Jerusalem, and they besieged it. And the Chaldeans burned the king's house and the houses of the people with fire, and brake down the walls of Jerusalem." (Jer. 39: 1, 8.)

"And it came to pass in the ninth year of his reign, in the tenth month, in the tenth day of the month, that Nebuchadnezzar king of Babylon came, he and all his army, against Jerusalem, and pitched against it, and *built forts against it* round about.

"So the city was besieged unto the eleventh year of king Zedekiah. And in the fourth month, in the ninth day of the month, the famine waxed sore in the city, so that there was no bread for the people of the land. *Then the city was broken up.*" (Jer. 52: 4-7.)

When we pause to consider the fact that Jeremiah, one of the witnesses quoted above, was among the captives, and, therefore, an eye witness to the events described, and the further fact that the "woe" described by this prophet occurred nearly one hundred and twenty years *after* the "woe" predicted against Jerusalem by the prophet Isaiah, there remains little room for any doubt that one prophet was but writing the history of an event predicted by the other.

At the risk of being regarded as somewhat tedious, I will venture to call attention to the striking similarity of the specific terms employed by the two writers.

1. ISAIAH says his "woe" was predicted of *Jerusalem*, "the city where David dwelt."

JEREMIAH says he was writing of a calamity which befell that city.

2. ISAIAH says, "There shall be heaviness and sorrow" (verse 2).

Jeremiah says, "The famine was sore in the city, so that there was no bread for the people of the land," thus causing *heaviness and sorrow* (verse 6).

3. Isaiah says, "I will *camp* against thee round about" (verse 3).

Jeremiah says, "Nebuchadnezzar king of Babylon came . . against Jerusalem and *pitched* (camped) against it" (verse 4).

4. Isaiah says, "I will lay siege against thee with a mount" (verse 3).

Jeremiah says, "So the city was *besieged* unto the eleventh year of king Zedekiah" (verse 5).

5. Isaiah says, "I will *raise forts* against thee" (verse 3).

Jeremiah says, "And . . . Nebuchadnezzer . . *built forts* against it round about" (verse 4).

6. Isaiah says, "Thou shalt be *brought down*" (verse 4).

Jeremiah says, "Then the city was *broken up.*"

7. Isaiah says, "Thou shalt be visited of the Lord of hosts with thunder, and with earthquake, and great noise, with storm and tempest, and the *flame of devouring fire*" (verse 6).

Jeremiah says the city was utterly destroyed by fire:

"Now, in the fifth month, and the tenth day of the month, which was the nineteenth year of Nebuchadnezzar, king of Babylon, came Nebuzar-adan, captain of the guard which served the king of Babylon, into Jerusalem, and burned the house of the Lord, and the king's house, and *all the houses of Jerusalem*, and all the houses of the great men, *burned he with fire*: And all the army of the Chaldeans, that were with the captain of the guard, brake kown the walls of Jerusalem round about." (Jer. 52: 12-14).

Here we have seven points of identity and agreement between the prophecy of Isaiah, and its fulfillment in the recorded history of its accomplishment by Jeremiah.

Add to the testimony of Jeremiah that of 2 Kings 25: 8-10—the language being exactly that of the prophet just quoted—and we have evidence *absolutely unquestionable*, so perfect is the agreement between the prophecy and its subsequent fulfillment, and proves, beyond the possibility of a reasonable doubt, that the prediction of Isaiah 29: 1-4 had its complete accomplishment in the utter destruction of "Ariel, the city where David dwelt," the captivity of the Jews, and the overthrow of their kingdom.

Should any additional proof be required, it may very readily be furnished in the history of the nations engaged in this terrible work of desolation. It is not infrequently the case that God punishes the wicked nations or individuals employed as a means in the execution of divine justice. Of this fact we have a very striking illustration in the subsequent overthrow and subjugation of the Babylonian Empire.

But before passing to a brief consideration of this bit of history, let us follow this prophecy of Isaiah a little further; for as I now view it, the prophecy of Babylon's destruction is recorded in verses seven and fourteen, inclusive, of the twenty-ninth chapter.

The particular reason offered for the careful examination of this matter may be found in the fact that the Saints place, as I think, an unwarranted construction upon the passages to be reviewed. Along with all their leading minds, such as Blair, Kelley,

Forscutt, Lambert and Derry, Latter Day Saints maintain that the later portions of this chapter refer to the spiritually *blind* and "drunken" condition of the religious world at the present age; while others think quite differently. To what, in reality, are but flights of Oriental imagery and *comparison*, they give a literal construction. But these things we may consider in their proper place, if time and space will permit.

At the close of the sixth verse, after declaring the utter destruction of Jerusalem by "flames of devouring fire," the prophet proceeds to unfold the destiny of the Chaldean army, and the overthrow of the Babylonian Empire, who were the direct instruments employed in the destruction of the "City of David," in the following graphic, yet highly poetic, style:

"And the multitude of all the nations that fight against Ariel, even all that fight against her and her munition [fortification], and that distress her, shall be *as a dream of a night vision*." (Isa. 29: 7).

Let us now inquire: *Who* are to become *as* the "dream of a night vision?" The answer cannot be misunderstood. It is "the multitude of all the nations that fight against Ariel"—Jerusalem—the nations of Babylon, Syria, Egypt and Assyria, who at different periods were engaged in war against Jerusalem and Judah, but specifically that of Babylon. Their extinction was to be so nearly absolute as to render them to future ages as "the dream of a night vision;" even as of "an hungry man," who thinks he is eating, but who only awakes to find himself hungry still. To show beyond doubt that this is a representation of the future condition of these nations, the prophet concludes the eighth verse by saying: "So shall *all* the nations be that fight against Mount Zion."

I wish to call particular attention to the fact that this prediction is made concerning the nations that should fight against "Mount Zion," and *not* against a people who, at some remote age of the past, may have lived and warred with one another upon the American continent. These nations have all passed away, and have become, indeed, as the "dream of a night vision." Not one of them remains to tell the story of their former greatness.

Continuing, at the ninth versee, the prophet exclaims: "Stay yourselves, and wonder; cry ye out and cry: they are drunken, but not with wine; they stagger, but not with strong drink."

Who are represented as being "drunken," and who "stagger?" Let the next verse answer; and remember, the language is addressed to the inhabitants of Jerusalem: "For the Lord hath poured out upon you (the Jews) the spirit of deep sleep, and hath closed your eyes: your prophets and your rulers, the seers hath he covered." (V. 10).

Here we have the fact, not only as to *who* were to be drunken and stagger, but the very *cause* of this condition. These Jews, at the time we are describing, were overcome by the "spirit of *deep sleep*," thus closing their eyes, so that to them their "prophets and seers" were "covered," or hidden from their view. None escaped the terrible drowsiness of this overpowering spirit of sleep. It included in its sombre folds every phase of Jewish life: even their "rulers and seers" were involved to a very remarkable degree. Oppressed by this "spirit of deep sleep," whenever they attempted to move they would inevitably and unavoidably "stagger."

Respecting the lamentable condition of both priest and people, the learned as well as the unlearned, the prophet, in the following verse says:

"And the vision of *all*, [including their "rulers and seers,"] is become unto you *as* the words of a book [the marginal reading is *letter*] that is sealed, which men delivered to one that is learned, saying, Read this, I pray thee; and he saith, I cannot, for it is sealed. And the book is delivered to him that is not learned, saying, Read this, I pray thee: and he saith, I am not learned." (Verses 11, 12.)

Let us now proceed to analyze this text and see if we can learn the real facts therein set forth. We learn:

1. That a certain people were reduced to a state of drunken stupor, not from wine or strong drink, but from a condition of "deep sleep" into which they had fallen, as the result of sin.

2. That this condition was general, including many of their prophets, their rulers and their seers.

3. The people referred to were the people of ancient Israel, but specifically the Jews.

4. That the "learned" were reduced to the same lamentable condition as that of the unlearned. They could neither see nor read the words of the letter.

Clearly, and undoubtedly, all that is meant by the eleventh verse is, that the people were morally debased and spiritually blind,—so blind, indeed, that they were as utterly incapable of reading the designs of God concerning themselves, as the learned man would be to "read a letter that is sealed," or for the "unlearned" man to read the same letter if the seal were broken and the letter laid open before his eyes.

The fact is perfectly clear that neither could read a letter under these conditions; and would, therefore, blindly stagger on to the end of the road that should ultimately lead to their destruction. Because of these conditions, the prophet continues thus:

"Wherefore the Lord said, Forasmuch as *this* people [the Jews] draw near me with their mouth, and with their lips do honor me, but have removed their heart far from me, and their fear toward me is taught by the precepts of men; therefore, behold I will proceed to do a marvelous work *among this people*, even a marvelous work and a wonder: for the wisdom of their wise men shall perish, and the understanding of their prudent men shall be hid." (Verses 13, 14.)

Notwithstanding their generally depraved and benighted condition, the Jewish people, at the time of their desolation, had a few "wise" and "prudent" men among them. A marvelous work, "even a marvelous work and a wonder," was to be performed "among this people," and these "wise men" fully understoood the nature of this work, and strove earnestly to avert the pending calamity by giving them wise counsel, and exhorting them to repentance. Prominently among their "wise men" were Jeremiah, Ezekiel and Hosea.

But the wisdom of their "wise men" was allowed to "perish," and the "understanding of their *prudent* men" was "hid" from this gainsaying people because of their great iniquity and their lamentable and hopeless state of blindness.

At the time Isaiah delivered this wonderful prophecy, not one of her rulers or princes believed Jerusalem could be taken by an enemy, so perfect was their confidence in the strength of her fortifications and the impregnability of her walls. From the time when David, the great warrior-king, first established his capital here, till the time of Isaiah's prophecy, it had successfully resisted the assaults of every enemy, no matter what his strength, till it had become the settled conviction that no power on earth could bring her under subjection, and render her tributary to a Gentile nation. But notwithstanding all this the Lord said, "Behold I will proceed to do a marvelous work, even a marvelous work and a wonder *among this people.*"

Even when the Chaldean army had encamped "round about" the city, and had proceeded to "raise forts" against her, building mounds, says Josephus, in height, equal to the height of the walls of the city, those within had no fears of being overpowered and defeated by this great "multitude of strangers." I quote from Josephus upon this point af follows:

"Now the King of Babylon was very intent and earnest upon the siege of Jerusalem; and he erected towers upon great banks of earth, and from them repelled those that stood upon the walls: he also made a great number of such banks round about the whole city, whose height was equal to those walls. However, those that were within bore the siege with courage and alacrity, for they were not discouraged, either by the famine or the pestilential distemper, but were of cheerful minds in the prosecution of the war. . . And this siege they endured for eighteen months, until they were destroyed by the famine, and by the darts which the enemy threw at them from the towers." (Antiq. Book 10, ch. 8, pp. 253, 254).

Nothing, perhaps, could appear more marvelous to this very confident people than to see the victorious Chaldean army enter the city, after having battered down her walls, and to witness the complete overthrow of their proud kingdom, and behold the desecration and destruction of their magnificent temple by "flames of devouring fire;" and yet it was done.

This "marvelous work and a wonder," predicted by Isaiah, was accomplished in a most striking and literal manner, as we have just seen by the testimony of both Jeremiah, the prophet, and Flavius Josephus, the historian.

Having witnessed the terrible devastation of his beloved city, and the reduction of his people to a state of servitude and bondage, the prophet mournfully exclaims, as if in great surprise: "How doth the city sit solitary that was full of people! how is she become as a widow! she that was great among the nations, and princess among the provinces, how is she become tributary!" (Lam. 1: 1).

As a reason assigned for this distressed condition of his people, Jeremiah says: "Jerusalem hath grievously sinned; therefore she is removed. . . . Her filthiness is in her skirts; she remembereth not her last end; therefore she came down wonderfully: she hath no comforter." (Vs. 8, 9).

Isaiah predicted of Jerusalem, "Thou shalt be brought down;" and Jeremiah records the fact that "she came down wonderfully."

That it is not forcing the sense of the passage in Isaiah to say the "marvelous work and a wonder" can be nothing more nor less than the work of desolation just described, will be rendered apparent from the following declaration of the prophet Jeremiah:

"The kings of the earth, and all the inhabitants of the world, would not have believed that the adversary and the enemy should have entered into the gates of Jerusalem." (Lam. 4: 12).

To Jeremiah, as well as to "the prophets, the rulers, and the seers," it was a "marvelous" thing that the "enemy" should have "entered into the gates of Jerusalem." Whatever is "marvelous" is at the same time a *wonder*. Hence, the Lord did a "marvelous work, even a marvelous work and a wonder," when he permitted the enemy to enter into the gates of the beloved city and batter down her walls, burn with "flames of devouring fire" the beautiful and costly temple; rob the house of the Lord of its magnificent treasure, and carry the daughters of Zion away captive into Babylon.

We venture the assertion that not in all history can there be found a circumstance that looks so much like a complete and circumstantial fulfillment of Isaiah's prophecy as this. Certainly the vague theory concerning the Book of Mormon does not contain one single element of its accomplishment. Every material point advanced in its support is seriously in question. Not one thing claimed by its advocates is conceded. Not a scholar of the century, the most advanced period of the world's history, has ever given it his support. The entire premise is founded in the most wild and reckless speculation of an uncultivated mind. Nothing is proved. All is assumed.

But this cannot be affirmed of the present argument. The premise is a clear, well-defined statement of prophecy, and the conclusion derived from the premise is supported by plain, unquestionable facts of history.

CHAPTER XXIV.

PROFESSOR ANTHON AND MARTIN HARRIS.

Professor Anthon and Martin Harris—The "words of a book"—Joseph Smith's transcript presented to the Professor—Read this, I pray thee—I cannot read a sealed book—Joseph Smith, not Martin Harris, made the statement—Times and Seasons for May 2, 1842—Mr. Kelley states the case—The Professor could not decipher the characters—Characters were Egyptian, Chaldaic, Assyrian and Arabic—Self-contradictory—Correctly translated—Professor Anthon's statement—Contradicts Mr. Harris—No other witnesses—The statements compared—Smith-Harris testimony incompetent.

HAVING discussed that portion of the question which relates to Isaiah's prophecy and its fulfillment in the history of the Israelitish people, I wish now to take up the claim respecting the presentation of certain characters by Martin Harris to Professor Charles Anthon, of New York City, for examination by that gentleman. These characters are said to have been transcribed from the plates of the Book of Mormon by Joseph Smith. This transcript was taken to the city and presented to the Professor, with the request to decipher them. This transcript is claimed to be the "words of a book," mentioned in Isaiah 29: 11, and hence the fulfillment of the prophecy.

As to the object of this interview all parties are agreed. But as to what was said and done at the time there is quite a difference. The statements of Professor Anthon differ very materially from those made by Mr. Harris. The statement of Mr. Harris has never been verified; in fact, there is no evidence that he ever made the statement attributed to him. The document is open to at least two serious objections, namely:

1. No competent witness has left his testimony concerning what transpired, except the Professor himself—no proof that "the words of a book" were presented to Mr. Anthon with a request to read them. If so, who is the witness? and where is his testimony?

2. No competent witness has ever said that Professor Anthon admitted that he could not read or decipher the characters presented to him. If so, who is the witness? when did he testify? and where is his testimony recorded?

These are questions material to the issue. If it transpires that no competent witness has ever testified to the material points in this controversy, the entire case must fail for want of proof. As to the first count in the allegation, it is claimed that, in accordance with Isaiah 29: 11, "the words of a book" were presented to Professor Anthon, who was asked to read them, but who, upon learning that a miracle was in some way connected with the discovery of the plates from which the characters were transcribed, and a part of which were sealed, said, "I cannot read a sealed book." (See Presidency and Priesthood, page 203.)

In the circumstances of this visit, it is claimed, were fulfilled that portion of Isaiah's prophecy which relates to "the book that is sealed."

The point we wish to examine in a fair, careful manner is this: Do the facts, as gleaned from the testimony of the witnesses, sustain the allegation? Did Professor Anthon *admit* that he could not decipher the characters presented to him, as claimed?

As a matter of fact, this is the only answer he could have made in order to meet the demands of this particular case. Had he professed to be able to "read" the words of the so-called "sealed book," the object of Mr. Harris' visit to the Professor would have been signally defeated, and no semblance to a fulfillment of Isaiah's prophecy would be discoverable.

The terms of this prediction are: "*Read this*, I pray thee: and he saith, *I cannot*, for it is sealed."

The most casual observer cannot fail to notice the striking similarity between the form of words used by Isaiah and that put into the mouth of Professor Anthon by the man who made the so-called report of what he said. This similarity of verbal construction becomes rather significant when we consider the *date* of the utterance of Professor Anthon and that of the individual by whom it was reported and published.

We have said no competent witness has ever testified to the statement attributed to Professor Anthon. In order to determine this point, let us go to the very bottom of the whole matter, and see if Martin Harris, the man who, it is said, made the visit to Professor Anthon, has ever said one word about it. The statement of Harris is of first importance, as that of any other person, except Professor Anthon himself, would come under the head of "hearsay" evidence, and would therefore be excluded by any court of law on the ground of incompetency.

This remarkable statement appeared for the first time in the church organ, at Nauvoo, Illinois, known as "The Times and Seasons," Vol. 3, No. 13, in the issue for May 2, 1842, and is made, *not* by Martin Harris, but by Joseph Smith, Jr. Instead of being the testimony of Harris, as it should be to give it validity, it is but a second-hand statement of Joseph Smith as to what Harris had told him.

If Martin Harris ever made such a statement as that attributed to him, why not produce that statement instead of Joseph Smith's version of it? The very fact of Harris' persistent silence upon a subject of so much importance to those concerned may very properly be construed to mean that he never made the statements attributed to him, and that as a matter of fact they may be, and probably are, but a "revised version" of what he did say, made and published some fourteen years later by an interested party to bolster up an error and a fraud which at the time had obtained a degree of currency that brought it into public prominence.

Produce the published statement of Martin Harris, well authenticated, and it will greatly strengthen this peculiar claim, and at the same time relieve its defenders of the necessity of quoting Joseph Smith's version of that statement. Produce it, and let the world see and read the well-attested statement of Martin Harris himself, over his own signature, that the judgment of an enlightened and intelligent public may be passed upon its merits. From an experience of some thirty-five or forty years in the church, I shall venture the assertion that no such statement of Martin Harris can be produced.

But, for the sake of the argument, let us admit that Harris did present the "words," or characters, to Prof. Anthon, and what do we have? Not a fulfillment of Isaiah 29: 11, but the exact opposite, as will appear as we proceed.

Joseph Smith makes Harris to put these words into

Prof. Anthon's mouth: "I cannot read a sealed book."

Every writer who has made any attempt to defend the claims of the Book of Mormon on this ground has urged as an argument full of potency, that the learned professor could not decipher the characters submitted to him. Upon this point Elder Wm. H. Kelley says:

"Both he [Prof. Anthon] and Dr. Mitchell were waited upon by Mr. Harris with a copy of the characters, and they examined them, just as affirmed by Mr. Harris, and as predicted in the twenty-ninth chapter of Isaiah, and eleventh verse, would be done, which is the main point in the investigation, and that neither of them was able to decipher them." (Presidency and Priesthood, p. 205.)

Here we have the affirmation of Mr. Kelley, (and he is considered good authority,) that the "characters" were presented to the Professor, and that neither he nor Dr. Mitchell was able to decipher them, and that their failure to do so is "the main point in the investigation." In this declaration Mr. Kelley but repeats the position, and reflects the sentiment of all the leading minds of the denomination from its rise to the present day. With this view of the case firmly fixed in the mind, let us recall the witness, Martin Harris, for re-direct examination:

Question. Mr. Harris, please state what you know of a conversation which is said to have taken place some time in February, 1828, in the city of New York, between yourself and one Prof. Charles Anthon, concerning the translation of certain characters, which it is claimed were presented to him.

Answer. "I went to the city of New York, and

presented the characters which had been transcribed, with the translation thereof to Prof. Anthon, a gentleman celebrated for his literary attainments. Prof. Anthon stated that the translation was correct; more so than any he had before seen translated from the *Egyptian*. I then showed him those that were not translated, and he said they were Egyptian, Chaldaic, Assyrian and Arabic, and he said they were the true characters." (Presidency and Priesthood, p. 202.)

The above statement is held up to the world as the testimony of Martin Harris, but which, as a matter of fact, as I shall show, is but the unsupported statement of Joseph Smith.

While, in their eagerness to make the prediction of Isaiah and the alleged fulfillment agree, they claim that Prof. Anthon could not decipher these characters, said to be Egyptian, Chaldaic, Assyrian and Arabic, yet Joseph Smith makes Mr. Harris to assert that Prof. Anthon was not only *able* to do so, but that he actually *did* "decipher the characters," and told the plain, "simple-hearted farmer" just what the characters were, and that they had been correctly translated, a thing utterly impossible had the professor not been able to "read," or translate, the characters presented to him.

If this part of the Smith-Harris "testimony" can be relied upon as valid, then the twenty-ninth chapter of Isaiah could not possibly have been fulfilled in this event, for the very good reason that the "learned" man of Isaiah's prophecy says, "*I cannot* read it, for it is sealed." Instead of Mr. Anthon saying, *I cannot*, he says, I CAN; and, Smith and Harris being the witnesses, *he did read it*. What, then, becomes of the claim of Mr. Kelley, and other prominent writers, that Prof. Authon "could not decipher the characters?"

Did it ever occur to you that this document, so much relied upon to support this claim for the Book of Mormon, is actually self-contradictory? And yet such is the case.

That part of the statement just quoted, says, in substance, that Prof. Anthon could, and in fact did, "read" the words or characters submitted to him by Martin Harris, while the latter part of the statement represents Mr. Anthon as saying, "I cannot read a sealed book."

If Prof. Anthon really examined the characters and declared them to have been "correctly translated," then it is clear to the most casual observer that he must have been able to decipher the characters in which the "sealed book" was said to have been written.

If by his great learning this distinguished professor of languages could translate the characters in which it is claimed the Book of Mormon was written, then it is absurd in the extreme to urge that Joseph Smith, or any other man, should be divinely inspired in order to their translation.

If Mr. Anthon did *not* decipher the characters presented to him, then his alleged statement or certificate, that said characters had been correctly translated, is absolutely worthless, and amounts to nothing by way of proving what is claimed for the Book of Mormon.

If he *did* decipher them—which he must have done in order to render the alleged certificate of any value —then it does not come within the range of Isaiah's prophecy, for he declares that when the "words" were presented, the "learned man" should say, "I cannot read them."

On which horn of the dilemma, think you, will the defenders of Mormonism prefer to fall? Either will prove fatal to their cause.

In view of the facts as they appear upon the face of this document, it seems clear that Prof. Anthon never could have made the statement put into his mouth by the Smith-Harris testimony, namely, "I cannot read a sealed book."

This bit of testimony—if the statement may be dignified by this title—is rendered incompetent, as the witness clearly and unmistakably contradicts himself upon what Mr. Kelley declares to be "the main point in this investigation." A witness who contradicts himself upon the principal point involved, invalidates his testimony, and is accounted as of no value in the establishment of the question in controversy.

The so-called testimony of Martin Harris having been examined, let us now call the next, and only other witness ever introduced upon this point. Strange as it may appear, this witness is none other than Prof. Anthon himself. His statement is introduced by another party, and for an entirely different purpose, namely, to disprove the very thing sought to be established by the advocates of Mormonism.

This witness was introduced by E. D. Howe, in a work called "Mormonism Unveiled," published in 1834. The object in publishing this statement of Prof. Anthon was to prove the Book of Mormon a fraud, and the "characters" but a bungling attempt to deceive the credulous.

As this entire case depends upon what both parties

to the controversy call the testimony of Prof. Anthon, it becomes necessary, in order to understand the true status of this question, to here quote such part of the testimony of this witness as relates directly to the subject under consideration. Relative to this matter, Prof. Anthon says:

"Some years ago a plain, apparently simple-hearted farmer, called on me with a note from Dr. Mitchell, of our city, now dead, requesting me to decipher, if possible, a paper which the farmer would hand me, and which Dr. Mitchell confessed he had been unable to understand. When I asked the person who brought it how he obtained the writing, he gave me, as far as I now recollect, the following account. A gold book, consisting of a number of plates of gold fastened together in the shape of a book by wires of the same metal, had been dug up in the northern part of the state of New York, and along with the book an enormous pair of gold spectacles. These spectacles were so large that if a person attempted to look through them, his two eyes would have to be turned toward one of the glasses merely, the spectacles in question being altogether too large for the human face.

"Whoever examined the plates through the spectacles was enabled not only to read them, but understand their meaning. All of this knowledge, however, was confined, at that time, to a young man who had the trunk containing the plates and spectacles in his sole possession. He put on the spectacles, or rather looked through one of the glasses, and deciphered the characters in the book, and having committed some of them to paper, handed copies to a person outside.

"This paper was in fact a singular scroll. It consisted of all kinds of crooked characters, disposed in columns, and had evidently been prepared by some person who had before him at the time a book containing various alphabets, Greek and Hebrew letters, crosses and flourishes. Roman letters inverted or placed sideways, were arranged in perpendicular columns, and the whole ended in a rude delineation of a circle, divided into various compartments, decked with various strange marks, and evidently copied after the Mexican Calendar given by Humboldt." (Presidency and Priesthood, pp. 203, 204, as quoted by W. H. Kelley from E. D. Howe's works, p. 272).

This quotation is made by Mr. Kelley with the view to strengthen the statement of Martin Harris concerning the latter's visit to Prof. Anthon, as will appear from the following:

"This statement of Martin Harris is corroborated and confirmed by Prof. Anthon himself." (Presidency and Priesthood, p. 203).

We now have before us two several statements, namely, one made by Martin Harris in a second-hand way through Joseph Smith, as touching the visit of Harris to Prof. Anthon in 1828, with a paper containing a transcript of the characters from the gold plates; and another declared to be the verified statement of the Professor concerning the same visit, and his conversation with the "simple-hearted farmer" concerning the plates and characters in question.

It will doubtless be observed that these statements differ materially as to what occurred on that occasion. Harris states that Prof. Anthon declared they were "the true characters," and that said characters were

"Egyptian, Chaldaic, Assyrian and Arabic," and that Smith's translation of them was correct.

But Prof. Anthon flatly contradicts this statement, as clearly appears from the above quotation. Instead of pronouncing them "true characters," he avers that the paper presented by Harris "was in fact a *strange scroll*," consisting of "all kinds of crooked characters," with some "Greek and Hebrew letters (as he remembered it) crosses and flourishes," but *not one word* about either Egyptian, Chaldaic, Assyrian or Arabic. Which of the statements are we to believe?

It is quite apparent that the witnesses radically disagree upon the material points in issue. When witnesses disagree upon a point material to the issue, the credibility of such witnesses must be taken into consideration in order to the arrival at just conclusions.

A witness who has no personal interest in the questions involved, and who is of good moral character, is entitled to full credence. But if the witness be an interested party, or if his general veracity is bad, then his testimony must be received with a degree of allowance commensurate with existing facts.

The only two witnesses in this case are Prof. Charles Anthon on the one hand, and Martin Harris on the other. To apply the above rule (and it is a rule by which courts of justice are invariably governed, and the justice of which is never questioned), let us inquire whether these witnesses, or either of them, were interested, directly or indirectly, in the question now under consideration.

It certainly cannot be maintained with any degree of candor that Joseph Smith and Martin Harris, the two moving spirits in the "golden plate" scheme, were not directly interested in a matter fraught with so much importance to themselves. If they succeed, bright prospects of both wealth and renown are before them. If they fail, poverty and ignominy are their lot. At the time of this interview they were unknown to the public, having nothing to lose, but everything to gain in the event of success.

On the other hand, Prof. Anthon was a scholar and linguist of great renown, and a gentleman of unquestionable veracity, having in view, as a man of letters, only the development of such facts as would tend to the general advancement of literature and science. Hence, his only interest in this paper handed him by the "simple-hearted farmer" was to arrive at the exact truth concerning the peculiar characters which the paper contained. He had no reputation either to make or to lose in this transaction. The result of the examination could not in the least affect his standing before the general public, either as a gentleman or scholar, and he cannot, therefore, be considered in any sense an interested witness in the case.

This, to the writer, seems to be a fair and impartial view of the matter as it now stands.

I am quite aware, however, that the genuineness of Mr. Anthon's statement, as published by E. D. Howe, is questioned by those interested in the defense of the Book of Mormon, on the ground that Howe was an enemy to the Latter Day Saints. But I confess I do not see how this enmity towards the church on the part of E. D. Howe could in the least affect the statement voluntarily made by the eminent professor. It is unreasonable to believe that an obscure editor of a village paper—a man whose reputation at the time scarcely exceeded the bounds of his State—could exercise such influence as to induce a man of Prof. Anthon's standing to make a statement utterly false and misleading.

Besides this, Prof. Anthon's statement appeared in Mr. Howe's work as early as 1834; and if it had been a vile fabrication—a malicious, misleading falsehood—perpetrated by Mr. Howe, as has been charged, the fact might easily have been determined by simply calling Mr. Anthon's attention to the matter, and securing his denial of its truthfulness. Although the professor lived thirty-three years after the publication of Howe's book, having died in 1867, no such denial was ever sought or obtained. The presumption would, therefore, naturally be that Mr. Anthon's statement, as published by E. D. Howe, is substantially, if not circumstantially correct.

Having briefly examined the testimony of the witness, and the source through which it has been transmitted to us, on the one hand, let us now proceed to examine the evidence as presented by the other side, and the channels through which it comes to us.

To begin with, and in order to be perfectly fair, I shall concede the witnesses on both sides to be of good moral character, and that their veracity has never been questioned. As we have already seen, the testimony of Martin Harris and that of Prof. Anthon differ materially on very important points, and hence both cannot be true. It is not deemed necessary to repeat the testimony of Mr. Harris, but merely to examine the channel through which we have received it.

I wish again to call attention to the fact that the statement attributed to Martin Harris concerning his interview with Prof. Anthon never saw the light of day, so far as the public is concerned, till May 2, 1842, fourteen years after the event is said to have taken place; and it was then made public, not by Martin Harris, but by Joseph Smith, the very man, above all others on earth, the most directly interested.

From the church organ, a weekly paper published at Nauvoo, Ill., of which Joseph Smith was the editor, the following extract is quoted. Joseph Smith says:

"Some time in the month of February [1828] the aforementioned Martin Harris came to our place [in Pennsylvania], got the characters which I had drawn from the plates, and started with them to the city of New York. For what took place relative to him and the characters, I refer to his own account of the circumstances, as he related them to me, after his return, which was as follows: 'I went to the city of New York, and presented the characters which had been translated, with the translation thereof, to Prof. Anthon, a gentleman celebrated for his literary attainments.'" etc., etc. (Times and Seasons, No. 13, Vol. 3, May 2, 1842.)

Thus it will be seen that the statement generally attributed to Martin Harris, is nothing more nor less than a repetition by Joseph Smith of what he says Harris told him of the alleged interview with Prof. Anthon. The legal value of this statement, as every intelligent reader knows, amounts to absolutely nothing, and, so far as the testimony of this witness is concerned, the fact is just as far from being proved as if he had never made the statement. Mr. Harris is the only competent witness on this side of the case, and he never testified—Mr. Smith simply speaks for him.

The best evidence, and, in fact, the *only* evidence, of which this case is susceptible, would be the solemn affirmation, or what would be still better, perhaps, the sworn statement of Mr. Harris. But no such statement or affirmation was ever obtained from him. Not a scrap of anything Martin Harris ever wrote—if he ever wrote anything on the subject—can be adduced in support of this claim concerning his interview with Prof. Anthon.

Every rule, either of law or usage, will exclude Joseph Smith's statement as to what Harris said concerning the Anthon-Harris interview, so long as the testimony of the latter was attainable. Harris lived nearly, or quite, *forty years* after Mr. Smith's death, in 1844, and his testimony was, therefore, easily obtainable, had he been willing to verify Mr. Smith's statement as made in the Times and Seasons. As he never did this, it is clearly presumable, as well as highly probable, that he never made the statement attributed to him. This view is rendered still more probable when the fact is considered that he denounced Smith and left the church several years before Mr. Smith's death.

The foregoing is a brief summary of the *facts* as we have them from authentic Mormon sources, and prove beyond all doubt or controversy that the statement always attributed to Martin Harris, as a matter of fact *came from Joseph Smith*, the so-called translator of the "gold plates."

The testimony is thus shown to be both ex parte and hearsay, and is, therefore incompetent, and hence inadmissible.

These objections do not, and indeed cannot, apply

to the testimony of Prof. Anthon, as presented to the public by E. D. Howe, for the very good reason that he made the statement himself—it is not Howe's version of it—directly to the public, and no competent witness has ever attempted to contradict him.

In fact, Joseph Smith, eight years after Prof. Anthon's statement, or affidavit, was made public, was the first and only man to attempt a denial of the matters and things therein set forth, and that, too, in the very face of the fact that he had no possible chance of knowing whether the statements were true or false, he having never met Prof. Anthon, nor corresponded with him on this very important subject.

Did it ever occur to you that the perpetual silence of Martin Harris, and the method of all the leading minds of the church to "fight shy" of Prof. Anthon on this point (not one of them, so far as I know, ever having made an effort to obtain from him a statement confirmatory of their claim), looks just a little suspicious? Does it not look just the least bit like they were afraid his testimony would upset the whole theory? It certainly looks so to me.

The foregoing analysis of the 29th chapter of Isaiah shows most conclusively that the prophecy has no reference whatever to America and its inhabitants, but to Jerusalem and the people of Israel. It is impossible, therefore, that the Book of Mormon can be a revelation from God, "brought forth" in fulfillment of Isaiah's prophecy, or any other Scripture.

All this talk, therefore, about "the book that is sealed," is simply and only "a cunningly devised fable," invented to bolster up a falsehood, and has no foundation in the truth. Not one *fact*—and facts are said to be stubborn things—can be adduced in its support.

The "*words* of a book that is sealed," as well as the "book" itself, were simply employed by the prophet as symbols to illustrate the utter blindness of the Israelitish people, as already shown, and can, therefore, have no possible reference to the visit of Martin Harris to Prof. Anthon, with the so-called words of a book, transcribed from the plates.

CHAPTER XXV.

TESTIMONY OF THE THREE WITNESSES.

The testimony of the three witnesses—A remarkable document—Apostle Pratt's view—An immense conclusion—The witnesses not deceived—Their testimony is true or they are impostors—The line is drawn by Mormon authority—Are the witnesses unimpeachable?—Direct and indirect evidence—The Mormon Church—Authority depends upon the veracity of these witnesses—An admission—A negative proposition—How established—An illustration.

FOLLOWING is the testimony of the three witnesses to the Book of Mormon, and whose declarations are regarded as absolutely unanswerable. These witnesses say:

"Be it known unto all nations, kindreds, tongues, and people, unto whom this work shall come, that we, through the grace of God the Father, and our Lord Jesus Christ, have seen the plates which contain this record, which is a record of the people of Nephi, and also of the Lamanites, his brethren, and also of the people of Jared, which came from the tower of which hath been spoken; and we also know that they have been translated by the gift and power of God, for his voice hath declared it unto us; wherefore we know of a surety, that the work is true. And we also testify that we have seen the engravings which are upon the plates; and that they have been shewn unto us by the power of God, and not of man. And we declare with words of soberness, that an angel of God came down from heaven, and he brought and

laid before our eyes, that we beheld and saw the plates, and the engravings thereon; and we know that it is by the grace of God the Father, and our Lord Jesus Christ, that we beheld and bear record that these things are true; and it is marvelous in our eyes: Nevertheless, the voice of the Lord commanded us that we should bear record of it; wherefore, to be obedient unto the commandments of God, we bear testimony of these things. And we know that if we are faithful in Christ, we shall rid our garments of the blood of all men, and be found spotless before the judgment seat of Christ, and shall dwell with him eternally in the heavens. And the honor be to the Father, and to the Son, and to the Holy Ghost, which is one God. Amen." OLIVER COWDERY.
DAVID WHITMER.
MARTIN HARRIS.

These three witnesses, it is maintained by the advocates of the Mormon hierarchy, stand alike unimpeached and unimpeachable. Whether the Saints are right in this claim remains to be seen. I am not aware that any attempt has ever been made to analyze the testimony of the "three witnesses," and test their utterances by the introduction of the testimony of other witnesses, but I shall do so in these pages.

So confident, indeed, are Latter Day Saints that the testimony of these three men cannot be invalidated, or made void, that Apostle Orson Pratt defies the world to refute their testimony concerning the Book of Mormon. He says:

"If he, [Joseph Smith] was sincere, then the Book of Mormon is a divine revelation, and this church must be 'the only true and living Church of Christ upon the face of the whole earth,' and there is no salvation in any other. This is an immense conclusion, but we can come to no other, the moment we admit his sincerity." (Pratt't Works, Evidences of the Book of Mormon and Bible Compared, page 55.)

Respecting the testimony of Joseph Smith and the three witnesses, Mr. Pratt says:

"No reasonable person will say that these persons were themselves deceived; the nature of their testimony is such that they must either be bold, daring impostors, or else the Book of Mormon is true." (Ibid, page 50.)

Relative to the same matter, President Joseph Smith of Lamoni, Iowa, says:

"The testimony of these witnesses is plain, and of a nature to preclude the possibility of their having been deceived. They could not have been mistaken, hence their testimony is true, or they are liars."— (Smith's History, page 48.)

Thus the line is drawn, and thinking people are forced to choose between Joseph and Mormonism on one hand, and the entire Christian world on the other; and when these are judged by the results, by their fruits, the choice may with safety be made. If these four men told the truth, then Mormonism is true, and men can only reject it "under the penalty of eternal damnation." Truly, as Mr. Pratt says, "this is an immense conclusion," and yet there is no middle ground. The aggressive methods of Mr. Pratt, Mr. Kelley, President Smith, and in fact all other well-informed Latter Day Saints, force us in dealing with this question, to treat Joseph Smith and the three witnesses, either as saints and absolutely right, or as base impostors and intentional deceivers.

It is rather painful to be driven to such extremes. Christian people would rather believe a man deceived and honestly in error than be forced to regard him as a designing impostor and an unmitigated fraud. But since President Smith and Mr. Pratt inform us that the facts claimed in the present instance preclude the possibility that "these four persons were themselves deceived," we are compelled—though ever so much against our will—to treat them as willful deceivers. Deceived or deceivers they most certainly must be, for Mr. Pratt declares, and very correctly as we must admit, that "the nature of their testimony is such that they must either be bold, daring impostors, or else the Book of Mormon is true."

ARE THE WITNESSES UNIMPEACHABLE?

With reference to the impeachability of the witnesses Apostle Pratt has this to say:

"But in order to prove that the witnesses of the Book of Mormon are all impostors, it will be necessary to prove that they did not see and hear an angel—that they did not see the plates in the angel's hand—that they did not hear the voice of the Lord declaring that they were translated correctly. All reasonable men will admit that it is impossible for any negative testimony to be found to prove *directly* that God did not send his angel to reveal and confirm the truth of the Book of Mormon; and as there is no *direct* evidence to negative their testimony and prove them impostors, therefore if it be possible to prove them such it can only be done by some *indirect* evidence arising from the circumstances of the case, or from the nature of the message itself, as being contradictory to some known truth." (Ibid, page 55.)

From the foregoing it may be seen that this renowned philosopher and apostle of Mormonism takes an intelligent and comprehensive view of the question he discusses. He fully realizes the fact that there is no room for the chief actors in this unique drama to be deceived, and that the authenticity of the Book of Mormon, as well as the authority of the Mormon Church, depends upon the veracity of these witnesses.

Confident he must be of his ability to sustain the veracity of his witnesses, as may be seen by the following:

"These witnesses have neither of them denied the bold and fearless, though humble, testimony which they have sent forth to all nations. No man living can prove that an angel did not appear to them. There is nothing in the nature of the event, *nor in any of the circumstances connected with it*, that would render it absurd, unscriptural, unreasonable or improbable. . . . Therefore, no man living has the least authority for condemning these witnesses as impostors. Indeed, there cannot be brought the least shadow of evidence, either direct or indirect, to prove that their testimony concerning the angel is false. Therefore, as their testimony cannot be proved false, the Book of Mormon stands upon a foundation as firm as the rock of ages, and as secure as the throne of the Almighty." (Ibid, page 56.)

Mr. Pratt then reaches his peroration as follows:

"All men among all nations, kindreds, tongues and people are required, under the penalty of eternal damnation, to believe, receive and obey the Book of Mormon, unless they can prove the witnesses thereof impostors. *And this they cannot do.*" (Ibid, page 56.) The italics are mine.

I am now about to admit a fact that I once believed would prove fatal to the position of any man making it, namely: I concede that if the testimony of these witnesses cannot be proved false, that their testimony is flatly contradicted by many known truths, their statement concerning the angel is unquestionably true, and the Book of Mormon, therefore, is a divine revelation.

The reader will doubtless have observed that our admission of Mr. Pratt's conclusions is as frank and unreserved as are the premises from which he derives them. We desire to meet this issue fairly and squarely, having perfect assurance that the truth is mighty and will prevail.

If Mormonism is the embodiment of a revelation from God, let it triumph; but if it be a fraud, a base deception, let it be crushed to earth to rise again no more forever.

Mr. Pratt, as do all defenders of this Mormon dogma, depends upon the inability of his opponents to prove a negative. If the testimony of these witnesses cannot be proved untrue, if these witnesses cannot be proved impostors, then, according to Mormon logic, the Book of Mormon must be true.

Two objections may, with all propriety, be urged against this mode of argument, namely:

First. Every known rule of logic or law requires the party who affirms a matter in dispute to *prove*, by competent testimony, that which he affirms to be true in a manner so clear as to leave no room for reasonable doubt. Failing in this he simply loses his case, with nobody to blame but himself.

Second. No man is required to prove a negative. This is but the consequence of the above rule.

While under no obligation to do so, yet negative propositions are quite often proved by defendants. Where this can be done it makes a strong case doubly strong.

A negative proposition can be established only by the introduction of evidence to prove a fact which is utterly incompatible with the alleged fact in question. Thus A swears he saw B kill C at a given *time* and *place*. This is called direct, or positive testimony.

To prove that he did *not* kill C as charged in the indictment, B shows by numerous witnesses whose veracity cannot be questioned that at the exact time he is charged with having committed the crime he was fifty miles distant from the place where the crime was committed. B thus proves that he did not kill C, and A's testimony is thereby rendered worthless, while A himself stands impeached. In this case B is said to have proved an *alibi*.

The circumstances of the case must harmonize in every detail with the facts as they are set up in the petition. If there is one material fact which is incompatible with what is alleged to have transpired, it materially weakens the plaintiff's cause; and if the point in question be fundamental, it utterly destroys it.

Governed by these rules, I shall proceed at once to examine each material point in the testimony of these witnesses, and see if they are in accord with known truths.

CHAPTER XXVI.

DID THEY SEE AN ANGEL?

The three witnesses—Did they see an angel?—Impeaching the witnesses—Seven counts in the indictment—Eight witnesses—Testimony unimportant—Their defection from the prophet in Missouri—Stick to their original story—The three witnesses did not recant—Reasons for adhering to the original story—Afraid to expose the fraud—Better die with a lie on their lips than to divulge the secret—The touch of angelic hands in holy ordination—How could they forsake the prophet?—If I had seen the angel—A visit to David Whitmer—Did the witnesses reaffirm?—A letter from Martin Harris.

In the examination of the testimony of "the three witnesses," please bear in mind the fact that we have undertaken to prove a negative,—or to put it in different form, to impeach these witnesses. Such points as we shall be able to sustain by suitable evidence will be regarded as so many counts in the articles of impeachment as having been proved.

The several counts in this indictment are as follows: These three witnesses claim:

1. That they saw an angel of God descend from heaven.

2. That said angel held in his hand the gold plates from which the Book of Mormon was translated.

3. That certain letters or characters were engraved upon these plates.

4. That said letters or characters were "translated by the gift and power of God," and therefore,

5. That the "voice of God" declared unto them that said plates had been translated correctly.

6. That this "record" contains the history of ancient America; and

7. That "the voice of God" commanded them "to bear testimony of these things."

These several points are either true or false. If true, the Book of Mormon is a divine revelation, and the Mormon Church the only church of Christ. If they are false, then the Book of Mormon is a fraud, Joseph Smith and "the three witnesses" were impostors, and the Church of Jesus Christ of Latter Day Saints a failure.

Mr. Pratt, as we have already seen, presents as a matter of first consideration and importance the fact that neither of the three witnesses ever "denied the bold and fearless testimony which they have sent forth to all nations."

Besides the three witnesses named there were also eight others, four of whom were Whitmers, and three were Smiths, with one Page. These witnesses merely testify to having seen "the plates of which hath been spoken," and which they declared had "the appearance of gold."

They also saw the engravings on the plates which had the appearance of ancient work, and of curious workmanship.

In the excerpt which follows, the "eight witnesses" are included. Concerning their defection from the prophet and withdrawal from the church, President Joseph Smith, in his Church History, says:

"It is true that some of them became disaffected during the troublesome times in Missouri, and that differences arose between them and Joseph Smith; but these differences did not occur on account of the Book of Mormon or the testimony before published

Their contention arose from other causes, real or supposed, and did not affect their attitude towards the book. . . .

"Some strong and perhaps harsh statements were made during this controversy, but this only argues that they were not afraid of retaliation by way of exposure of previous frauds." (Smith's History, Vol. 1, page 49.)

I quote the foregoing to show that all Mormon writers of eminence regard the circumstance of these witnesses having remained steadfast to their original declaration concerning the angel and the plates, as being a very strong presumptive evidence of their sincerity, and the truthfulness of what they affirm. This by no means follows. Thousands of men guilty of greater offenses than that of these witnesses (allowing them to have been guilty of perpetrating a fraud) have gone into eternity protesting their innocence when they had been proved guilty beyond the shadow of doubt.

Does the fact that these witnesses stuck to their original story told about the angel prove the story true? By no means. No reasonable man can claim that it can do more than raise the presumption that they may have been sincere; but it by no means proves their sincerity.

If good reason can be shown for believing that silence, or even a reaffirmation of the original story, would be more profitable to them, then instead of confirming the presumption of sincerity, it would most certainly raise a presumption of fraud.

It will readily be granted that if their testimony be true, nothing would be more natural than that they should adhere to their original declarations until the day of their death. But let us suppose the whole thing was a conspiracy and a fraud; then what would be the probable course of these witnesses?

Would one of them, because he had disagreement with the arch-conspirator, be likely to go out on the streets and denounce his co-conspirator as a cheat, a liar and a fraud, knowing that while doing so he would lay his own hypocritical, fraudulent conduct bare to the gaze of an indignant public? Would he be likely to uncork the vials of his own guilty wrath against his followers, when he knew it would be but the signal for his own exposure to the righteous contempt of an injured public? Hardly.

No such course would be in the least probable. The interest of these four men in keeping their own counsel was mutual. If one suffered, they must all suffer. If one was exposed, all must be exposed. If there is anything in this wide world that a criminal fears and dreads, it is exposure.

The character of this fraud, if fraud it be, is such as to forever ruin the prospects and blast the hopes of any man, or set of men, once the fraud should be made public. For a man to confess his complicity in such a nefarious transaction, would be to confess himself capable of any crime in the catalogue, and would set the mark of Cain upon his brow, and brand his posterity with the ineradicable mark of infamy.

Could either of the witnesses afford to do this? Better, far, to smother their conscience, or at least put it to sleep, than face the storm of indignation that must inevitably follow exposure. So such men would view it.

That these witnesses, during a serious difficulty between themselves, did not expose one another, but continued to tell the same old story concerning the angel and the plates, proves nothing beyond the fact that the secret that formed the bond of their union was common to them all, and could not with impunity be divulged by either.

Better go down to their graves with a lie upon their lips, than to divulge a secret, the revelation of which would cover their names with infamy, and mantle the cheeks of their innocent children with the blush of shame and regret.

That these witnesses turned away from the church and denounced their leader, is already in evidence. To believe that these men saw an angel, and heard the voice of God to declare that Joseph Smith, by the power of God, had correctly translated the characters on the plates, and then in a very short time turn away from him and denounce him, is incredible. It is unreasonable that any ordinary matter of disagreement should produce such a result. If in company with Joseph Smith these witnesses saw the angel and heard the voice of God, they would have been willing to condone his faults and stand by him through any trial and in any emergency. But understanding his secret, they were unable and unwilling to make allowance for his faults.

Who can be made to believe that, if Oliver Cowdery with Joseph Smith bowed in the lonely wood at noon-tide, and there, in the sweet solitude and grandeur of nature's great temple, received the divine impress of angelic hands in holy ordination, he could ever be induced to turn away and forsake him?

Who can believe that after all this he could bring himself to denounce the prophet called of God to open up the work of the seventh and last dispensation—even the "dispensation of the fullness of times?"

It is impossible to believe that these witnesses, and especially Oliver Cowdery, knowing that the church organized by Joseph and Oliver, if their testimony is true, must be the only Church of Christ on earth, would deliberately withdraw from it, and live and die without its protecting fold? And yet this is exactly what they did.

If I had seen an angel; if I had heard the voice of God; if I had bowed by Joseph's Smith's side and felt the touch of angel hands in ordination, and heard the declaration that he was a prophet of the living God, all the combined powers of earth and hell could never have induced me to forsake him. And yet this is exactly what Oliver Cowdery did.

No, sir, I cannot believe it—it is too absurd. These witnesses never saw the angel; they heard not the voice of God, or they never could have pursued the course they did later in life.

President Joseph Smith and apostles W. H. Kelley and Heman C. Smith, are particular to state that they saw David Whitmer and talked with him concerning Oliver Cowdery and Martin Harris, the other two witnesses, and their attitude towards the Book of Mormon.

I am glad to be able to state that I, too, visited David Whitmer and talked with him on the same subject many years before either of the above named gentlemen had seen him. During the interview I made special inquiry concerning Oliver Cowdery, as I had been informed that he died an infidel. This he informed me was incorrect. He apologized for Oliver's persistent refusal to return to the fellowship of the church by saying that Joseph Smith's conduct during the troubles in Missouri had rendered Oliver, his brother-in-law, very skeptical, but that he was not an infidel.

It seems impossible that Oliver should become skeptical respecting divine things, or even indifferent towards them, if he had in reality seen what he claimed to have witnessed. Upon the whole the conduct of these witnesses certainly raises the presumption of fraud respecting their connection with the origin of Mormonism.

It is an old saying and a true one, that "actions speak louder than words;" and in this case the *actions* of these witnesses certainly give the lie to their words.

DID THE WITNESSES REAFFIRM?

As to whether these witnesses did or did not reaffirm their former testimony is a matter of indifference, for the reasons already assigned. That David Whitmer did so, and for reasons which directly concerned himself, may not be questioned; but that Oliver Cowdery ever did so is extremely doubtful.

President Smith, in his church history, undertakes to prove that both Cowdery and Harris reaffirm their statement concerning the angel and the plates, but his authority is questionable.

He reproduces from George Reynolds' "Mith of the Manuscript Found," a quotation from the *Deseret News*, the Brighamite organ of Salt Lake City, a journal by no means reliable in matters of this kind, as the people of the Reorganized Church have ever maintained. The extract refers to a conference of the Brighamite Church held at Council Bluffs, Iowa, Oct. 21, 1848, when Oliver Cowdery, it is claimed, was present, and, in a short address, reaffirmed his former testimony. In this roundabout way he is reported to have said:

"In the early history of this church I stood identified with her, and one in her councils. . . . I wrote, with my own pen, the entire Book of Mormon (save a few pages), as it fell from the lips of the prophet, Joseph Smith, as he translated it by the gift and power of God, by the means of the Urim and Thummim, or, as it is called by that book, 'holy interpreters.' I beheld with my own eyes and handled with my hands the gold plates from which it was translated. I also saw with my eyes and handled with my hands the 'holy interpreters.' That book is *true*. Sidney Rigdon did not write it. Mr. Spaulding did not write it. I wrote it myself as it fell from the lips of the prophet." (Smith's History, Vol. 1, page 50.)

Allowing that Oliver Cowdery uttered the exact words as reported, it lacks every important element of his original testimony. His original declaration was that he saw an heavenly angel and heard the voice of God, the only two things in his testimony which are of any value. In his so-called reaffirmation he makes not the slightest reference to either. He simply affirms what I have heard a thousand Latter Day Saints declare, that the Book of Mormon was translated by "the gift and power of God," and was therefore true.

He says not one word about seeing an angel nor hearing the voice of God, the only means of rendering his knowledge absolute and unmistakable.

If Oliver Cowdery ever made that speech—which is extremely doubtful—why did he omit the only two points that are of the least historical or legal importance? Evidently it was because he knew the "testimony of the three witnesses" was false, and he did not care to repeat it.

Now a word concerning Martin Harris. Following is the manner in which this witness reaffirms his testimony. In a private letter to one H. B. Emerson, of New Richmond, Ohio, and as it seems, in answer to questions touching the matter, Mr. Harris is represented as saying:

"SMITHFIELD, UTAH, Nov. 23, 1870.

"MR. EMERSON, *Sir:*—I received your favor. In reply I will say concerning the plates: I do say that the angel did show me the plates containing the Book of Mormon. Further, the translation that I carried to Prof. Anthon was copied from these same plates; also, that the professor did testify to it being a correct translation." (Ibid, pages 50, 51.)

Except in a letter to the same person written the year following "by a borrowed hand," in which he reaffirms his testimony concerning the angel and the plates, the above is the only time, so far as the writer is aware, that Martin has ever said anything for the public respecting the matter; and it is the only reference he has ever made, in writing, to his visit to Professor Anthon. Compare the language of this letter with the statement attributed to him by Joseph Smith, on page 224, and you will see at a glance that the language is that of Joseph Smith and not that of the illiterate and "simple-hearted farmer."

David Whitmer was compelled, in order to keep up appearances, to reaffirm his testimony, for the reason that he was himself the president of a Mormon church whose authority was dependent upon the validity of ordinations performed by Joseph Smith. And to deny his former testimony would be to proclaim himself an impostor, and his church a fraud. And this, for prudential reasons, he could not afford to do.

All the circumstances considered, it would be the wise but selfish policy of those witnesses to allow their secret to die with them, and thus save themselves from ignominy while living, and their posterity from shame and disgrace after their death.

The foregoing facts form the basis for a strong presumption in the minds of persons not previously committed to a belief in the story, that the whole thing was a conspiracy to deceive and mislead the unwary, for the purpose of achieving wealth and renown.

CHAPTER XXVII.

THEY DID NOT SEE THE ANGEL.

They did not see the angel—The reasons given—Egyptology little understood in 1830—Under the light of recent discoveries—The veil removed—Book of Mormon written in Egyptian—Orson Pratt's testimony—Testimony of Martin Harris—Were the characters on the plates Egyptian?—Fac-simile of the characters—Genuineness verified by Mormon authority.

In the preceding chapter we have presented facts which are of such a character as to create not only a grave doubt as to the sincerity of the four witnesses to the Book of Mormon, but to actually raise a very strong presumption of guilt.

As already quoted, Mr. Pratt has sought to assure us that "no man living can prove that an angel did not appear to them." The reason assigned by this astute defender of Mormonism is this:

"There is nothing in the nature of the event itself, nor in any of the circumstances connected with it, that would render it absurd, unscriptural, unreasonable or improbable. . . . Indeed, there cannot be brought the least shadow of evidence, either direct or indirect, to prove that their testimony concerning the angel is false."

As an additional reason why the witnesses cannot be proved impostors, Mr. Pratt tells us just what he thinks must be proved, and which, in his opinion, was utterly impossible. On page 35 of the work last quoted he says that in order to prove these witnesses to be impostors it will be necessary to show:

1. That the four witnesses (which include Joseph Smith) "did not see and hear an angel."
2. "That they did not see the plates in the angel's hand;" and,
3. "That they did not hear the voice of the Lord declaring that they were not translated correctly."

These propositions, being of a negative character, are more difficult of proof; and at the time he made them (1850) Mr. Pratt no doubt considered it a matter of impossibility that they could be disproved. And this was probably the case at that early day. But the last half of the present century has wrought miracles in the way of revealing the secrets of the remote past.

Keys have been discovered in recent years by which the tombs and temples of ancient Egypt have been made to yield up their hidden treasures of knowledge greatly to the benefit and enlightenment of the modern world.

In 1830, when the Book of Mormon appeared, and in 1850, when Mr. Pratt threw down his challenge to the scholarship of the world to prove the testimony of the witnesses false, comparatively little was known concerning the language and literature of the world's most ancient civilization. A dense veil of mystery, deep and seemingly impenetrable, hung, like the pall of death, over all ancient Egypt. This veil has at last been lifted, the gloom of centuries penetrated, and ancient Egypt to-day stands revealed to the admiring gaze of the nineteenth century. Her language is now as easily read as are the languages of ancient Babylon and Assyria.

The Book of Mormon, while professedly written by Hebrews and their descendants, is said to have been written in Egyptian. A very unusual thing, indeed, for a writer to abandon his own language and adopt one of a foreign nation, and especially one so little understood as that of the Egyptians.

Relative to this the Book of Mormon says:

"I, Nephi, having been born of goodly parents, therefore I was taught somewhat in all the learning of my father; . . . [and] I make a record in the language of my father, which consists of the learning of the Jews and *the language of the Egyptians.*" (1 Nephi 1: 1, page 1.)

Again:

"For he [Lehi], having been taught in *the language of the Egyptians*, therefore he could read these engravings, and teach them to his children." (B. of M., page 154.)

Concerning the plates of the Book of Mormon and the engravings upon them, Mr. Pratt says:

"Each plate was not far from seven by eight inches in width and length, being not quite as thick as common tin. Each was filled on both sides with *engraved* Egyptian characters." (Pratt's works, Evidences of the B. of M. and Bible Compared, page 49.)

Martin Harris, it will be remembered, says that the characters were *Egyptian*. Moroni, who "hid up the record unto the Lord," (see Mormon, chapter 4, page 532) says:

"And now behold, we have written this record according to our knowledge of the characters, which are called among us the *reformed Egyptian*, being handed down and *altered* by us, according to our manner of speech." (Ibid, page 538.)

Although altered somewhat, the characters were Egyptian, nevertheless.

There can be no question, then, that the language of the plates was Egyptian. Not the slightest intimation that any other language was ever employed in keeping these records, and hence no other letters, signs or characters could possibly have been used.

The reader will please bear this in mind, as it forms the basis upon which the argument now to be offered is predicated. If the plates were engraved with some other characters or letters, Greek and Hebrew, for instance, the testimony of the witnesses is thereby proved false.

Again, if it should be claimed that not only Egyptian, but other characters or letters, were employed, such as Assyrian, Arabic and Aramaic, and none of these characters are found on the plates, then it follows as an unanswerable fact that the plates are a fraud, and the testimony of the "four witnesses" to the Book of Mormon is therefore proved false beyond question or doubt.

I wish now to lay down as the major premise in this argument a proposition which no man, I care not what his religious faith may be, will care to dispute, namely: Neither God himself nor an angel of his presence can be made a party to fraud and deception; that they can neither by voice nor by their presence give countenance and encouragement to falsehood; that what they shall utter must be absolutely and undoubtedly true.

This fact being conceded, then it must follow as a logical necessity that if God or an angel be represented by men as having sanctioned, approved and affirmed an alleged fact, and the thing alleged or affirmed shall afterwards be proved untrue, then the men who bore such testimony have testified falsely, and are therefore proved impostors; the very thing that Mr. Pratt says cannot be done.

There remains, therefore, but one question now to be decided, which, in the very nature of the case, must finally and forever settle this matter concerning the testimony of these "four witnesses," and that question is this:

WERE THE CHARACTERS ON THE PLATES EGYPTIAN?

In his eagerness to give face to his fraud, Joseph Smith transcribed some of his signs, letters, or characters, and sent them by Martin Harris to Professor Charles Anthon to be translated. This one act of daring egotism has rendered it possible to test this marvelous claim, as it could in no other possible manner ever have been tested.

This identical transcript fell into the hands of David Whitmer, along with the original manuscript of the Book of Mormon (and how this happened the writer has never learned) and was by him carefully preserved. Photographic copies were made of the original, some of which are now extant. Plates have been made and fac-similes printed in various books published by the Mormon Church, among them Smith's Church History and Kelley's Presidency and Priesthood. Concerning its genuineness Mr. Kelley remarks:

"Here is presented a fac-simile of the characters sent by Mr. Smith to Prof. Anthon and Dr. Mitchell by Martin Harris. . . . These characters were photographed from the original document borne by Mr. Harris at the direction of David Whitmer, who had in his possession at the time said paper. They were carefully examined and compared by the author."

Relative to the same matter, President Joseph Smith says:

"The paper containing the characters (not translated) which Martin Harris carried to Professor Anthon was carefully preserved, copied and photographed. We have examined them when in the hands of the late David Whitmer. Without further comment we herewith present a fac-similie from a plate used in Presidency and Priesthood by W. H. Kelley. The reader can examine them, compare them with Professor Anthon's statements, examine the evidence, and form conclusions accordingly." (Smith's History, Vol. 1, page 22.)

There can be no possibility of any mistake as to the genuineness of the characters. Made by Joseph Smith's own hand, preserved by David Whitmer, one of the "three witnesses," photographed, printed and published by Mormon authority, precludes the possibility of doubt as to their genuineness.

But one point now remains to be settled, namely: Are these characters Egyptian?

CHAPTER XXVIII.

THE CHARACTERS ARE NOT EGYPTIAN—THE TESTIMONY OF SCHOLARS.

The characters are not Egyptian—The testimony of scholars—Mr. Kelley's fac-simile—Submitted to scholars for examination—Explanatory letter—President James B. Angell's reply—A moral, not a linguistic question—Characters fraudulent—Chas. H. S. Davis, M. D., Ph. D.—Characters put down at random—Resemble nothing, not even shorthand—Not an Egyptian letter or character in it—A letter from Jerusalem—Dr. Charles E. Moldenke—The plates of the Book of Mormon a fraud—Egyptian and Arabic side by side—Is ridiculous and impossible—Characters bear no resemblance to Egyptian or Assyrian—Testimony of the witnesses compared—Scholarship vs. ignorance—Conclusion of the whole matter.

IN the very nature of the case, the entire question is narrowed down to one of language. Everything now depends upon the one question, *Were the characters on the plates Egyptian?* If they were, then I am free to admit that the Mormon Church is the Church of Christ. If they were not Egyptian, then the church of the Saints is not the Church of Christ, and they should honestly admit the fact.

In order to satisfactorily determine this important question—important because fundamental—the writer pursued the only course by which it is possible to settle a linguistic question, and that is to submit the fac-simile to the most eminent scholars of our time for careful examination.

Unwilling to trust to the accuracy of a transcript made in the ordinary way, I cut the plate out of a copy of Mr. Kelley's book, and submitted it to a few of the best Egytologists of the present time, with a request for each to pass his professional opinion upon the unique document. Each of the gentlemen addressed returned a prompt answer, neither of them knowing what the other had said; or, to be more accurate, neither knew that anybody else was to answer the questions, and hence there could be no possibility that the statement of one could be influenced by that of another.

In this manner each depended entirely upon his own knowledge of the question to be considered, and was, therefore, entirely free from any bias that might arise from having previously read the opinions of another, thus securing the independent opinion of some of the finest scholars in the Oriental languages that our country affords.

The accompanying plate, an exact reproduction of Mr. Kelley's photographic copy, will give the reader an opportunity to make a more extended examination should he desire to do so.

To each of the gentlemen whose testimony is submitted herewith, was addressed a letter of explanation and inquiry, substantially as follows:

"DEAR SIR: I herewith inclose what purports to be a fac-simile of the characters found upon the gold plates from which it is claimed the Book of Mormon was translated. The advocates of Mormonism maintain that these characters are 'Egyptian, Chaldaic, Assyrian and Arabic.'

"So far as I am informed, these characters have never been submitted to scholars of eminence for examination; and as the languages named fall within your province, including Egyptology and Archeology,

[Fac simile of the charactors claimed by the Mormons to have been found on the original plates from which the Book of Mormon was translated.]

your professional opinion as to their genuineness will be of great value to the general reader, in determining the exact truth with respect to this remarkable claim. I would also like your opinion upon the following questions, namely:

"1. Did Hebrew scholars at any time, either before or since Christ, keep their records on tablets, or plates of brass?

"2. If so, did they ever write in the Egyptian language?

"3. Is there any evidence to show that the Pentateuch was ever written upon such plates of brass?

"4. Is there any proof that the law of Moses, or even the Decalogue, was ever written in the Egyptian language?"

In response to this communication, President James B. Angell, of the University of Michigan, at Ann Arbor, writes:

"REV. D. H. BAYS, *Dear Sir:* I have submitted your letter and inclosure to our Professor of Oriental languages, who is more familiar with the subjects raised by your questions than I am. He is a man of large learning in Semitic languages and archeology. The substance of what he has to say is:

"'1. The document which you enclose raises a *moral* rather than a *linguistic* problem. A few letters or signs are noticeable which correspond more or less closely to the Aramaic, sometimes called Chaldee language; for example, s, h, g, t, l, b, n. There are no Assyrian characters in it, and the impression made is that *the document is fraudulent.*

"'2. There is no evidence that the Hebrews kept their records upon plates or tablets of brass; but the Assyrians, in the eighth century before Christ, did.

"'3. There is no evidence whatever to show that the Pentateuch was ever written on such plates of brass.'   Yours Truly,
"JAMES B. ANGELL."
Ann Arbor, Mich.   (Italics are mine).

The question raised by this document is not one of *language*, but of *morals;* and why of morals. The answer is obvious. If the characters were *Egyptian*, as claimed, the question would evidently be one of language rather than of morals. In the careful language of a scholar the writer says, "the impression made is *that the document is fraudulent.*"

A few of the letters, or signs, bear some resemblance to the Aramaic, or Chaldee, yet there is not a word of Egyptian in it. If the story told by these witnesses concerning the angel be true, the characters on these plates must be Egyptian; otherwise the witnesses are proved to be impostors.

Relative to the characters on the plates, Chas. H. S. Davis, M. D. Ph. D., of Meriden, Conn, author of "ANCIENT EGYPT *in the Light of Recent Discoveries*," and a member of the American Oriental Society, American Philological Society, Society of Biblical Archeology of London, Royal Archeological Institute of Great Britain and Ireland, etc., etc., in answer to the letter of inquiry addressed to him, writes as follows:

"REV. D. H. BAYS, *Dear Sir:* I am familiar with Egyptian, Chaldaic, Assyrian and Arabic, and have considerable acquaintance with all of the Oriental languages, and I can *positively assert* that there is not a letter to be found in the fac-simile submitted that can be found in the alphabet of any Oriental language, particularly of those you refer to—namely, Egyptian, Chaldaic, Assyrian and Arabic.

"A careful study of the fac-simile shows that they are characters put down at random by an ignorant person—with no resemblance to anything, not even shorthand.

"No record has ever shown that the Hebrews, or any other Eastern nation, kept their records upon plates or tablets of brass, but thousands upon thousands of tablets of baked clay have been brought to light, antedating two or three thousands years, before the time of Moses, while libraries of these baked clay tablets have been found, like those at Tell el Amara. At the time the Old Testament was written paper made from papyrus was in use, and as documents have been found in Egypt of the times of Moses, written on papyri, it is not unreasonable to suppose that we may find yet portions of the Old Testament.

"The treasures of Egypt and Palestine are only just being brought to light. Remarkable discoveries are yet to be made. Respectfully,

"CHAS. H. S. DAVIS."

Comment seems useless. Here we have the testimony of one of the most profound scholars of our times, who declares positively, upon his reputation as a gentleman and scholar, that there is not a letter to be found in the fac-simile submitted that can be found in the alphabet of any Oriental language, especially naming the "Egyptian, Chaldaic, Assyrian and Arabic."

This declaration is so perfectly clear and unequivocal that no misunderstanding can possibly arise concerning its meaning.

Dr. Charles E. Moldenke, of New York, now in the Orient, and concerning whom Dr. Davis says, "He is probably the best Egyptian scholar in the country," confirms the statements above presented, as the following letter shows:

"JERUSALEM [Palestine], DEC. 27, 1896.

"REV. D. H. BAYS, *Dear Sir and Brother:* Your letter dated Nov. 23rd I have just received. I will try to answer your questions as far as I am able. I believe the plates of the Book of Mormon to be a fraud.

"In the first place it is impossible to find in any old inscription, 'Egyptian, Arabic, Chaldaic and Assyrian,' characters mixed together. The simple idea of finding Egyptian and Arabic side by side is ridiculous and impossible.

"In the second place, though some signs remind one of those on the Mesa Inscription, yet none bear a resemblance to Egyptian or Assyrian.

"As far as I know there is no evidence that the Hebrews kept records on plates of brass, or ever wrote on such plates. About the prophecy contained in Isa. 29:1-14, I can venture no opinion, as I am not a Biblical scholar, and only concern myself about Egyptology.   Very Truly Yours,

"CHARLES E. MOLDENKE."

TESTIMONY OF THE WITNESSES COMPARED—SCHOLARSHIP VS. IGNORANCE.

The witnesses, four in number, which include Joseph Smith, all agree in their declaration that an angel of God appeared to them, holding the plates in his hand, and that they heard the voice of God out of heaven, declaring that Joseph Smith had translated the plates correctly. These witnesses say that the plates contained " Egyptian, Chaldaic, Assyrian and Arabic " characters. (See pages 224, 225.)

Orson Pratt says that these plates were " filled on *both sides* with engraved Egyptian characters." Hence, the Egyptian, Assyrian, Chaldaic and Arabic characters were necessarily found mixed together— found side by side. Concerning this Dr. Moldenke, a specialist in Egyptology, says:

" The simple idea of finding *Egyptian* and *Arabic* side by side, *is ridiculous and impossible.*"

This proves that the document presented to Professor Anthon by Martin Harris was fraudulent. As it is impossible for Egyptian and Arabic to be found " side by side," Egyptian and Arabic were not found on the plates; and if they were not found " side by side " on the plates, then the three witnesses were deceivers and Joseph Smith an impostor.

Two of these witnesses, namely, Joseph Smith and Martin Harris, say that some of the characters transcribed from the plates were " Assyrian." But this is flatly contradicted by President James B. Angell, who says: " *There are no Assyrian characters in it.*"

Relative to the characters submitted to him Dr. Davis declares:

" I can *positively assert* that there is *not a letter* to be found in the fac-simile submitted that can be found in *any* Oriental language, particularly those you refer to, namely, *Egyptian, Chaldaic, Assyrian* and *Arabic,*" and concludes by saying:

" A careful study of the fac-simile shows that they are characters *put down at random* by an ignorant person, *with no resemblance to anything,* not even short-hand."

All these scholars agree that the characters are fraudulent, and that there is not a single character, letter, or sign, in the fac-simile made by Joseph Smith that has even the slightest resemblance to the Egyptian.

Thus the testimony of three witnesses to the Book of Mormon is flatly contradicted by the testimony of an equal number of the best scholars of our country and our times.

Three men say an angel exhibited certain "plates" to them, and that these plates were "engraved with Egyptian characters" (Pratt) and contained the record of events that are said to have transpired upon this continent,—that these plates had been translated by the "gift and power of God," and that the Book of Mormon is the result of this translation.

The Book of Mormon confirms this declaration by saying the plates from which it was translated were engraved or written *in Egyptian*.

These three men also state that the voice of God commanded them to "bear record of these things." The testimony of three scholars of great eminence shows most conclusively that not one word, not one character, found in the fac-simile is Egyptian, thus proving, not only that the characters were fraudulent, but that the witnesses testified *falsely*, thus proving exactly what Mr. Pratt and all Latter Day Saints declare could not be proved, namely, *that the witnesses were impostors.*

The witnesses having sworn falsely, their testimony is invalidated—they stand impeached before God and man; and their names must go down in history as being the most daring, wicked impostors the world ever knew.

In conclusion upon this part of our subject, we simply submit that this whole Mormon question is purely a question of veracity? Mormonism comes to us and demands recognition as a revelation from heaven, upon the testimony of three interested witnesses—witnesses whose ignorance of the facts raised by the question of language involved renders them wholly incompetent.

The witnesses, however, did not pretend to be Egyptian scholars, and therefore say that God told them by his own voice that the plates had been translated correctly. This, they urge, was their only means of obtaining the knowledge which they claim to possess. As there is no possibility that these witnesses could themselves be deceived, their statement is either unquestionably true or absolutely false.

Three witnesses, whose veracity and competency is simply placed beyond question, have testified that there is not a word of Egyptian found among the characters submitted to them for examination.

All Mormon authority unites in declaring that the plates of the Book of Mormon were written in Egyptian. Joseph Smith says he made a transcript of the characters found on the plates.

These characters were submitted to Professor Anthon, who, according to the Smith-Harris statement, declared them to be Egyptian. But this the Professor denied. The fac-simile made by Joseph Smith was carefully preserved by David Whitmer. Mr. Kelley secured the photographic copy from which his plate was made. This identical fac-simile plate was submitted to three eminent scholars, whose testimony is herewith submitted, and these scholars declare there is not an Egyptian character in the entire transcript.

The Book of Mormon says the plates taken from Laban by Nephi contained the "five books of Moses" (see B. of M. page 15; also page 149) and that they were *written on plates of brass.* The scholars, in answer to questions as to whether the Hebrews ever kept their records on such plates, uniformly declare they never did, and that there is no evidence to show that the Pentateuch was ever written on such metallic plates. They further say the Pentateuch was never written in Egyptian.

THE PLATES OF BRASS.

The Book of Mormon minutely describes the circumstance of Nephi's return to Jerusalem, in company with his brothers, and the means employed to obtain possession of certain "plates of brass" which were the private property of a prominent Jew named Laban. In order to get these plates, Nephi slew Laban with his own sword, literally severing his head from his body, and then quietly donned the murdered man's apparel. In this disguise he returned to the palace, and by assuming Laban's voice, succeeded in deceiving the servant who had charge of the keys to his master's treasury, and through him obtained the coveted prize.

Zoram, Laban's servant, accompanied Nephi to the place where his brethren were concealed outside the walls of the city, where he was seized by Nephi, who gave the unfortunate man his choice between death and captivity. Rather than forfeit his life, the servant of Laban accompanied them into the wilderness, and became one of their number. (See Book of Mormon, pages 12-14.)

These plates were said to contain "the five Books of Moses," and "also a record of the Jews from the beginning, even down to the commencement of the reign of Zedekiah, king of Judah; and also the prophecies of the Holy prophets, from the beginning, even down to the commencement of the reign of Zedekiah; and also many prophecies which have been spoken by the mouth of Jeremiah." (Ibid, page 15.)

This circumstance would not in itself appear remarkable were it not for two alleged facts connected with it, namely:

1. That the Pentateuch, together with the prophecies, were written on "plates of brass;" and
2. That they were written in Egyptian.

If this so-called record had stopped at this, the fraud would have been less transparent, and not so easily detected, but, as if to cap the climax of historical absurdity, it goes back to the period of Joseph's sojourn in Egypt, and represents the favorite son of Jacob as having written a wonderful prophecy relative to the deliverance of the Israelites from bondage under the leadership of Moses.

These "plates of brass" revealed the further fact that Lehi was himself a descendant of Joseph. Not only did Joseph prophecy that God would raise up Moses, through whom Israel should be redeemed from the bondage of Egypt, but he told also of "a choice seer" who should arise in the last days to lead his posterity out of bondage. Concerning this modern Moses, Lehi says:

"Yea, Joseph truly said, thus saith the Lord unto me: a choice seer will I raise up out of the fruit of thy loins, . . . and I will make him great in mine eyes. . . . And he shall be great like unto Moses." "And thus prophesied Joseph, saying: Behold, that seer will the Lord bless, and they that seek to destroy him shall be confounded. . . . And his name shall be called after me; and it shall be after the name of his father. And he shall be like unto me." (Book of Mormon, pages 66, 67.)

Thus it is made plain that this wonderful "seer" should be known among his fellows as *Joseph*, which was also to be the name of his father.

With the addition of the rare and euphoneous cognomen of "Smith," this remarkable prophecy of Jacob's fortunate son could, by no possible means, have been misunderstood. But even as it is, no reader of ordinary intelligence can fail to understand that "my servant, Joseph Smith, Jr.," was the individual whom the original Joseph had in mind at the time he engraved the burning words of this great prophecy upon these "plates of brass." How fortunate that the words of this prophecy have been thus miraculously preserved, and handed down from father to son in a direct line from the great progenitor, to bless the inhabitants of the earth in the closing decade of the nineteenth century! Who can now wonder that the prophet-angel Moroni should gladly leave the shining courts of glory and joyously wend his way to earth, to make known the hiding-place of such a treasure?

That this prophecy was written on the plates of brass which Nephi murdered Laban to obtain, may be seen from the following:

"And now, I, Nephi, speak concerning the prophecies of which my father hath spoken, concerning

Joseph, who was carried into Egypt. For behold, he prophesied concerning his seed . . . and they are written upon the plates of brass." (Ibid, page 68.)

One would naturally suppose that the Israelites would keep their records in the language of their fathers—the Hebrew. But not so. Joseph, the son of Jacob, wrote this prophecy in Egyptian, and both the Pentateuch and the prophecies, which were said to have been found on these plates, were written in the Egyptian language, as may be seen from the following:

"And he [King Benjamin] also taught them [his three sons] concerning the records which were engraven on the plates of brass, saying, My sons, I would that ye should remember, that were it not for these plates, . . . we must have suffered in ignorance, even at the present time, not knowing the mysteries of God: for it were not possible that our father Lehi could have remembered all these things, to have taught them to his children, except it were for the help of these plates: for he having been taught in the language of the Egyptians, THEREFORE he could read these engravings, and teach them to his children." (Ibid, pages 153, 154.)

From the foregoing it is impossible to dodge the fact that the brass plates under consideration were written in the Egyptian language, and contained the "five Books of Moses" and the writings of all the prophets, including Isaiah, down to the time of the Babylonian captivity. This claim is either true or false. If the Hebrews kept their records on "plates of brass," and if such records were written in Egyptian and not in Hebrew, then the Book of Mormon may be true. But if it can be shown that brass tablets were never used by the Hebrews in keeping their records, and that they never wrote in the Egyptian language, then the statement made concerning the brass plates in question cannot be true, and the Book of Mormon must, therefore, be a transparent fraud. In order to determine this matter, we have but to ascertain what are the facts relative to the following questions:

1. Is it historically true that the Hebrews ever wrote on tablets or "plates of brass?"

2. If so, did they ever write in the Egyptian language?

3. Were the "five books of Moses" ever written upon such plates of brass?

4. Were the "law and the prophets," or any portion of them, ever written in Egyptian?

In answer to a letter of inquiry addressed to President William R. Harper, of the University of Chicago, that distinguished scholar says:

"To your first three questions I would give the answer, NO. With regard to the fourth, the Pentateuch was transmitted in Coptic some time between the third and tenth centuries, A. D., but was *never written in Egyptian before that time.*" (Italics mine).

With the above statement Ira Maurice Price, Ph. D., of the University of Chicago, is in perfect accord. He says:

"There is no such instance on record among the Hebrews, nor among other nations about the Hebrews. No evidence that they ever did write in the Egyptian language."

Relative to the same questions President James B. Angell, University of Michigan, says:

"There is no evidence that the Hebrews kept their

records upon plates or tablets of brass. There is no evidence whatever to show that the Pentateuch was ever written on such plates of brass."

To the testimony of these gentlemen we might add that of a number of others, but to do so would be wholly superfluous, as their reputation for ripe scholarship is world-wide and unquestionable.

From the foregoing we glean the following facts:

1. The Hebrews never kept their records on "plates of brass."
2. No Hebrew records were ever kept on tablets of brass, or any other substance, in the Egyptian language, and
3. The Pentateuch was never written in Egyptian prior to the Christian era.

Conclusion: As the Book of Mormon declares the Pentateuch was written on plates of brass, and in the Egyptian language in the year 600, B. C., and as no such thing was ever done, the Book of Mormon is thereby proved a fraud, and Mormonism a delusion.

If the "five books of Moses" (a purely modern phrase) were never written on "plates of brass," this fact furnishes another link in the chain of evidence that the Book of Mormon is a fraud. The question now stands thus:

THE TESTIMONY OF THREE GREAT SCHOLARS,
vs.
THE TESTIMONY OF THE THREE WITNESSES.

Reader, in the light of all the facts, whose word will you take in this case? The whole question may be summed up in a single proposition. If Mormonism is true, the plates *must have been written in Egyptian*. The plates were not written in Egyptian. Therefore

Mormonism is not true. And if Mormonism is not true, then the three witnesses were deceivers, Joseph Smith was an impostor, and the Mormon Church a fraud. There is no possible means of escape from this conclusion. "Choose ye this day whom ye will serve."

CHAPTER XXIX.

THE DOCTRINES OF MORMONISM.

The Doctrines of Mormonism—What the Saints believe—The only way to be saved—Erroneous exegesis—Faith towards God—Repentance from dead works—Works of the law—Must leave them—Cannot perfect the believer—Character of the Hebrew letter—Hebrews 6: 1, 2 paraphrased—The doctrine of baptisms—Divers washings of the law—Baptize—Born—The difference—The law of life—The law of sin and death—Summary.

HAVING in a previous chapter reviewed the doctrine of the Mormon Church with respect to church organization, I will now proceed to examine what they are pleased to term the plan of salvation. The Saints believe that, in order to be received into the "celestial glory," a man must obey that form of doctrine which they teach. If he comes short of this, that is, if he does not formally obey the Gospel *as they teach it*, he must be damned. The logical conclusion is, that none but Latter Day Saints will "be saved in the celestial kingdom."

Man fell through disobedience to a *specific law*, we are told, and he can only be redeemed through obedience to a law whose terms are equally definite. The particular elements of this law, they assure us, may be found in the following Scriptures:

"Whosoever transgresseth and abideth not in the doctrine of Christ, hath not God. He that abideth in the doctrine of Christ, he hath both the Father and the Son." (2 John 9.)

"Therefore leaving the principles of the doctrine of Christ, let us go on unto perfection; not laying again the foundation of *repentance* from dead works, and of *faith* towards God, of the doctrine of *baptisms*, and of *laying on of hands*, and of *resurrection* of the dead, and of eternal *judgment*." (Heb. 6: 1, 2.)

As taught in Mormon theology, the "doctrine of Christ," mentioned by John, is analyzed by Paul in his letter to the Hebrews, who names the six *principles* or elements entering into the doctrine of Christ as a completed whole. Anything short of these six principles, called by the Saints the "first principles of the Gospel," will not suffice to save a man.

The passage, as usually quoted and defined by the teachers among the Saints, stands thus:

1. "Faith towards God."
2. "Repentance from dead works."
3. "The doctrine of baptisms,"—*i. e.* of water and of the Spirit.
4. "The laying on of hands,"—for the gift of the Holy Ghost.
5. "The resurrection of the dead," and
6. "Eternal judgment."

NOTE.—There has long existed a difference of opinion among scholars as to the authorship of the epistle to the Hebrews. It is worthy of remark that while the *Western* or *Roman* division of the church rejected the epistle both as Pauline and canonical, the *Eastern* division, including Asia Minor and Palestine, accepted it as Pauline, and therefore canonical. Those who oppose its claim to Pauline authorship seem to "confound a matter of historical *fact*, namely, the true authorship by Paul, with a matter of opinion," and base their opposition principally, if not altogether, upon the question of style. The Alexandrian and Palestinian churches seem never to have questioned what to them was historically true, namely, that Paul was the author of the Hebrew letter.

Origen, who was perhaps the most eminent biblical scholar of his age, while he thought the style un-Pauline, yet he was willing to

These six principles constitute the "doctrine of Christ," in which a man must believe and abide, exactly as the Saints teach and practice it, or he cannot be saved. From a doctrinal point of view this is the citadel of the Saints, and is regarded as a veritable Gibraltar, and absolutely impregnable.

If the premise assumed by their teachers be granted, why, of course we should be compelled to admit their conclusions; but I do not admit their premise. It is assumed; not *proved*. Let us now reconnoitre this stronghold of the Saints, and see whether it be invulnerable.

In the first place, the rendering of this passage in the common version does not suit the Saints, and so their "translator," Joseph Smith, has furnished them a better one. It reads thus:

"Therefore *not* leaving the principles of the doctrine of Christ,"—that is to say, you must not *leave* the principles of the *doctrine of Christ;* and that the *six principles* enumerated immediately following, are the principles *taught by Christ*, and are, therefore, his doctrine. Let us see about this. Is it a tenable position? I think not, and for the following reasons:

First: Nowhere in all the teachings of Christ, as they are recorded in the Scriptures—not even in the "Inspired Translation"—do we find that he either *taught* or *practiced* that form of doctrine urged by the Saints as being necessary to salvation.

---

admit the epistle to have been Paul's, and habitually quoted it as such. It is not my purpose, however, to offer any proofs or make any argument in support of the Pauline authorship of the epistle, but merely to call attention to the fact that, as the question is an open one between biblical scholars, I have not hesitated to treat it as being of Pauline origin.

Second: Paul does not even *hint* that the six propositions named in the two verses quoted are to be observed as a means of salvation.

Third: The apostle does not declare these six propositions to be "*principles* of the doctrine of Christ." This is only the construction put upon the passage by the Saints, Paul's allusion to them being purely incidental.

Fourth: The six propositions named are *propositions of the Mosaic law*, and not " principles of the doctrine of Christ."

If this view be the correct one, it will be needless to say Latter Day Saints are wrong; but if I am mistaken, they may be right, but not necessarily so.

It must be regarded as a fact not to be questioned, that what Christ did not *authorize* cannot be made legally binding. Hence, since Christ has nowhere authorized such a system as that taught by the Saints, it cannot be urged as a necessary means of salvation; and if not necessary to salvation, then why teach it? Paul does not say that we are to observe the six propositions named in order to salvation; and if neither Christ nor Paul enjoins such observance, then certainly nobody else has any authority to do so. This seems unquestionable.

I have said that the six propositions named in Hebrews 6: 1, 2, are propositions of the law. This, as a matter of course, will be denied by the Saints. I do not expect their teachers to admit the fact, but I believe we shall be able to show that this is the more reasonable view, as it frees the text from all theological technicalities, and renders it more practical.

If there is any one thing in the teachings of our Lord that may be regarded as particularly phenomenal, it is to be found in the eminently practical character of his doctrines, of which the following may serve as an example:

"Therefore all things whatsoever ye would that men should do to you, do ye even so unto them. For this is the law and the prophets." (Matt. 7: 12.)

Let us now proceed to a careful examination of the language of this peculiar text upon which Latter Day Saints rely for proof of their position. It reads thus:

"Therefore *leaving* the principles of the doctrine of Christ, let us go on unto perfection."

Whatever these "principles" may be, they are to be left behind in the onward march to perfection. This brings us to inquire: Can any *principle*, or constituent part, of the Christian religion be omitted from the Christian system with impunity? In answer to this question every consistent Latter Day Saint must say,—No, we cannot do away with any primal truth upon which Christianity rests. To do this will be to destroy its foundation, and thus endanger the whole superstructure.

With this primal truth admitted, there can be but one legitimate, logical conclusion, namely: The principles referred to by Paul cannot be the fundamental truths of Christianity. Why? Because *leaving* the principles referred to, is declared to be the only possible means by which they could "*go on unto perfection.*"

To say that by *leaving*—i. e. "quitting;" "withdrawing from;" "relinquishing," the truths of Christianity, we may "go on unto perfection" in the Christian character, is as palpably absurd as it would be to affirm that we may abandon the fundamental principles of mathematics, and yet be able to solve the more abstruce problems of that science.

The apostle, therefore, does not refer to the underlying truths of Christianity, but to the principles of some other law, or system of religion; for the Hebrews were required to *leave* certain principles which they had espoused, and which were a hindrance to their spiritual progress, and *go on to perfection.*

To the Bible student it is scarcely necessary for me to say that Paul was addressing Hebrew Christians, who, as the history of early Christianity abundantly shows, were constantly being hampered and perplexed by the Judaism of those days, their teachers insisting, as many of them did, that they must still observe much of the ritualism of the law. Against these heresies Paul was constantly warning these Judaizing Christians, as the following Scriptures will plainly show:

"Where is boasting then? It is excluded. By what law? of works? Nay: but by the law of faith. Therefore we conclude that a man is justified by faith *without the deeds of the law.*" (Rom. 3: 27, 28.)

"Therefore by the deeds of the law there shall no flesh be justified in his sight." (Ibid, verse 20.)

"But that no man is justified by the *law* in the sight of God, it is evident; for the just shall live by faith. And the law is not of faith." (Gal. 3: 11, 12.)

These, with many other Scriptures, show that there was a uniform and constant tendency among Hebrew Christians to adhere to their old Jewish notions and traditions, and in his letter to them Paul declares that they must *leave* them behind—cut loose from all these hindering causes—and *go on unto perfection* in Christ.

That this is the obvious meaning of Heb. 6: 1, 2 is

also apparent from the following considerations:

1. The principles enumerated are all principles of the law, as we shall show, and are not, therefore, fundamental truths of the Christian system.

2. Heb. 6: 1, 2 omits *faith in Christ*, which is the chief distinguishing characteristic feature of the Christian religion, and hence can have no reference to the doctrines taught by Christ and the apostles. Let us carefully go over the ground and see if we shall not be able to get at the bottom truths of this passage.

"FAITH TOWARDS GOD."

This is specifically a doctrine of the law. One God, the God of Abraham, of Isaac and of Jacob, stands out prominently in the law as being the God of Israel. "Thou shalt have none other gods before me," was written on tables of stone, thus becoming a fundamental principle of the law. Not so with the Gospel. Jesus said to the disciples, "Let not your heart be troubled: ye believe in God, *believe also in me*." (John 14: 1.)

Thus it appears that "faith towards God," enjoined by the law, is not sufficient, but that faith in Jesus Christ also is required. Had Paul been talking about the doctrine taught in the Gospel, he would have emphasized "faith in Christ" as being fundamental, as he was determined to know nothing among men, save "Jesus Christ and him crucified."

Not one word does the apostle say about the death, the burial and the resurrection of Jesus, and yet these are the foundation facts of the Gospel. (See 1 Cor. 15: 1-4.) These are the fundamental principles of Christianity—"the first principles of the oracles of God." (Heb. 5: 12.) While these Hebrews ought now to be teachers, they had, through their adherance to the rites of Judaism, so far departed from first principles as to render it necessary to *again* be taught the rudiments of the Christian religion.

In the fifth chapter Paul invites attention to Christ as the great high priest, who "became the author of eternal salvation unto all them that obey him" (verse 9).

In the sixth chapter he calls attention to the fact that, having departed from these "first principles," they had *again* laid the foundation of "repentance from dead works."

Having received the Gospel and afterwards leaving or departing from its fundamental truths and returning to "the works of the law," they laid *again* the foundation of "repentance from dead works." The apostle, therefore, is exhorting the Hebrews to leave behind them the law of "dead works" and of "faith towards God" only, as enjoined by the law, and include Christ, the great High Priest, as the *author* and *finisher* of our faith—"the author of eternal salvation" (chapter 5: 9).

REPENTANCE FROM DEAD WORKS.

What is meant by "repentance from dead works?" This exhortation, it will be observed, is to a *special* repentance—repentance from particular things. It is not of a general character, such as that of Peter on Pentecost, "Repent, every one of you," but an injunction to turn away from and forsake all "dead works," including the "baptisms" associated with the works of the law. That the dead works from which they were to turn or repent are the works of the law is rendered apparent from the following:

"Wherefore, my brethren, ye are become *dead to the law* by the body of Christ. . . . But now we are *delivered from the law*, that [law] being *dead* wherein we were held." (Rom. 7: 4-6.)

If these people were dead to the law, then the works prescribed by the law could no longer be binding upon them; and hence all works enjoined by a dead law must of necessity be "dead works." The apostle further declares that the law "wherein we were held"—that is to say, "the law of sin and death"—(Rom. 8: 2) "being dead," they were "delivered" from its bondage.

If the law was dead to the people, and if the people were *dead to the law*, then certainly the "works of the law" must necessarily be "dead works." To render it absolutely certain that the works of the law are the "dead works" referred to in Heb. 6: 1, 2, we have but to go with the apostle through a few chapters immediately following. He first calls the attention of these Hebrew Christians to the great dangers of apostasy involved in their return to Judaism. He assures them of the absolute justice of God, and that their "good works," manifested in their "ministering to the saints," would be amply rewarded. He finally commends them to Christ, who was "made a priest forever after the order of Melchizedek."

The seventh chapter is devoted to explaining the peculiarities of this priesthood, and the character of Christ as the great High Priest; that, having annulled "the commandment going before"—the law—he had himself become the "surety of a *better covenant*."

The eighth chapter deals with the establishment of the "better covenant," and assures these Judaizing

Christians that God had set up "the *true* tabernacle," of which the old was but the shadow, and that Jesus was the "minister of the sanctuary." The apostle seeks to assure them that the entire law of Moses, with the tabernacle and its peculiar service, was composed very largely of but mere "shadows," pointing to Christ as "the mediator of a *better covenant*, established upon better promises."

In the ninth chapter the various "gifts and sacrifices" of the tabernacle service are pointed out, which he informed them were to continue *only* till "the time of reformation."

Step by step the apostle leads them from the law of Moses to the law of life in Christ, contrasting the bloody rites of the one with the higher spiritual sacrifices of the other, leading them from the "dead works" of the law to the "good works" of the Gospel, in which "God had before ordained they should walk." (Eph. 2: 10).

To clinch his argument with respect to the necessity for *leaving behind them* the "dead works" mentioned in chapter six, the apostle says:

"For if the *blood of bulls* and of goats, and the ashes of an heifer sprinkling the unclean sanctifieth to the purifying of the flesh, how much more shall *the blood of Christ*, who through the eternal Spirit offered himself without spot to God, *purge your conscience from dead works.*" (Heb. 9: 13, 14.)

The difference between "the law of works" and "the law of the Spirit of life in Christ" is measured by the difference between "the blood of bulls and of goats" and "the blood of Christ," which "cleanseth us from all sin" (1 John 1: 7). The one sanctified to "the purifying of the flesh," while the other was to "purge the conscience" from the "dead works" of the law.

Nothing can be plainer, therefore, than that the dead works referred to in Heb. 6:1, are "the works of the law." From these dead works, by which the apostles declares *no man can be made perfect*, they were to repent. Hence the passage may be paraphrased thus:

"Therefore in leaving the principles of the doctrine of Christ, and returning to the observance of the law, you are laying again the foundation of repentance from the dead works of the law, of faith towards God only, of the doctrine of divers washings, and of laying on of hands, and of resurrection of the dead and eternal judgment, as taught in the law."

THE DOCTRINE OF BAPTISMS.

Since the apostle is writing of the law and not of the Gospel, the "baptisms" here mentioned are the baptisms, or divers washings, imposed by law, they can, therefore, have no possible reference to Christian baptism. Nowhere do the Scriptures mention *two* Christian baptisms.

Not even two *modes* of baptism are suggested. If *two baptisms* had been taught either by Christ or the apostles, it seems quite reasonable to suppose that some allusion to the fact would have been made by some of the evangelists in relating the acts of the apostles. Since no such baptisms are mentioned, it is perfectly legitimate to conclude that no two baptisms ever occurred: and the only reason why they did not occur was clearly because they had never been authorized. Hence "the doctrine of *baptisms*" is no part of the "doctrine of Christ."

At this particular juncture we are met by the objection that "baptisms" refer not to two immersions in water, but rather to *one* immersion in water and to *one* in the Holy Spirit. To prove this position we are referred to the conversation with Nicodemus, to whom Jesus said:

"Verily, verily, I say unto thee, Except a man be born of water, and of the Spirit, he cannot enter into the kingdom of God." (John 3: 5.)

The argument adduced in support of the theory of two baptisms, proceeds upon the assumption that "born" and "baptize" are synonyms, and may, therefore, be used interchangeably; but this position is not supported by the facts, as the definitions of the two words will clearly show:

"BAPTIZE. To administer the sacrament of baptism to. By some denominations of Christians baptism is performed by plunging or immersing the whole body in water."—*Webster*.

"BORN. Brought forth. *To be born*, is to be produced or brought into life."—*Webster*.

Thus *baptism* is a plunging or immersion in water, while a *birth* is the act of producing or bringing into life. In a Scriptural sense, both may be regarded as transitional, passing from one state of being to another in which there is a corresponding change of environment.

In Christian baptism we are said to have "put on Christ" (Gal. 3: 27.) As Christ came forth from the grave to enter upon a new state of being, "so we also should walk in newness of life" (Rom. 6: 4.)

Baptism involves the conscious and voluntary change of an intelligent, accountable, human being from one set of environments to another; while a birth involves an unconscious and involuntary change of surroundings. Baptism is the continuation of life *under changed conditions,* while a birth is a condition *which marks the beginning of life.*

Baptism represents the death, burial and resurrection of Christ (Rom. 6: 3, 4), while the birth of the Spirit marks the beginning of a new life in Christ.

To be "buried with Christ in baptism" (Col. 2: 12) is to reach the *close* of the old life of sin. To be born of the Spirit is to *begin* the new life in Christ. Hence, there exists no similarity between a baptism and a birth. This being true the language of Jesus to Nicodemus can have no possible reference to Heb. 6: 1, 2, and to rely upon it to prove *two baptisms,* as "a principle of the doctrine of Christ," and, therefore, a part of the "plan of salvation," is, to say the least, unfortunate. The apostle doubtless has reference to the baptisms or "divers washings" of the law.

In order to render this position indisputable we again advert to the fact that the apostle, in his letter to the Hebrews, was trying to impress upon their minds the importance and supremacy of the "law of life" as in contradistinction to "the law of sin and death;" and to show them the utter worthlessness of the dead works of the law.

Referring them to the law of Christ, he desires them to understand that it is supreme, and permanent; while the law of Moses was but a "figure" of better things to come.

Touching the ceremonies imposed by the law, the apostle continues:

"Which was a *figure* of the time then present, in which were offered both gifts and sacrifices, that could not make him that did the service perfect, as pertaining to conscience, which stood only in meats and drinks, *and divers washings,* [numerous baptisms] and carnal ordinances, imposed on them until the time of reformation." (Heb. 9: 9, 10.)

From the foregoing we learn the following facts:

1. That the service of the tabernacle was but a " figure" pointing to or representing " the true tabernacle," which God had set up, and of which Jesus was the minister.

2. That this service stood in meats and drinks, and " divers washings " or " baptisms," and carnal ordinances.

3. That the " gifts and sacrifices " of the law could not make him that did the service *perfect.*"

4. That because of the imperfections of both the law and its service, they were to cease at " the time of reformation," when the " better covenant," with its better service, should be established.

5. That all these things, including " the doctrine of baptisms," they were to *leave behind them,* as they were but so many parts of " the law of sin and death," and " abiding in the doctrine of Christ" (2 John 9), they must " go on unto perfection."

Upon a careful study of the question this seems the only view that will harmonize with all the material facts relative to the matter, and hence " baptisms " can have no possible reference to the doctrine required by Christ.

CHAPTER XXX.

THE LAYING ON OF HANDS.

The laying on of hands—Is it an ordinance of the Gospel?—Neither Christ nor the apostles enjoin it—Not a principle of the doctrine of Christ—Peter and John give the Holy Spirit—Paul at Ephesus—Classed among apostolic miracles—Not necessary to salvation—It is of Hebrew origin—The scape-goat—Sins laid upon the goat—Sins of the world laid upon Christ.

WITH Latter Day Saints the laying on of hands is reckoned among the ordinances of the Gospel, and actually necessary to salvation. The fact that Paul names it with what they believe to be "the principles of the doctrine of Christ," is regarded as positive proof that it is an ordinance of the Gospel, and therefore indispensable.

This view is much strengthened by the fact that, in two instances, the ordinance of baptism is followed by the laying on of apostolic hands. It is therefore maintained that the object or design of this rite was to impart the Holy Spirit to baptized believers.

That the Holy Spirit was received *after* the laying on of apostolic hands, none will deny; but that this peculiar ceremony was performed for that purpose, is, to say the least, questionable.

Latter Day Saints teach, and no doubt honestly believe, that the laying on of hands is an ordinance through obedience to which the Holy Spirit is given, that this was its original design; and since nothing can be gained by an unfair statement of a proposition, or by its improper treatment in discussion, I have endeavored to state the question substantially as its friends will be willing to defend it; and shall now try to answer, fairly and squarely, the arguments adduced in its support.

In the examination of this question it is important to observe the following points, namely:

1. Is the laying on of hands taught either by Christ or the apostles as an ordinance to be observed in the church?

2. Do the Scriptures teach that the laying on of hands was instituted for the purpose of giving the Holy Spirit to baptized believers in Christ?

3. Is its observance, like baptism, one of the requirements of the Gospel?

4. Is it necessary to salvation?

With these questions fairly and Scripturally answered the question may be regarded as settled.

First. Is the laying on of hands taught either by Christ or the apostles as an ordinance to be observed in the church?

I think it may be laid down as a principle not to be questioned that a doctrine not taught either by Christ himself or by his apostles cannot be regarded as binding upon Christians, or in any sense necessary to salvation.

Commencing with the baptism of John and carefully following him through his entire ministry, it is a very significant fact that Jesus nowhere, either by precept or example, ever taught the laying on of hands as a means of giving the Holy Spirit, not even to his disciples.

When Christ commissioned his apostles to go into all the world and preach the Gospel, he specifically mentioned the fact that all believers *must be baptized*, but he does not even hint that such persons were to be confirmed by the laying on of hands before they could receive the Holy Spirit. Thus we see that Jesus did not teach the laying on of hands, and now let us see if the apostles taught it.

Under the great commission no apostle ever informed the people that the laying on of hands was enjoined in the Gospel, much less tell them that it was the means, and the only means, of obtaining the Holy Spirit after baptism.

When Peter on the day of Pentecost stood up with the eleven to declare in a public manner "the doctrine of Christ," it is a remarkable and a very significant fact that not one word is said about the laying on of hands, not a syllable to intimate that it was in any sense whatever to be regarded as an ordinance of the Gospel. When, pricked in their hearts by the strong declarations of Peter, they cried out, saying, "Men and brethren, what shall we do?" Peter said unto them:

"*Repent*, every one of you, and be *baptized* in the name of Jesus Christ, for the remission of sins, and ye shall receive the gift of the Holy Ghost.

"Then they that gladly received his word were baptized: and the same day there were added unto them about three thousand souls." (Acts 2: 38, 41.)

Following the example of his Lord and Master, Peter, in this remarkable and historic initiatory sermon of the Gospel dispensation, says not one word about the laying on of hands as an ordinance of the Gospel to be perpetuated in the church. Neither Peter at Pentecost, nor any other apostle subsequently, has ever enjoined the laying on of hands.

If this be a principle of such vital importance as

the Saints declare it to be, why did the Great Teacher of mankind so utterly ignore it all through his ministry? And why did the apostles omit it when answering the question of questions, "What shall I do to be saved?" (Acts 2: 37; 16: 30.)

If this principle be necessary in order to the reception of the Holy Spirit, why was it not mentioned in the commission? *Faith* in God the Father, in the Son, and in the Holy Spirit (Matt. 28: 19), *Repentance* (Luke 24: 47; Acts 2: 38), *Confession* (Rom. 10: 10), and *Baptism* (Mark 16: 16; Acts 2: 28), are all taught by both Christ and the apostles in a plain, direct and unmistakable manner.

If the laying on of hands had been of equal importance it would doubtless have received the same consideration. Had it been of vital importance it would have been included in the commission to the disciples, and would have been faithfully taught by them.

It is incredible to believe that if this so-called ordinance had been intended as an ordinance to be perpetuated in the church, Peter would have failed to declare it on Pentecost while filled with the Spirit to proclaim the saving truths of the Gospel at the very opening of the new dispensation. That he made no reference to the laying on of hands when answering the questions of inquiring penitents may be regarded as proof that Peter did not consider it to be a matter that in any way related to their salvation.

The laying on of hands never having been enjoined either by Christ or the apostles, it cannot, therefore, be a "principle of the doctrine of Christ," and hence is not an ordinance to be perpetuated in the church.

Second. Do the Scriptures teach that the laying on

of hands is for the purpose of imparting the Holy Spirit to baptized believers in Christ?

If, as the Saints declare, this is the *law* through obedience to which men are to receive the Holy Spirit after baptism, why is it not somewhere so explained? Why do Christ and the apostles so uniformly and so persistently omit a principle of such grave importance? There is but one answer, and that is, it was never intended to be so understood.

It is true that when the people of Samaria had received the word of God under the preaching of Philip, they did not receive the Holy Spirit until *after* the apostles, Peter and John, had laid their hands upon them. But this by no means proves that this was the law through which they were to receive it. There is nothing in this circumstance to warrant the belief that the Samaritans could not and would not have received the Spirit without the performance of such a ceremony.

Latter Day Saints argue that Philip, being a deacon at that time, was not authorized to perform the rite of the laying on of hands; and the fact that Peter and John were sent down to lay their hands upon them, proves that it was necessary that the ceremony should be performed.

The following is the Scripture upon which they rely to prove this position:

"Now when the apostles which were at Jerusalem heard that Samaria had received the word of God, they sent unto them Peter and John: who, when they were come down, *prayed for them*, that they might receive the Holy Ghost: (for as yet he was fallen upon none of them, only they were baptized in the name of the Lord Jesus.) Then laid they their hands on them, and they received the Holy Ghost." (Acts 8: 14-17.)

The defenders of this peculiar dogma are in error upon two points at least, namely:

1. They maintain that Philip had no authority to administer in this supposed ordinance, being at the time only a deacon.

2. That Peter and John were sent expressly to perform the laying on of hands.

Two objections may be urged against this position, as follows: In the first place, there is no proof that Philip was at that time a deacon. He was doing "the work of an *evangelist*" (see 2 Tim. 4: 5), which is wholly incompatible with the duties of a deacon. He probably held the same office as did Timothy, Titus, Barnabas, Apollos, and others of that class. And in the next place, there is nothing to indicate that Peter and John were sent to Samaria for the specific purpose of laying their hands upon these new converts, but rather to pray for them, as the record clearly shows:

"Who, when they were come down, *prayed for them*." What did they pray for? "*That they might receive the Holy Ghost.*"

To pray for the Samaritans that they might receive the Holy Spirit seems to have been the prime object of the visit of the apostles to Samaria, while the laying on of hands was purely incidental, and the *object* of it is not mentioned. Just why the apostles laid their hands upon these new converts does not appear; but that the reception of the Holy Spirit followed there can be no question.

It is a well known fact that all the apostles were schooled under the law among whose ceremonies was found the laying on of hands. This rite was formerly employed in the consecration of men and things for divine service. In this manner Joshua was set apart as a leader to succeed Moses (see Num. 27: 15-20), and in like manner Aaron and his sons were consecrated to minister in the priest's office (see Exod. 29: 10). Even animals were in the same manner set apart as sacrificial offerings (see Lev. 1: 4; 3: 8).

So it is by no means improbable that it was designed in this case as a special consecration of the Samaritans to the service of God. This view is confirmed by the additional fact that they had been given to idolatry; and this impressive service, while it was not required under the Gospel, served as a means of confirmation.

A similar incident occurred at Ephesus, under the ministry of St. Paul. Like the Samaritans, these Gentile converts had been idolaters, and did not receive the Holy Spirit till after Paul had laid his hands upon them (see Acts 19: 1-6.) But as in the case of the Samaritans, there is not the slightest intimation given as to why the ceremony was performed.

Not only in the two cases just cited do the writers fail to name the purpose of this ceremony, but nowhere in all the New Testament is the object stated. The nearest approach to it is in the incident first named. There it is said:

"And when Simon saw that through laying on of the apostles' hands the Holy Ghost was given, he offered them money, saying, Give me also this power, that on whomsoever I lay hands he may receive the Holy Ghost." (Acts 8: 18, 19.)

That the apostles on this particular occasion gave the Holy Spirit, as did also the apostle Paul at Ephesus, by the laying on of hands, even the unregenerate Simon could plainly see, and which, therefore, we may not question. But to say that it was therefore an *ordinance* of the Church of Christ to be handed down side by side with Christian baptism is wholly gratuitous, having not the shadow of support in the Word of God.

These incidents are clearly classed among the miracles of the apostles, extraordinary in character, and are not to be classed among the ordinary requirements of the Gospel, as, for example, are baptism and the Lord's Supper.

We repeat with emphasis that nowhere in all the New Testament is there a single passage which declares that the laying on of hands is an ordinance of the Church of Christ, or that its purpose is to impart the Holy Spirit to believers after baptism.

Even if we admit that the apostles were sent from Jerusalem for the specific purpose of laying their hands upon the Samaritan converts, still the fact remains that it was a special dispensation, and not a general provision of law. This brings us to consider:

Third. Is its observance, like baptism, one of the requirements of the Gospel?

The discussion of the two preceding propositions has clearly developed the fact that observance of the laying on of hands is nowhere enjoined by either Christ or his apostles. Being nowhere enjoined, it is not a requirement; and what is not required is not to be perpetuated, and hence, not a requirement of the Gospel.

Fourth. Is it necessary to salvation?

If the laying on of hands is taught neither by Christ nor his apostles; if the Scriptures nowhere teach that it is necessary in order to receive the Holy Spirit; and if its observance is nowhere commanded, then certainly it is no part of the Gospel; and if no part of the Gospel, it is not necessary to salvation.

OF HEBREW ORIGIN.

The laying on of hands being of Jewish origin, the Hebrew Christians were very tenacious of its observance. Having been accustomed to it all their lives, it was, like any other habit or tradition, very difficult, indeed, for them to break away from it. With characteristic tenacity, they clung to the traditions of their fathers so closely that Jesus often rebuked them very sharply. To their teachers he at one time said, "Why do ye also transgress the commandment of God by your traditions?" (Matt. 15: 3.)

And at another:

"Howbeit, in vain do they worship me, teaching for *doctrines* the commandments of men. . . . Full well ye reject the commandment of God, that ye may keep your own tradition." (Mark 7: 7, 9.)

Many of these traditions, as well as the observance of the works of the law, were carried by the Hebrews into the Church of Christ. And it was against these that Paul directed his polished shafts of argument in his letter to the Hebrews. They not only insisted that the "dead works of the law," with its divers "baptisms," and the keeping of its Sabbaths, must be observed, but that the "laying on of hands," which originated with the law, must also be recognized.

The first reference to the laying on of hands as an ordinance is that commanded when the burnt offerings were to be made, at the consecration of Aaron and his sons to the priest's office. (See Ex. 29: 10.)

Later it became the custom that when a man brought his offering unto the Lord, he should present it at the door of the tabernacle, and there "lay his hand upon the head of the burnt offering, and it shall be accepted for him to make an atonement for him." (See Lev. 1: 4; 3: 8.)

In laying the hand upon his offering before killing it, there was a symbolical transfer of sin from the individual to the offering. Not only were there individual offerings of this character, but there was also an offering made annually for the sins of the whole people. (See Lev. 16: 23-26, 34.)

Immediately preceding this annual offering for the sins of the people, is another, which is peculiar, but very significant.

THE SCAPEGOAT.

For the purposes of this peculiar ceremony, a bullock and two goats are selected. Choice is made between the two goats, one for a sin offering, and the other for the scapegoat. The bullock is first offered for the sins of Aaron and his household, and then the goat is offered for the sins of the whole people.

When Aaron shall have made "an atonement for the holy place," and for the "altar," and for "the tabernacle of the congregation," he shall bring the live goat:

"And Aaron shall lay both his hands upon the head of the live goat, and confess over him all the iniquities of the children of Israel, and all their transgressions in all their sins, putting them upon the head of the goat, and shall send him away by the hand of a fit man into the wilderness:

"And the goat shall bear upon him all their iniquities into a land not inhabited: and he shall let go the goat into the wilderness." (Lev. 16: 21, 22.)

This is perhaps one of the most remarkable, as well as one of the most significant, ceremonies connected with the Mosaic law. It points in a most unmistakable manner to Christ, who should bear the sins of the entire world.

Seemingly in a manner to apply this great type to the sacrificial offering to be made by Christ, Isaiah says:

"Surely he hath borne our griefs, and carried our sorrows: yet we did esteem him stricken, smitten of God, and afflicted. But he was wounded for our transgression, he was bruised for our iniquities: the chastisement of our peace was upon him, and with his stripes we are healed.

"All we like sheep have gone astray; we have turned every one to his own way; and the Lord hath laid upon him the iniquity of us all. He was oppressed, and he was afflicted, yet he opened not his mouth: he is brought as a lamb to the slaughter, and as a sheep before her shearers is dumb, so he openeth not his mouth." (Isa. 53: 4-7.)

That this Scripture was understood to refer directly to Christ is clearly shown by the following:

"And the place of the Scripture which he read was this: He was led as a sheep to the slaughter, and like a lamb, dumb before his shearer, so opened he not his mouth. Then Philip opened his mouth, and began

at the same scripture, and preached unto him Jesus."
(Acts 8: 32, 35).

Let us now pause to inquire: What have we learned from these lessons of the law? Summarized, we glean the following facts:

1. The laying on of hands originated with the law and formed a conspicuous part of its service.

2. It was employed as a means of consecration; such as separating, or setting apart, men to perform important services.

3. It was a symbol representing the transfer of sin from one being to another, as the transfer of individual sin to the individual sacrifice, or the transfer of collective sin to the individual sacrifice, as in the case of the scapegoat.

4. As the scapegoat represents Christ, so the pressing down with both of Aaron's hands upon the head of the goat represents the great weight, or burden, of the sins of the world as they were laid upon Christ.

Thus it is rendered reasonably clear that the laying on of hands, referred to by Paul in his letter to the Hebrews, has its place among the ordinances of the law, and as such was repealed when, upon the establishment of Christianity, the Mosaic system was abolished. Hence, the laying on of hands cannot be regarded as a "principle of the doctrine of Christ."

CHAPTER XXXI.

TESTIMONY OF THE BOOK OF MORMON—DOES IT TEACH THE LAYING ON OF HANDS?

Testimony of the Book of Mormon—Does it teach the laying on of hands?—Contains the fullness of the Gospel—The first Nephite Church—Alma the first high priest—No laying on of hands—One faith and one baptism—First appearance of Christ—His Doctrine —Taught his disciples—He neither taught nor practiced the laying on of hands—Holy Spirit received without it—Nephite twelve disciples did not teach the doctrine—Its practice—Not an instance in the Book of Mormon—It is mentioned but once—Faith, Repentance, Confession and Baptism—More than this cometh of evil— Joseph and Oliver received the Holy Spirit without the laying on of hands—Resurrection of the dead and eternal judgment—Leaving the principles of the doctrine of Christ—What is meant by it? —Conclusion.

THE revelations of Joseph Smith, as found in the book of Doctrine and Covenants, the recognized discipline of the Mormon Church, declare that the Book of Mormon contains

" The fullness of the Gospel of Jesus Christ to the Gentiles, and to the Jews also, which was given by inspiration." (D. and C. 7:2, page 93. See also 26:2, page 112.)

From this quotation we learn not only that the Book of Mormon contains the "*fullness* of the Gospel," but that such fullness was " given by inspiration," and was, therefore, complete in all its appointments.

That which contains a fullness is necessarily complete; and being complete, it needs nothing more.

What is taught in the Book of Mormon respecting "the principles of my Gospel" (D. and C., page 142) must, therefore, be regarded as sufficient,—that whatever is not therein contained and required is unnecessary, and should not be observed.

In view of this remarkable claim for the perfect character of its teachings, let us now make a brief examination of the teachings of the Book of Mormon, as to its requirements respecting the plan of salvation.

Alma, at one time the priest of the very wicked King Noah, but who later renounced his allegiance to the king and his wicked priests, became a believer in Christ.

"And it came to pass that Alma, who had fled from the servants of King Noah, repented of his sins and iniquities, and went about privately among the people, and began to teach the words of Abinadi." [A prophet whom King Noah had put to death.] (B. of M. Mosiah 9: 4, page 191.)

Alma continued his preaching till many converts were made. These were baptized in the "waters of Mormon," and by Alma organized into a church. The particulars are given as follows:

"And now it came to pass that Alma took Helam, he being one of the first, and went and stood forth in the water, and cried, saying, O Lord, pour out thy Spirit upon thy servant, that he may do this work with holiness of heart. And when he had said these words, *the Spirit of the Lord was upon him*, and he said, Helam, I baptize thee, having authority from Almighty God, *as a testimony* that ye have entered into a covenant to serve him until you are dead, as to the mortal body; and may the Spirit of the Lord be poured out upon you; and may he grant unto you eternal life, through the redemption of Christ, which he hath prepared from the foundation of the world. And after Alma had said these words, both Alma and Helam were buried in the water; and they arose and came forth out of the water rejoicing, *being filled with the Spirit*. And again, Alma took another, and went forth a second time into the water, and baptized him according to the first, only he did not bury himself again in the water. And after this manner he did baptize every one that went forth to the place of Mormon; and they were in number about two hundred and four souls; yea, they were baptized in the waters of Mormon, and were filled with the grace of God; and they were called the Church of God, or *the Church of Christ*, from that time forward." (Ibid, page 192.)

In this manner was the first church organized among the people of Nephi. Alma proved to be the St. Paul of those times, building up churches all over the land. He also "ordained priests" and set them to watch over these churches. In giving his charge he instructed them "concerning the things pertaining to the kingdom of God." He commanded them that they "should preach nothing save it were *repentance* and *faith* on the Lord," and that they should be united, "having *one* faith and *one* baptism." . . . And *thus* he commanded them to preach. And *thus* they became the children of God." (Ibid, page 193.)

Here we have the Church of Christ, organized according to Book of Mormon chronology, in the year 124 B. C. No Latter Day Saint will care to question either the correctness of its organic structure, or the completeness of its doctrine.

Several very interesting facts are apparent in the above brief story of the first Nephite Church and its founder, namely:

1. Its founder, Alma, was the priest of a foreign and very wicked king, and hence, utterly without authority, according to every known rule of Mormon theology, to baptize penitent believers, he having never been ordained either by the hands of angels or men.

2. This unordained and unauthorized alien priest baptized first himself and then other " strangers and foreigners " into the Church of Christ.

3. These aliens became members of " the Church of Christ," through *faith*, *repentance* and *baptism*.

4. That they received the Holy Spirit in baptism, and *not by the laying on of hands*.

5. That they had but *one* faith and but " one baptism,"—*not two*.

6. That the priests whom he ordained were to " preach *nothing* save it were *repentance* and *faith* on the Lord."

7. That this " *one* faith and *one* baptism " were sufficient to constitute all believers " the children of God."

If the Book of Mormon contains " the fullness of the Gospel;" and if Alma taught that Gospel in its fullness, then it follows as a fact not to be questioned, that the laying on of hands is no part of the Gospel.

But it may be urged that this was long before the birth of Christ, and that the "fullness" was not taught till after Christ had appeared.

Very well; and in order to remove all doubt upon this point, let us move down the stream of time one hundred and twenty-four years, and examine the record of those times.

The Book of Nephi, the son of Nephi, opens its first page with the year A. D. 1. (See B. of M., page 452.) In the fifth chapter of this book is given a detailed account of the appearance of Christ, after his resurrection, to the people of Nephi; and his instructions to them concerning his doctrine, and how to conduct the affairs of the church, is related in the six following chapters.

The first appearance of Christ was to a vast multitude; and calling Nephi from among the multitude he said unto him:

"I give unto you power that ye shall baptize this people, when I am again ascended into heaven." (Ibid, 477.)

Then follows the formula to be used, and the baptism shall be " in the name of the Father, and of the Son, and of the Holy Ghost." As to the doctrine to be taught and obeyed, we have the following:

"And again I say unto you, ye must repent and be baptized in my name, and become as a little child, or ye can in no wise inherit the kingdom of God. Verily, verily, I say unto you that *this is my* doctrine. . . And whoso shall declare *more* or *less*, and establish it for my doctrine, *the same cometh of evil*, and is not built upon my rock, but he buildeth upon a *sandy foundation*, and the gates of hell standeth open to receive such, when the floods come, and the winds beat upon them." (Ibid, 479.)

The above language was addressed to Nephi and the twelve, whom Jesus had just commanded to preach and baptize, and may, therefore, be regarded as the Nephite commission. So far, in this investigation, we find no reference whatever to "the laying on of hands for the gift of the Holy Spirit."

We now pass to the administrations of these disciples and see if we can determine just how they received the Holy Spirit. The vast multitude was divided "into twelve bodies," and the twelve thus taught the multitude:

"And it came to pass that they arose and ministered unto the people. And when they had ministered those same words which Jesus had spoken, . . . behold, they knelt again, and prayed to the Father in the name of Jesus; and they did pray for that which they most desired; and *they desired that the Holy Ghost should be given unto them.* And when they had thus prayed, they went down unto the water's edge, and the multitude followed them. And it came to pass that Nephi went down into the water, and was baptized. And he came up out of the water, and began to baptize. And he baptized all they whom Jesus had chosen." (Ibid, page 494.)

We have carefully followed these disciples through the different stages of their progress, till they have come to the point where Latter Day Saints tell us the laying on of hands must be performed for the purpose of giving the Holy Spirit to baptized believers in Christ.

These disciples prayed for what they most desired, namely, that the Holy Spirit should be given unto them. If the laying on of hands be a principle of the doctrine of Christ, we have now reached the very point where it should be performed. Did these disciples receive the Holy Spirit by the laying on of hands? Let the record answer:

"And it came to pass when they were all baptized,

and had come up out of the water, the Holy Ghost did fall upon them, and they were filled with the Holy Ghost, and with fire." (Ibid.)

Thus in A. D. 34, the twelve disciples among the Nephites, preached the Gospel to the people, and required only *faith, repentance and baptism*. Not a word did either Christ or the twelve disciples say about the laying on of hands for the gift of the Holy Spirit, but quite to the contrary, they were "filled with the Holy Ghost" immediately after their baptism *without the laying on of hands*.

So pleasing, indeed, was this unto the Lord that he again approvingly appeared to them in the presence of the multitude, and bowing "a little way off from them," said: "Father, I thank thee that thou hast given the Holy Ghost unto these whom I have chosen." (Ibid, page 494.)

If the laying on of hands is a matter of such grave importance as the Saints claim it to be, why did not Jesus, during some of his visits, instruct them to observe it? But instead of this, nothing was required except faith, repentance, confession and baptism. (See Helaman, chapter 5, page 450.)

"And they which were baptized in the name of Jesus, were called the Church of Christ." (B. of M., Nephi, chapter 12, page 507.)

Again Jesus tells the disciples just what they should do to be saved:

"Now this is the commandment: Repent, all ye ends of the earth, and come unto me and be baptized in my name, that ye may be sanctified by the reception of the Holy Ghost. . . . Verily, verily, I say unto you, this is my Gospel; and ye know the things that ye must do in my church." (Ibid, page 508.)

And thus Jesus presents the *fullness* of his Gospel, and the laying on of hands is never once named. Such quotations might be multiplied, but one more will be sufficient, as follows:

"And as many as did come unto them, and did truly *repent* of their sins, were *baptized* in the name of Jesus; *and they did also receive the Holy Ghost.*" (B. of M., Nephi, chap. 1, page 514.)

Thus it appears that Jesus, when among the Nephites, utterly ignored the doctrine of the laying on of hands as taught by the Saints, never once having referred to it in all his teachings.

Perhaps some of their wise men may explain why a book which contains "the fullness of the everlasting Gospel" is as silent as the grave upon a subject of such grave importance. Why did neither Jesus nor his disciples teach it? and why was it never performed as an ordinance of the Gospel to follow baptism? Echo answers, Why?

I am now about to make a statement which will perhaps surprise even some of the teachers among the Saints, and possibly provoke incredulity in the minds of others; but we make it advisedly, knowing whereof we affirm. The statement is simply this: Not a single instance can be found in all the Book of Mormon, from its opening page to the closing chapter, where any man ever received the Holy Spirit by the laying on of hands. No man ever taught or practiced the doctrine. Jesus never once alluded to it. The twelve disciples of Jesus neither *taught* nor *practiced* the laying on of hands.

As a matter of fact, it is never once mentioned by any of the so-called writers of the Book of Mormon, except by Moroni, who wrote his little book about the year A. D. 420 (see Moroni, chap. 10, page 585), when there was not a Nephite living, except himself, to tell the story of the virtues and vices of a once powerful race. Relative to this Moroni says:

"And now it came to pass that after the great and tremendous battle at Camorah, behold the Nephites which had escaped into the country southward were hunted by the Lamanites *until they were all destroyed;* and my father also was killed by them; and I, even I remain alone to write the sad tale of the destruction of my people." (Ibid, page 532.)

Following is the only passage in the Book of Mormon that in any way relates to the laying on of hands for the gift of the Holy Spirit. Concerning it Moroni says:

"The words of Christ which he spake unto his disciples [four hundred years previously. See Book of Nephi, chap. 8, page 493] the twelve whom he had chosen, *as he laid his hands upon them.* And he called them by name, saying, Ye shall call on the Father in my name in mighty prayer; and after that ye have done this ye shall have power that on whom ye shall *lay your hands ye shall give the Holy Ghost;* and in my name shall ye give it: for thus do mine apostles [referring to the apostles at Jerusalem].

"Now Christ spake these words unto them at the time of his first appearing; and the multitude heard it not, but the disciples heard it; *and on as many as they laid their hands fell the Holy Ghost."* (B. of M., Moroni, chap. 2, page 574.)

The language quoted above constitutes one entire chapter, and is the only passage in the book that even hints at the doctrine so persistently urged by the Saints.

Upon a careful examination of the events and teachings referred to not one word is uttered concerning the laying on of hands. As my readers, many of them, will not have the Book of Mormon to which they may refer, I will here give the language of the record. It reads thus:

"And it came to pass that when Jesus had made an end of these sayings, he *touched* with his hand the disciples whom he had chosen, one by one, even until he had touched them all, and spake unto them as he touched them; and the multitude heard not the words which he spake, therefore they did not bear record; but the disciples bear record that he gave them power to *give the Holy Ghost*. And I will show unto you hereafter that this record is true." (B. of M., Nephi, 2, page 493.)

Thus it will be seen that not one word is said either by Christ or by the evangelist making the record concerning the giving of the Holy Spirit by the laying on of hands. But Nephi says, "I will show unto you hereafter that the record is true." As already shown by the passages quoted from this writer and those who succeeded him, the Holy Spirit was given by the twelve, *but never in a single instance* by the laying on of hands, as the incident recorded on the following page clearly shows:

"And it came to pass that Nephi went down into the water and was baptized. And he baptized all whom Jesus had chosen. And it came to pass that when they were all baptized and had come up out of the water, *the Holy Ghost did fall upon them*." (Ibid, page 494.)

Thus every passage shows that the Holy Spirit was received through faith, repentance, confession and baptism, and never once by the laying on of hands.

The Book of Mormon being the witness, then, "the fullness of the everlasting Gospel" consists of *faith, repentance, confession* and *baptism*, without a single word concerning the laying on of hands, thus proving that it is *not* a principle of the doctrine of Christ. What will the Saints do about this perplexing state of affairs? After stating that faith, repentance and baptism were the principles of his doctrine, the Book of Mormon represents Jesus to have said:

"And whoso shall declare *more* or *less*, and establish it for *my doctrine*, the same cometh of *evil*, . . and the *gates of hell standeth open to receive such*." (Page 479.)

Thus it is rendered conclusive that the Book of Mormon not only fails to provide for the laying on of hands as a principle of the doctrine of Christ, but by excluding everything else under penalty of eternal damnation, actually forbids it.

Forbidden by the Book of Mormon, which contains the *fullness* of the everlasting Gospel, this afterthought of the prophet must be regarded as an innovation, unsupported alike by the Bible and the Book of Mormon.

Not only is this true, but it is likewise a fact that this peculiarity of Mormonism was not conceived till sometime between May 15th, 1829, and April 6th, 1830. When Joseph and Oliver baptized one another, upon the date first above given, which immediately preceded their ordination by the hand of an angel, it is specifically declared that they received the Holy Spirit without the laying on of hands, as the following extract, written by Joseph Smith himself, clearly shows:

"No sooner had I baptized Oliver Cowdery than the Holy Ghost fell upon him, and he stood up and prophecied many things which should shortly come to pass. And again, as soon as I had been baptized by him, I also had the spirit of prophecy, when, standing up, I prophecied concerning the rise of the church. . . . *We were filled with the Holy Ghost*, and rejoiced in the God of our salvation." (Smith's History, Vol. 1, page 36. Also Tullidge's History, page 44).

In like manner Samuel H. Smith, brother of the prophet, was baptized by Oliver Cowdery, and received the Holy Spirit without the laying on of hands. Referring to the event Joseph says:

"And he returned to his father's house greatly glorifying and praising God, *being filled with the Holy Spirit.*" (Ibid, page 37).

These incidents would amount to but little were it not for the further fact that Joseph Smith and Oliver Cowdery, neither of them, ever received the laying on of hands for confirmation and the gift of the Holy Spirit. They baptized and ordained one another, and I have searched all available history to find the record of their laying hands on one another to confirm them members of the church and give the Holy Spirit, but I searched in vain. No such history can be found.

Query: If Joseph and Oliver, not to mention Samuel H. Smith, could, and did, receive the Holy Spirit immediately upon being baptized, as in every case recorded in the Book of Mormon, why may not every other baptized believer receive it in the same way?

If the laying on of hands was not necessary in the cases of Joseph and Oliver and Samuel, why should it be considered necessary in the case of others? God is no respecter of persons.

Mormon history records not an instance of the laying on of hands to give the Holy Spirit, till the day the church was organized in April, 1830. By this time Joseph and Oliver had conceived the idea that an elder, who, in Mormon parlance, "holds the Melchizedek priesthood," could officiate in this "ordinance;" and so they first ordained one another to the office of elder, and then proceeded to lay their hands on those who had previously been baptized "that they might receive the gift of the Holy Ghost, and be confirmed members of the Church of Christ." (Ibid, page 77.)

Thus Joseph and Oliver received the Holy Spirit *without the laying on of hands;* the Book of Mormon converts received it without submitting to that "ordinance;" the Bible nowhere enjoins its observance, and hence, the laying on of hands cannot be a "principle of the doctrine of Christ," and necessary to salvation.

THE RESURRECTION OF THE DEAD, AND ETERNAL JUDGMENT.

These two principles were taught in the law and the prophets as being in prospect—something to be revealed in the dim, distant future; but now the apostle wishes to assure these Hebrew Christians that the *resurrection of the dead* has been demonstrated in the resurrection of Christ, and must, therefore, be regarded as an established *fact* of the Gospel.

Since the sins of the entire world had been laid upon Christ, as symbolized by laying on of both Aaron's hands in the ceremony conferring the sins of all Israel upon the head of the scapegoat, it now becomes possible for every man to enter into his rest, through the atonement made in the sacrificial offering of Christ. Hence, every man is held accountable for his own transgressions, and, in the *eternal judgment*, must be "judged according to his works." (Rev. 20: 12, 13).

Relative to this doctrinal question, we have gleaned the following facts:

1. The Hebrews had forsaken what the apostle terms "the first principles of the oracles of God," the Gospel, and had returned to their former practice of the works of the law.

2. That in turning away from the rudiments of Christianity they had laid *again* (as they had done before) the foundation of repentance from dead works—that is, they must *leave* these practices; *abandon* their observances of the law, and return to the simplicity of the Gospel.

3. That "faith towards God," to the exclusion of Christ, "repentance from dead works," the "doctrine of baptisms," or "divers washings," the laying on of hands, the resurrection of the dead and eternal judgment as taught in the law, are all to be abandoned as obsolete.

4. The substance having appeared, the shadow is no longer to be followed.

We conclude, therefore, that in *leaving* "the first principles of the oracles of God," as they evidently had done, and returning to the dead works of the law, which the apostle then proceeds to enumerate, they had laid *again* the foundation of a second repentance from the "dead works" of the law.

What are these dead works from which these

Hebrews were required to repent? The apostle names them as follows:

1. "Faith towards God" *only*, as required by the law, thus excluding Christ as an object of faith.

2. "Of the doctrine of baptisms,"—that is, the "divers washings" of the law.

3. "Of laying on of hands," one of the most specific and significant of the works of the law.

4. The "resurrection of the dead" and "eternal judgment," as they were taught under the law and the prophets.

In short, the entire Mosaic system was but a series of types and shadows pointing to Christ; and now that the substance had been revealed, the Hebrews were to forsake, turn away from, all these useless, if not actually hurtful, practices, and looking to Christ as their only hope of salvation, and abiding steadfastly in "the doctrine of Christ," they were exhorted to "go on unto perfection."

Evidently this, and nothing more, is the doctrine which the apostle, in his Hebrew letter, was trying to enforce.

CHAPTER XXXII.

MORMON POLYGAMY—WAS JOSEPH SMITH ITS AUTHOR?

Mormon polygamy—Was Joseph Smith its author?—Became public soon after the prophet's death—Joseph's power over his people—An illustration—"Thou shalt give heed to all his words"—Doctrine and Covenants accepted—Polygamy practiced before Joseph's death—Questioned only by the Reorganized Church—The son guards the good name of his father—Polygamy a gradual growth—Book of Mormon condemns the doctrine—Early suspicions—Charged with polygamy in 1835—Article on marriage—Does not exclude the practice—One man one wife—One woman *but* one husband—John C. Bennett—The secret wife system—Trouble between Smith and Bennett—The Nauvoo Legion—A sham battle.

THAT polygamy early became a tenet of the Mormon Church is a fact too well established to require proof. That it was taught and practiced in Nauvoo, Illinois, and other places before the death of Joseph and Hyrum Smith, in June, 1844, is equally apparent; but where it was first suggested, or by whom, is not so clear. Whether justly so or not, Joseph Smith has ever, until in recent years, been charged with being its author.

The writer has had ample opportunity to observe the practical workings of the system under the auspices of two different and widely separated Mormon churches, namely, Lyman Wight, in Texas, in 1847, and James J. Strang, of Beaver Island, Mich., in 1854.

Lyman Wight was one of Joseph's trusted apostles. He believed in nothing and in nobody quite as firmly as he believed in the prophet, in whom he reposed the utmost confidence. While the prophet lived "Brother Lyman" would do nothing without his approval, and would dare anything Joseph Smith counseled him to undertake. The following characteristic remark serves to illustrate the blind confidence this apostle reposed in his leader. One one occasion, while extolling the virtues of the prophet, Lyman Wight said:

"Why, brethren, I *know* Joseph Smith was a prophet of God; and if he had told me to go to hell on horseback and preach to the 'spirits in prison,' I should have started at once, believing it to be the will of God."

This well illustrates the power which Joseph Smith exercised over the vast majority of his followers. Men who would not submit to the prophet's will, and especially when that will was expressed in the form of a revelation from God, as most of his principal schemes were, sooner or later sought a more genial atmosphere and withdrew from the church, as did Oliver Cowdery, the Whitmers, the Laws, and other prominent men of the church.

Immediately after the church was organized on April 6, 1830, Joseph, in order to secure and retain the absolute control of all matters pertaining to the church, received the following revelation

"Behold, there shall be a record kept among you, and in it thou shalt be called a seer, a translator, a prophet, an apostle of Jesus Christ, an elder of the church through the will of God the Father, and the grace of our Lord Jesus Christ. Wherefore, meaning the church, *thou shalt give heed to all his words*, and commandments, which he shall give unto you, as he receiveth them, walking in all holiness before me;

for his word ye shall receive, as if from mine own mouth, in all patience and faith." (Doc. and Cov., sec. 19, par. 1, 2, page 102.)

A few years later such of Joseph's revelations as were considered of general importance were compiled by a committee, of which the prophet himself was chairman, and published in a volume known as the book of "Doctrine and Covenants." (See Smith's History, vol. 1, page 578.)

In August, 1835, these revelations were received and made binding upon the membership of the church by the action of a "general assembly" held at Kirtland, Ohio, as the following excerpt shows:

"The assembly being duly organized, and after transacting certain business of the church, proceeded to appoint a committee to arrange the items of doctrine of Jesus Christ, for the government of his church of Latter Day Saints." (Ibid, page 572.)

"Afternoon.—President Cowdery arose and introduced the 'Book of Doctrine and Covenants of the Church of Latter Day Saints,' in behalf of the committee. He was followed by President Rigdon." (Ibid, page 573.)

The presidents of the different Quorums, and others, each "bore record to the truth of the book," declaring he knew the revelations were from God; and finally,

"The venerable Assistant President, Thomas Gates, then bore record of the truth of the book, and with his five silver-headed assistants *and the whole congregation*, accepted and acknowledged it as the doctrine and covenants of their faith by a unanimous vote." (Ibid, page 575. See also Doc. and Cov., page 4, General Assembly.)

At a semi-annual General Conference of the Reorganized Church, held at Galland's Grove, Iowa, Sept. 20, 1877, similar action was had. By the actions of these assemblies every member is bound to accept Joseph Smith's word as the word of God. To question what he says with a "thus saith the Lord" attached to it, is to question the word of the Lord, and few Latter Day Saints have the moral courage to do this. Hence the servility of the Saints to the mandates of the prophet.

Under such circumstances it is not a matter of astonishment that people can be led into believing anything a prophet may declare. When a people can bring themselves to that point where they are willing to accept the word of a man as being equivalent to the word of God, they have reached a condition of mental servitude fitting them for a willing submission to anything and everything the prophet may declare in the name of the Lord, it matters not how wicked or how absurd. Thus the women of Utah were willing to submit to the heart-crushing sorrows and shame which polygamy entailed, simply and only because they believed the "revelation" (!) which authorized the abomination came through a prophet of God. Their higher and better natures protested against it; their souls abhorred it; the higher and nobler instincts of their pure womanhood cried out against the abomination; but, believing their eternal salvation depended upon submission to the wicked mandates of the soul-destroying monstrosity, they yielded; for what sacrifice will a faithful Christian woman not make in order to secure everlasting life?

That Joseph Smith both taught and practiced polygamy was never doubted, so far as I am aware, till it was questioned by the people of the Reorganized Church, of which Joseph Smith, son of the prophet, is the president. If his father was in no way responsible for the introduction of a practice into the church which would stain the fair name of both his family and the church, it is eminently proper that a devoted son should do all in his power to repel the calumny and place the responsibility where it rightfully belongs.

And, on the other hand, had Joseph Smith either from the volitions of his own nature, or through the over-weening influence of wicked and designing men, been led into error and sin, it is but natural that the son should seek, in an honorable way, to parry the fatal blow, and let it fall as lightly as possible upon the heads of the innocent. For doing this President Smith will not be censured by fair-minded people, for in doing so he is but pursuing a course which would be adopted by almost anybody else under like circumstances. From a long personal acquaintance with President Smith I take great pleasure in saying I regard him as a most excellent and sincere Christian gentleman, and worthy of the respect and esteem of all good people. If he believed his father to have been the author of the infamous revelation on polygamy, he possesses both moral courage and Christian manhood to denounce it in the roundest terms, and would neither by word nor deed seek to justify even his father, whose memory he holds sacred, in the introduction of a doctrine alike soul-destroying to men and dishonoring to God.

It matters not what the father may have done, for his deeds the son must not be held responsible. Eating sour grapes can no longer set the children's teeth on edge. We live in an age of progress, and of individual responsibility.

In the discussion of this question I shall endeavor to present such facts as are in my possession, together with my personal observations, and let the reader judge for himself as to whether Joseph Smith, Jr., was the author of Mormon polygamy.

A GRADUAL GROWTH.

Mormon polygamy did not spring suddenly into existence, as a tenet of the church, but, like many other ideas and dogmas of the Saints, it was an afterthought, if not an evolution. The seed from which the pernicious weed sprang, was certainly planted after the publication of the Book of Mormon, in which it is most strongly denounced, as will appear from the following:

"Behold, David and Solomon truly had many wives and concubines, which thing was abominable before me, saith the Lord. . . . Wherefore, my brethren, hear me, and hearken unto the word of the Lord: for there shall not any man among you have save it be one wife; and concubines you shall have none: for I, the Lord God, delighteth in the chastity of women." (B. of M., Jacob, chapter 2, page 127.)

Joseph Smith here represents his ideal Nephites as seeking to justify themselves in the practice of polygamy on the ground that David and Solomon had many wives and concubines; but the good prophet Jacob assured them that it was an abomination in the Lord's sight, and ever had been; and that God would not tolerate the evil. How Latter Day Saints, while professing to believe in the divinity of the Book of Mormon, could so soon lose sight of its teachings and endorse a principle so clearly antagonistic to its precepts, is one of the anomalies of Mormonism, and shows that the word of a so-called inspired prophet has a vastly greater influence over Latter Day Saints than does the written Word of God.

At just what period this excrescence of Mormonism appeared and became the dream of its leaders, may never be known; but of one thing we are quite sure, and that is the Saints were at an early date reproached by their enemies, as they deemed the people of all other churches, with "the crime of fornication and polygamy." What gave rise to this reproach is very largely a matter of conjecture; but it is probable that something either in their teachings or their conduct (probably the latter) led people, who viewed things from the outside, to believe that the lives of their leaders were not as pure as the title, "Latter Day *Saints*," would lead one to suppose them to be. This feeling was, no doubt, materially intensified by the strong prejudices of the people generally, but that their suspicions were wholly groundless, subsequent developments forbid us to believe.

A prejudice nearly as strong as that which existed against the Saints was also fostered by other denominations towards the Disciples of Christ, a denomination of Christians which had its rise about the same time, under the leadership of Alexander Campbell; yet these people were never reproached with the crime of polygamy, or any other form of vice and immorality. Hence, we feel warranted in the belief that had there been nothing in the conduct of the Saints to give rise to such suspicions, no such charges of immorality would ever have been made. And then again, had there been no foundation in fact for these charges, it is altogether probable the sentiment would ultimately have died out, and polygamy among the Mormons would never have become one of the established facts of history. But since the belief of their guilt only grew stronger with the passing years; and since polygamy became an acknowledged fact in Mormon history as early as 1843, it amounts to a very strong presumptive evidence that the charge so early made against the Saints had its foundation in fact. They were charged with polygamy at as early a day as August, 1835, as may be seen from the following article on marriage:

"MARRIAGE."

"1. According to the custom of all civilized nations, marriage is regulated by laws and ceremonies; therefore we believe that all marriages in this Church of Christ of Latter Day Saints should be solemnized in a public meeting, or feast, prepared for that purpose; and that the solemnization should be performed by a presiding high priest, high priest, bishop, elder or priest, not even prohibiting those persons who are desirous to get married of being married by other authority. We believe that it is not right to prohibit members of this church from marrying out of the chnrch if it be their determination to do so, but such persons will be considered weak in the faith of our Lord and Saviour Jesus Christ.

"2. Marriage should be celebrated with prayer and thanksgiving; and at the solemnization, the persons to be married, standing together, the man on the right, and the woman on the left, shall be addressed by the person officiating, as he shall be directed by the Holy Spirit; and if there be no legal objections, he shall say, calling each by their names: 'You both mutually agree to be each other's companion, husband and wife, observing the legal rights belonging to this condition; that is, keeping yourselves wholly for each other, and from all others, during your lives.' And when they have answered 'Yes,' he shall pronounce them ' husband and wife ' in the name of the Lord Jesus Christ, and by virtue of the laws of the country and authority vested in him: 'May God add his blessings and keep you to fulfill your covenants from henceforth and forever. Amen.'

"3. The clerk of every church should keep a record of all marriages solemnized in his branch.

"4. All legal contracts of marriage made before a person is baptized into this church should be held sacred and fulfilled. *Inasmuch as this Church of Christ has been reproached with the crime of fornication and* POLYGAMY: we declare that we believe that one man should have one wife, and one woman but one husband, except in case of death, when either is at liberty to marry again. It is not right to persuade a woman to be baptized contrary to the will of her husband, neither is it lawful to influence her to leave her husband. All children are bound by law to obey their parents; and to influence them to embrace any religious faith, or to be baptized, or to leave their parents without their consent, is unlawful and unjust. We believe that husbands, parents and masters who exercise control over their wives, children and servants and prevent them from embracing the truth, will have to answer for that sin." (Smith's History, Vol. 1, pages 575-6. Also Doc. and Cov., Sec. 111, page 329.)

This article on marriage—which I have quoted

entire—was presented before a "General Assembly" at Kirtland, Ohio, August 17, 1835, and by the action of that body became one of the articles of church government, and was ordered printed as a part of the "Doctrine and Covenants" of the church.

This article shows that at that early day the church had been charged with "the crime of fornication and polygamy." The adoption and publication of this article on marriage was designed to serve the two-fold purpose of refuting the charges of polygamy, and at the same time counteract the influence of the charge upon the public mind. Upon its face, the article, especially that portion which includes the marriage ceremony, seems absolutely to prohibit polygamy; and yet, strange to say, this identical ceremony has been employed in every polygamous marriage performed in the endowment house in Salt Lake City during the palmy days of Brigham Young, and, in fact, by every other polygamous branch of the Mormon Church.

Upon the surface there seems no possible loop-hole to admit polygamy, but upon a careful examination it will be seen that such is not the case. Let us examine the document a little more closely.

Why should all marriages be "solemnized in a *public meeting*," or a feast prepared for that purpose, which is also public? Clearly it was for the purpose of creating the impression that no secret marriages ever had been or ever would be performed with the approval of the church. All polygamous marriages, up to the time of the exodus to Utah, were of necessity performed in secret, in order to evade the punishment which the law of every State prescribed.

Church clerks were to make a record of every marriage performed in the manner described, but of clandestine marriages he could make no record, not having *legal* knowledge that such marriage had been performed.

Again, you may have observed the ingenious phraseology of that part of the document which is designed to convey the impression that the assembly, as well as the entire church, was opposed to polygamy, but which, as a matter of fact, leaves the way open for its introduction and practice. The language I refer to is this:

"We believe that one man shall have *one* wife; and one woman *but one husband.*" Why use the restrictive adverb in the case of the woman, and ingeniously omit it with reference to the man? Why not employ the same form of words in the one case as in the other? Of the woman it is said she shall have *but one husband.* Why not say of the man, he shall have "*but one wife,* except in case of death, when either is at liberty to marry again." We repeat the question with emphasis, Why not restrict the man to *one* wife in the same manner that the woman is restricted to *one* husband? The reason seems obvious.

As we have already stated, polygamy was a plant whose seed was rather slow to germinate, but which soon sprang into vigorous life when once its head was above ground. As early as October, 1842, the existence of what was called the "secret wife system," was made public at Nauvoo, Ill., through the apostasy of Gen. John C. Bennett, who was about that time expelled from the church. General Bennett was a man of prominence in the church, and a personal friend of Joseph Smith's up to within a short time before the trouble originated which separated them.

Just what caused the difficulty I have never been able to learn, but that it was of a very grave character may be seen from the history of those times.

The "Nauvoo Legion," of which Joseph Smith was the General-in-Chief, was said to be the finest military organization in the State of Illinois. On the 9th of May, 1842, the Legion was on parade, and was reviewed by "Lieutenant-General Joseph Smith, who commanded through the day." There were present at this grand review of the Legion a number of prominent men, among whom were Judge Stephen A. Douglas, of Illinois, and James Arlington Bennett, of the *New York Herald.* "In the afternoon the Legion was separated into cohorts, and fought an animated sham battle," during which General John C. Bennett commanded. Concerning the incident that occurred on this occasion, Tullidge, Joseph's historian, says:

"But a somewhat startling view is also brought to light in the significant fact that Gen. John C. Bennett repeatedly requested the Prophet to take part in the sham battle, urging him in one instance to command the first cohort in person, without his staff." (Tullidge's History, page 394.)

The interpretation which the prophet put upon the conduct of Gen. Bennett, is shown by his own words, as follows:

"If General Bennett's true feelings towards me are not made manifest to the world in a very short time, then it may be possible that the gentle breathings of that Spirit, which whispered me on parade that there was mischief concealed in that sham battle, were false. A short time will determine the point. Let John C. Bennett answer at the day of judgment: Why did you request me to command one of the cohorts, and also to take my position without my staff during the sham battle on the 7th of May, 1842, where my life might have been the forfeit, and no man have known who did the deed?" (Ibid, page 395.)

CHAPTER XXXIII.

SIDE-LIGHTS.

Side-lights—A. H. Smith on polygamy—Those certificates—Dr. Bennett's apostasy—He divulges the secret wife system—Joseph denies—Hyrum Brown cut off from the church—Hyrum Smith denies—Denials examined—Priesthood and polygamy—Testimony of William Marks—Joseph Smith knew polygamy existed—A thus saith the Lord would have stopped it—Joseph alone responsible.

THE following historic facts throw a strong side-light upon the trouble between Joseph Smith and General Bennett. In a tract against polygamy, by Alexander H. Smith, an apostle of the Reorganized Church, the writer quotes from the *Times and Seasons*, the official organ of the church of which his father, Joseph Smith, was at the time editor, to show that polygamy was not a tenet of the church at the time of the prophet's death.

One of the objects in making the quotations is stated by Mr. Smith as follows:

"To rebut some affidavits of some who have sworn that a different marriage ceremony [from that given in the article on Marriage, already quoted] was known and practiced as early as 1840." (POLYGAMY, Was it an Original Tenet of the Church? by A. H. Smith, page 5).

But the documents quoted, so far from proving what he undertakes to establish, only serve to confirm the rumors which had been currently circulated for several years concerning the secret existence of polygamy, which will abundantly appear as we proceed.

Commenting upon the editorial, Mr. Smith says:

"The note of the editor (Joseph Smith) reads thus:

"'We have given the above rule of marriage as the only one practiced in the church, to show that Dr. J. C. Bennett's *secret wife system* is a matter of his own manufacture; and further, to disabuse the public ear, and to show that the said Bennett and his misanthropic friend, Origen Bachelor, are perpetrating a foul and infamous slander upon an innocent people, and need but be known to be hated and despised.'

"In support of this position we present the following certificates.

"'We, the undersigned, members of the Church of Jesus Christ of Latter Day Saints, and residents of the city of Nauvoo, persons of families, do hereby certify and declare that we know of no other rule or system of marriage than the one published from the Book of Doctrine and Covenants, and we give this certificate to show that Dr. John C. Bennett's *secret wife system* is a creature of his own make, *as we know of no such society* in this place, nor never did.

  S. Bennett.   N. K. Whitney.
  George Miller.   Albert Perry.
  Alpheus Cutler.   Elias Higbee.
  Reynolds Cahoon.   John Taylor.
  Wilson Law.   E. Robinson.
  Wilford Woodruff.   Aaron Johnson.'

"I also give the following:

"We, the undersigned, members of the Ladies' Relief Society, and married females, do certify and declare, that we know of no system of marriage being practiced in the Church of Jesus Christ of Latter Day Saints, save the one contained in the Book of Doctrine and Covenants; and we give this certificate to the public, to show that J. C. Bennett's *secret wife system* is a *disclosure* of his own make.

Emma Smith, President.
Elizabeth Ann Whitney, Counselor.
Sarah M. Cleveland, Counselor.
Eliza R. Snow, Secretary.

Mary C. Miller.	Catherine Petty.
Lois Cutler.	Sarah Higbee.
Thyrsa Cahoon.	Phebe Woodruff.
Ann Hunter.	Leonora Taylor.
Jane Law.	Sarah Hillman.
Sophia R. Marks.	Rosannah Marks.
Polly Z. Johnson.	Angeline Robinson.

Abigail Works."—(Ibid. pages 5 and 6, as quoted from *Times and Seasons*, Vol. 3, page 939, for Oct. 1, 1842.)

From the foregoing it will be seen that General Bennett, having left the church, was the first to make a "disclosure" of the "secret wife system," which is said to have existed since 1840. The statement of Dr. John C. Bennett, and others, was made under oath, and sets forth the fact that a "society" existed at Nauvoo, in which this "secret wife system" was practiced by the church leaders.

To counteract the effect produced upon the public mind by these affidavits, Joseph Smith published the entire article on marriage in the *Times and Seasons*, the official organ of the church, together with the certificates of *twelve* men and *nineteen* women. This array of witnesses would, under proper conditions, be quite sufficient to impeach Gen. John C. Bennett, et al, but which, under the circumstances, is of no legal value whatever. Three serious objections to the testimony of these witnesses may be urged, as follows:

1. The witnesses were not under oath when they made their statements, and they were not sworn to afterwards, and hence are incompetent to impeach witnesses who have made a statement of alleged facts under oath.

2. Neither set of witnesses have shown themselves competent to testify upon the questions in issue.

3. The witnesses do not contradict the material facts set forth in the allegation of the affiants.

To render a witness competent to testify in a given case, it must appear that the witness *knows* something pertinent to the issue. An *absence* of knowledge upon the question in controversy does not, and in the very nature of the case cannot, render a witness competent to testify. The witnesses whose testimony is given above simply content themselves by certifying,

1. That they " know of no other rule or system of marriage than that contained in the Book of Doctrine and Covenants," but they do not assert that they are in position to know, and that another rule or system does not exist.

2. They do not certify and declare that no such " system " as that sworn to by Gen. Bennett and others *did not at the time exist;* but content themselves by saying, " we know of no such rule," and that " Dr. John C. Bennett's secret wife system is a *disclosure* of his own make," and that " we know of no such *society* in this place."

While these witnesses all agree that " Dr. Bennett's secret wife system " was a creature "of his own make," *not one of them denies that he made it.* It matters but little whether the "system" was originated by General John C. Bennett, or "Lieutenant-General Joseph Smith." That it *existed* is a fact established by the concurrent testimony of *thirty-one* leading men and women of the Mormon Church.

You will doubtless have observed that Joseph Smith, in the editorial quoted above, charges the system up to Gen. Bennett, saying that "Dr. J. C. Bennett's secret wife system is a matter of his own manufacture;" but many of these same witnesses, both men and women, have since declared that Gen. Joseph Smith was himself the author of the "system," which was afterwards known as the "spiritual wife system," or "celestial marriage," but in plain English, polygamy.

Several of the men whose names appear in the list of witnesses became noted advocates of polygamy. George Miller, also a general in the Nauvoo Legion, and the second man on the list, was a polygamist with *two* wives, when first I knew him in 1847, but five years after his testimony was made public, and only *three* years after the death of the prophet; and Wilford Woodruff, N. K. Whitney and John Taylor—and possibly others of less note—all became advocates of polygamy, and declare that Joseph received the "revelation" on "celestial marriage," *only nine months later*.

Of the women who testified, Miss Eliza R. Snow, the poetess of the church, in later years made affidavit that she had been Joseph's "spiritual wife," but whose statement I have been unable to obtain, but the sworn statements of two of the witnesses, namely, Ebenezer Robinson and his wife Angeline, will be given later.

I will now take up other matters presented by Apostle A. H. Smith, in his effort to prove that polygamy was not in any manner sanctioned by the prophet and patriarch up to within a few months of their death. It is but fair that I should state that President Joseph Smith and his two brothers, Alexander and David, the only living sons of the prophet, have, each in a well-written tract, placed themselves on record as being strongly opposed to polygamy, and stoutly maintain that their father was not, as has been charged, "the putative father of 'polygamy.'"

That the seeds of polygamy had, like the thistledown, spread far into adjacent territory, as early as February, 1842 (only four months after John C. Bennett's disclosures) may be seen from the following:

"NOTICE.

"As we have been credibly informed that an elder of the Church of Jesus Christ of Latter Day Saints, by the name of Hyrum Brown, has been preaching polygamy and other false and corrupt doctrines in the county of Lapeer, State of Michigan, this is to notify him and the church in general, that he has been cut off from the church for his iniquity; and he is further notified to appear at the special conference on the 6th of April next, to make answer to these charges. Signed, Joseph Smith and Hyrum Smith, presidents of said church." (*Times and Seasons*, Vol. 5, page 423, as quoted by A. H. Smith, in his tract on polygamy, page 6.)

While it is true that Joseph and Hyrum Smith in this public manner denounce "polygamy and other false and corrupt doctrines," and summarily deal with

Elder Brown for preaching it, yet it remains a fact that the doctrine was taught by an authorized representative of the church, which fairly raises the presumption that the said elder believed he had the *right* to teach the "secret wife system." The trouble was that Elder Brown preached it to the wrong party, and was reported to headquarters, and as a matter of course something had to be done to appease the wrath of an offended public.

The "secret wife system," or polygamy, could not be openly taught and practiced in the States, for the reason that the laws of the several States were specifically opposed to every form of bigamy, and would punish the offender with imprisonment in the penitentiary. If Joseph Smith was a party to what he calls "J. C. Bennett's secret wife system," the only possible way he could escape public censure was to publicly condemn it, just as he did. But if he had no part nor lot in the matter, then it seems quite reasonable to conclude that no subsequent act or circumstance could have been coerced into even a seeming support of the theory of complicity in the nefarious transaction. Not only would he have denounced the abomination, but every subsequent act of his life would have given it the lie, and no friend of his, or of the cause for which he stood, would ever have been found to besmirch his name, or that of the church, by declaring him to be the author of a revelation enjoining its practice. But all the facts and circumstances immediately connected with the affair conspire to show that the prophet in some way lent his sanction to the evil, as we shall see a little later, all public denials to the contrary notwithstanding.

Alexander makes another quotation from the

church organ to prove that Joseph and Hyrum were not parties to the "secret wife system," as follows:

"NAUVOO, MARCH 8, 1844.

"To the brethren of the Church of Jesus Christ of Latter Day Saints, living on China Creek, in Hancock County, Greeting: Whereas, Brother Richard Hewitt has call on me to-day to know my views concerning some doctrines that are preached in your place, and states to me that some of your elders say that a man having a certain priesthood may have as many wives as he pleases, and that that doctrine is taught here, I say unto you that that man teaches false doctrine, for there is *no such doctrine* taught here, neither is there any such thing practiced here. Any man that is found teaching, privately or publicly, any such doctrine is culpable, and will stand a chance to be brought before the high council, and lose his license and membership also; therefore, he had better beware what he is about.

"HYRUM SMITH."

(*Times and Seasons*, Vol. 5, page 474. Also quoted by A. H. Smith, pages 6 and 7.)

In the above quotation I have italicized some of the words, in order to invite the reader's special attention to their import. The people of the Reorganized Church regard this as an unreserved denial by Hyrum Smith that the doctrine of polygamy was either taught or practiced in Nauvoo at that time.

That the doctrine in Hyrum Smith's mind at the time he wrote is most positively denied by him, as being taught in Nauvoo, is certainly true; and it is also a fact that he does not say polygamy, or "spiritual marriage" is not taught or practiced there. He says with emphasis, "*no such doctrine* is taught here." No such doctrine as what? Polygamy? Not a word of the kind! The doctrine Hyrum Smith referred to, and which he so vehemently denounced, is this: that a man holding a certain priesthood, may have as many wives as he pleases. That doctrine was denied; and that doctrine was not taught in Nauvoo. This could be strictly true, and yet polygamy may flourish as the green bay tree. As a matter of fact, such a doctrine was probably never taught in Nauvoo, nor yet in Salt Lake City, by Brigham Young, or on Beaver Island, by James J. Strang. Priesthood was never taken into consideration. The number of a man's wives was never limited to the grade of his priesthood. This, and nothing more, is what Hyrum Smith denied.

Hence, the patriarch's statement can never be tortured into a denial of polygamy. It is exactly what it was intended to be when penned by the writer, namely, *an ingenious evasion of the truth*, as it was known to exist at that very moment, as I shall hereafter show.

Notwithstanding all the so-called denials of the existence of polygamy in the Mormon Church, the doctrine continued to spread until the time of the prophet's death.

Only three months after Hyrum Smith published his "denial" that polygamy was either taught or practiced at Nauvoo, Joseph had an interview with President William Marks, in which he admitted that polygamy was practiced, and that it would eventually prove the overthrow of the church, unless it was speedily put down. Following is a certified copy of Elder Mark's statement as copied from the files of The *Saint'sHerald*, Lamoni, Iowa, but through an inadvertancy of the writer, the volume and number were not given, but this is immaterial. Following is Secretary Stebbin's letter:

"LAMONI, IOWA, July 5, 1895.
"BRO. D. H. BAYS, Hastings, Mich: I regret the delay in writing to you, but have been busy and have not written as early as I intended to do. The following is a copy of the writing of Elder William Marks that you ask for:

"'OPPOSITION TO POLYGAMY BY THE PROPHET JOSEPH.

"'About the first of June, 1884, situated as I was at that time, being the Presiding Elder of the stake at Nauvoo, and, by appointment, the presiding officer of the High Council, I had a very good opportunity to know the affairs of the church, and my convictions at that time were that the church, in a great measure, had departed from the pure principles and doctrine of Jesus Christ. I felt much troubled in mind about the condition of the church. I prayed earnestly to my Heavenly Father to show me something in regard to it, when I was wrapt in vision and it was shown me by the Spirit that the top or branches had overcome the root *in sin and wickedness*, and that the only way to cleanse and purify it was to disorganize it, and in due time the Lord would reorganize it again. There were many other things suggested to my mind, but the lapse of time has erased them from my memory.

"'A few days after this occurrence I met with Bro. Joseph. He said that he wanted to converse with me on the affairs of the church, and we retired by ourselves. I will give his words verbatim, for they were indelibly stamped upon my mind. He said that he had desired for a long time to talk with me *on the subject of polygamy*. He said it would eventually prove the overthrow of the church, and we should be obliged to leave the United States, unless it could speedily be put down. He was satisfied that it was a cursed doctrine, and there must be every exertion made to put it down. He said that he would go before the congregation and proclaim against it, and I must go to the High Council, and he would prefer charges against those in transgression, and I must sever them from the church unless they made ample satisfaction. There was much more said, but this was the substance.

"'The mob commenced to gather about Carthage a few days after, therefore nothing was done concerning it. After the prophet's death I made mention of this conversation to several, hoping and believing that it would have a good effect; but, to my great disappointment, it was soon rumored about that Bro. Marks was about to apostatize, and that all he said about the conversation with the prophet *was a tissue of lies*.

"'From that time I was satisfied that the church would be disorganized, and the death of the prophet and patriarch tended to confirm me in that opinion. From that time I was looking for a reorganization of the church and kingdom of God. I am thankful that I have lived to again behold the day when the basis of the church is the revelations of Jesus Christ, which is the only sure foundation to build upon. I feel to invite all my brethren to become identified with us, for the Lord is truly in our midst.'

"Dated Shabbona, DeKalb County, Illinois, Oct. 23, 1850, and signed, WILLIAM MARKS.

"If you receive this all right, please inform me by return mail.   Your friend and well-wisher,
"H. A. STEBBINS,
"Secretary of the Reorganized Church."

Believing it to be of some historic importance I have given Elder Stebbins' letter in full.

From this communication of Elder Marks we glean the following facts.

1. That about June 1, 1844, only about three weeks before the death of Joseph and Hyrum Smith, polygamy, or the "secret wife system," (divulged two years previously by Dr. John C. Bennett) had taken such deep root in the Mormon Church that the prophet himself became alarmed, lest they should be driven from the United States in consequence of it.

2. That the spirit of the doctrine had so permeated the entire church as to cause it to *depart* from the pure principles of the doctrine of Christ.

3. That the *top* had overcome the *root* "in sin and wickedness." That is to say, the leaders, through their licentious indulgences had corrupted and overpowered the membership of the church.

4. That it had reached such immense proportions as to render secrecy longer impossible.

5. That the leaders were all so imbued with the spirit of polygamy that the statement of Elder Marks concerning the prophet's mode of procedure, had he lived, was denounced as "a tissue of lies."

In view of these facts it is simply impossible that this monster of iniquity could have developed to such gigantic proportions under the very eyes of Joseph Smith, wholly unobserved by him. It requires a remarkable degree of credulity to believe that a man of the prophet's native mental astuteness was blind to the facts as they were known to exist. It is equally incredible that an evil of this character could have grown up without at least the tacit approval of the prophet, for the reason that his word was at that time, and ever had been, both law and Gospel to the entire people, leaders and all.

They had long since bound themselves, as we have already seen, to "give heed unto all his words, . . . for his words ye shall receive, as if from mine [the Lord's] own mouth." Hence, a "thus saith the Lord" from the prophet would have put an eternal quietus on the question of polygamy. But it never came; and so Joseph Smith, and Joseph Smith only, must be held responsible for the prevalence of the most abominable system that ever cursed and degraded a free people.

Instead of getting a "revelation" absolutely and peremptorily prohibiting polygamy, and thus lay the foundation of a pure society, he received one enjoining a practice under the penalty of eternal damnation, which served to drag the people of his church down to a moral level far below that of the heathen nations of the earth. In the following chapter we give the document in its entirety, although somewhat lengthy, that the reader may be able to judge of its merits and origin.

CHAPTER XXXIV.

REVELATION ON CELESTIAL MARRIAGE, GIVEN TO JOSEPH SMITH, NAUVOO, JULY 12, 1843.

Revelation on celestial marriage—Joseph Smith its author—A house of order—If any man marry him a wife—For time and all eternity—Passing the angels and the gods—Then shall they be gods—All manner of sins and blasphemies shall be forgiven—Shedding innocent blood the unpardonable sin—Abraham's wives—Sarah and Hager—Isaac and Jacob—David and Solomon—Sealed on earth and sealed in heaven—Emma Smith—Must accept the celestial law or be destroyed—If a man espouse a virgin—If he espouse another he is justified—If he have ten virgins given him—The original wife—She must procure other wives for her lord, or be destroyed—Will reveal more hereafter—Mrs. Stenhouse—Celestial law, indeed!—Joseph must have written it.

1. VERILY, thus saith the Lord unto you, my servant Joseph, that inasmuch as you have enquired of my hand, to know and understand wherein I, the Lord, justified Abraham, Isaac and Jacob; as also Moses, David and Solomon, my servants, as touching the principle and doctrine of their having many wives and concubines: Behold! and lo, I am the Lord thy God, and will answer thee as touching this matter: Therefore, prepare thy heart to receive and obey the instructions which I am about to give unto you; for all those who have this law revealed unto them must obey the same; for behold! I reveal unto you a new and an everlasting covenant; and if ye abide not in that covenant, then are ye damned; for no one can reject this covenant, and be permitted to enter into my glory; for all who will have a blessing at my

hands shall abide the law which was appointed for that blessing, and the conditions thereof, as was instituted from before the foundation of the world: and as pertaining to the new and everlasting covenant it was instituted for the fullness of my glory; and he that receiveth a fullness thereof, must and shall abide the law, or he shall be damned, saith the Lord God.

2. And verily I say unto you, that the conditions of this law are these: All covenants, contracts, bonds, obligations, oaths, vows, performances, connections, associations or expectations that are not made and entered into, and sealed by the Holy Spirit of promise, of him who is anointed, both as well for time and for all eternity, and that too most holy by revelation and commandment, through the medium of mine anointed whom I have appointed on the earth to hold this power, (and I have appointed unto my servant Joseph to hold this power in the last days, and there is never but one on the earth at a time on whom this power and the keys of this priesthood are conferred) are of no efficacy, virtue or force in and after the resurrection from the dead; for all contracts that are not made unto this end, have an end when men are dead.

3. Behold! mine house is a house of order, saith the Lord God, and not a house of confusion. Will I accept of an offering, saith the Lord, that is not made in my name? Or, will I receive at your hands that which I have not appointed? And will I appoint unto you, saith the Lord, except it be by law, even as I and my Father ordained unto you before the world was? I am the Lord thy God, and I give unto you this commandment, that no man shall come unto the Father but me, or by my word which

is my law, saith the Lord; and every thing that is in the world, whether it be ordained of men, by thrones, or principalities, or powers, or things of name, whatever they may be, that are not by me or by my word, saith the Lord, shall be thrown down and shall not stand after men are dead, neither in nor after the resurrection, saith the Lord your God; for whatsoever things remaineth are by me; and whatsoever things are not by me shall be shaken and destroyed.

4. Therefore, if any man marry him a wife in the world, and he marry her not by me, nor by my word; and he covenant with her so long as he is in the world, and she with him, their covenant and marriage is not of force when they are dead and when they are out of the world; therefore, they are not bound by any law when they are out of the world; therefore, when they are out of the world they neither marry nor are given in marriage, but are appointed angels in heaven, which angels are ministering servants, to minister for those who are worthy of a far more and an exceeding, and an eternal weight of glory; for these angels did not abide my law, therefore they cannot be enlarged, but remain separately and singly, without exaltation in their saved condition, to [all eternity, and from henceforth are not gods, but are angels of God forever and ever.

5. And again, verily I say unto you, if a man marry a wife, and make a covenant with her for time and for all eternity, if that covenant is not by me, or by my word, which is my law, and is not sealed by the Holy Spirit of promise, through him whom I have anointed and appointed unto this power, then it is not valid, neither of course when they are out of

the world, because they are not joined by me, saith the Lord, neither by my word; when they are out of the world, it cannot be received there, because the angels and the gods are appointed there, by whom they cannot pass; they cannot, therefore, inherit my glory, for my house is a house of order, saith the Lord God.

6. And again, verily I say unto you, if a man marry a wife by my word, which is my law, and by the new and everlasting covenant, and it is sealed unto them by the Holy Spirit of promise, by him who is anointed, unto whom I have appointed this power, and the keys of this priesthood; and it shall be said unto them, ye shall come forth in the first resurrection; and if it be after the first resurrection, in the next resurrection; and shall inherit thrones, kingdoms, principalities, and powers, dominions, all heights and depths—then shall it be written in the Lamb's Book of Life, that he shall commit no murder whereby to shed innocent blood, and if ye abide in my covenant, and commit no murder whereby to shed innocent blood, it shall be done into them in all things whatsoever my servant hath put upon them, in time, and through all eternity, and shall be of full force when they are out of the world; and they shall pass by the angels, and the Gods, which are set there, to their exaltation and glory, in all things, as hath been sealed upon their heads, which glory shall be a fullness and a continuation of the seeds forever and ever.

7. Then shall they be Gods, because they have no end; therefore shall they be from everlasting to everlasting, because they continue; then shall they be above all, because all things are subject unto them.

Then shall they be Gods, because they have all power, and the angels are subject unto them.

8. Verily, verily, I say unto you, except ye abide my law, ye cannot attain to this glory; for strait is the gate and narrow the way that leadeth unto the exaltation and continuation of the lives, and few there be that find it, because ye receive me not in the world, neither do ye know me. But if ye receive me in the world, then shall ye know me, and shall receive your exaltation, that where I am, ye shall be also. This is eternal lives, to know the only wise and true God and Jesus Christ whom he hath sent. I am He. Receive ye, therefore, my law. Broad is the gate, and wide is the way that leadeth to the death; and many there are that go in thereat; because they receive me not, neither do they abide in my law.

9. Verily, verily, I say unto you, if a man marry a wife according to my word, and they are sealed by the Holy Spirit of promise, according to mine appointment, and he or she shall commit any sin or transgression of the new and everlasting covenant whatever, and all manner of blasphemies, and if they commit no murder, wherein they shed innocent blood— yet they shall come forth in the first resurrection, and enter into their exaltation; but they shall be destroyed in the flesh, and shall be delivered unto the buffetings of Satan unto the day of redemption, saith the Lord God.

10. The blasphemy against the Holy Ghost, which shall not be forgiven in the world, nor out of the world, is in that ye commit murder, wherein ye shed innocent blood, and assent unto my death, after ye have received my new and everlasting covenant, saith

the Lord God; and he that abideth not this law, can in no wise enter into my glory, but shall be damned, saith the Lord.

11. I am the Lord thy God, and will give unto thee the law of my Holy Priesthood, as was ordained by me and my Father, before the world was. Abraham received all things, whatsoever he received, by revelation and commandment, by my word, saith the Lord, and hath entered into his exaltation, and sitteth upon his throne.

12. Abraham received promise concerning his seed, and of the fruit of his loins—from whose loins ye are, namely, my servant Joseph—which were to continue so long as they were in the world; and as touching Abraham and his seed, out of the world they should continue; both in the world and out of the world should they continue as innumerable as the stars; or, if ye were to count the sand upon the sea shore, ye could not number them. This promise is yours, also, because ye are of Abraham, and the promise was made unto Abraham; and by this law are the continuation of the works of my Father, wherein he glorifieth himself. Go ye, therefore, and do the works of Abraham; enter ye into my law, and ye shall be saved. But if ye enter not into my law, ye cannot receive the promise of my Father, which he made unto Abraham.

13. God commanded Abraham, and Sarah gave Hager to Abraham to wife. And why did she do it? Because this was the law, and from Hager sprang many people. This, therefore, was fulfilling, among other things, the promise. Was Abraham, therefore, under condemnation? Verily I say unto you, *Nay;* for I, the Lord, commanded it. Abraham was com-

manded to offer his son Isaac; nevertheless, it is written, Thou shalt not kill. Abraham, however, did not refuse, and it was accounted unto him for righteousness.

14. Abraham received concubines, and they bare him children, and it was accounted unto him for righteousness, because they were given unto him, and he abode in my law, as Isaac also, and Jacob did none other things than that which they were commanded; and because they did none other things than that which they were commanded, they have entered into their exaltation, according to the promise, and sit upon thrones, and are not angels, but are Gods. David also received many wives and concubines, as also Solomon and Moses my servants; as also many others of my servants, from the beginning of creation until this time; and in nothing did they sin, save in those things which they received not of me.

15. David's wives and concubines were given unto him, of me, by the hand of Nathan, my servant, and others of the Prophets who had the keys of this power; and in none of these things did he sin against me, save in the case of Uriah and his wife; and, therefore, he hath fallen from his exaltation, and received his portion; and he shall not inherit them out of the world; for I gave them unto another, saith the Lord.

16. I am the Lord thy God, and I gave unto thee, my servant Joseph, an appointment; and restore all things; ask what ye will, and it shall be given unto you according to my word: and as ye have asked concerning adultery—verily, verily, I say unto you, if a man receive a wife in the new and everlasting covenant, and if she be with another man, and I have not

appointed unto her by the holy anointing, she hath committed adultery, and shall be destroyed. If she be not in the new and everlasting covenant, and she be with another man, she has committed adultery; and if her husband be with another woman, and he was under a vow, he hath broken his vow, and hath committed adultery, and if she hath not committed adultery, but is innocent, and hath not broken her vow, and she knoweth it, and I reveal it unto you, my servant Joseph, then shall you have power, by the power of my Holy Priesthood, to take her, and give her unto him that hath not committed adultery, but hath been faithful; for he shall be made ruler over many; for I have conferred upon you the keys and power of the Priesthood, wherein I restore all things, and make known unto you all things in due time.

17. And verily, verily, I say unto you, that whatsoever you seal on earth, shall be sealed in heaven; and whatsoever you bind on earth, in my name, and by my word, saith the Lord, it shall be eternally bound in the heavens; and whosesoever sins you remit on earth, shall be remitted eternally in the heavens; and whosesoever sins you retain on earth, shall be retained in heaven.

18. And again, verily I say, whomsoever you bless, I will bless, and whomsoever you curse, I will curse, saith the Lord; for I, the Lord, am thy God.

19. And again, verily I say into you, my servant Joseph, that whatsoever you give on earth, and to whomsoever you give any one on earth, by my word, and according to my law, it shall be visited with blessings, and not cursings, and with my power, saith the Lord, and shall be without condemnation on earth, and in heaven; for I am the Lord thy God, and will

be with thee even unto the end of the world, and through all eternity; for verily, I seal upon you your exaltation, and prepare a throne for you in the kingdom of my Father, with Abraham your father. Behold, I have seen your sacrifices, and will forgive all your sins; I have seen your sacrifices, in obedience to that which I have told you; go, therefore, and I make a way for your escape, as I accepted the offering of Abraham, of his son Isaac.

20. Verily I say unto you, a commandment I give unto mine handmaid, Emma Smith, your wife, whom I have given unto you, that she stay herself, and partake not of that which I commanded you to offer unto her; for I did it, saith the Lord, to prove you all, as I did Abraham; and that I might require an offering at your hand, by covenant and sacrifice: and let mine handmaid, Emma Smith, receive all those that have been given unto my servant, Joseph, and who are virtuous and pure before me; and those who are not pure, and have said they were pure, shall be destroyed, saith the Lord God; for I am the Lord thy God, and ye shall obey my voice; and I give unto my servant Joseph, that he shall be made ruler over many things, for he hath been faithful over a few things, and from henceforth I will strengthen him.

21. And I command my handmaid, Emma Smith, to abide and cleave unto my servant Joseph, and to none else. But if she will not abide this commandment, she shall be destroyed, saith the Lord; for I am the Lord thy God, and will destroy her, if she abide not in my law; but if she will not abide this commandment, then shall my servant Joseph do all things for her, even as he hath said; and I will bless him and multiply him, and give unto him an hundred

fold in this world, of fathers and mothers, brothers and sisters, houses and lands, wives and children, and crowns of eternal lives in the eternal worlds. And again, verily I say, let mine handmaid forgive my servant Joseph his trespasses; and then shall she be forgiven her trespasses, wherein she hath trespassed against me; and I, the Lord thy God will bless her, and multiply her, and make her heart to rejoice.

22. And again, I say, let not my servant put his property out of his hands, lest an enemy come and destroy him, for Satan seeketh to destroy; for I am the Lord thy God, and he is my servant; and behold! and lo, I am with him, as I was with Abraham, thy father, even unto his exaltation and glory.

23. Now, as touching the law of the priesthood, there are many things pertaining thereunto. Verily, if a man be called of my Father, as was Aaron, by mine own voice, and by the voice of him that sent me: and I have endowed him with the keys of the power of this Priesthood, if he do anything in my name, and according to my law, and by my word, he will not commit sin, and I will justify him. Let no one, therefore, set on my servant Joseph; for I will justify him; for he shall do the sacrifice which I require at his hands, for his transgressions, saith the Lord your God.

24. And again, as pertaining to the law of the Priesthood: If any man espouse a virgin, and desire to espouse another, and the first give her consent; and he espouse the second, and they are virgins, and have vowed to no other man, then he is justified; he cannot commit adultery, for they are given unto him; for he cannot commit adultery with that that belongeth unto him and to no one else; and if he have ten

virgins given unto him by this law, he cannot commit adultery, for they belong to him, and they are given unto him, therefore he is justified. But if one or either of the ten virgins, after she is espoused, shall be with another man, she has committed adultery, and shall be destroyed; for they are given unto him to multiply and replenish the earth, according to my commandment, and to fulfill the promise which was given by my Father before the foundation of the world; and for their exaltation in the eternal worlds, that they may bear the souls of men; for herein is the work of my Father continued, that he may be glorified.

25. And again, verily, verily I say unto you, if any man have a wife who holds the keys of this power, and he teaches unto her the law of my priesthood as pertaining to these things, then shall she believe, and administer unto him, or she shall be destroyed, saith the Lord your God; for I will destroy her; for I will magnify my name upon all those who receive and abide in my law. Therefore, it shall be lawful in me, if she receive not this law, for him to receive all things whatsoever I, the Lord his God, will give unto him, because she did not minister unto him according to my word; and she then becomes the transgressor; and he is exempt from the law of Sarah, who administered unto Abraham according to the law, when I commanded Abraham to take Hagar to wife. And now, as pertaining unto this law, verily, verily I say unto you, I will reveal more unto you hereafter; therefore, let this suffice for the present. Behold, I am Alpha and Omega. Amen." (See *Millennial Star*, January, 1853.)

After quoting the more important parts of the

above document in her work (omitting only such portions as had no special reference to the question,) Mrs. Stenhouse comments thus:

"And this was the 'revelation!'—this mass of confusion, cunning, absurdity, falsehood and bad grammar! *This* was the celebrated document which was henceforth to be the law to the confiding men and women who had embraced Mormonism! Looking at it now, noting its inconsistencies and its flagrant outrage upon common decency and morality, I can hardly credit that I should ever have been such a silly dupe as to give it a second thought. And yet, what *could* I do? . . . Unquestioning obedience, we had been taught, was the highest virtue; rebellion was as the sin of witchcraft. I had been convinced of the truth of some of the tenets of the Mormon faith, and confident in them, I accepted without question all the rest. . . . The 'revelation' aroused within me feelings of horror and dismay, *but I did not dare to question its authenticity.*" (Tell it All, pages 138 and 139.)

I have italicized the last clause in the closing sentence, in order to call attention to a sentiment that at the time prevailed throughout the entire Mormon Church. None dared to question what the prophet declared in the name of the Lord, it mattered not how soul-crushing or absurd it may have been. Of all the "revelations" that Joseph Smith ever received, this one "caps the climax." As to the spirit and tone of the document I have nothing to say; it speaks for itself, and is doubtless the most damnable, soul-destroying, woman-oppressing, happiness-crushing system of marriage that man, in his most depraved condition, ever attempted to foist upon the human race. "*Celestial law*," indeed!

Who is the author of this immoral, degrading document? Was it Brigham Young, as the Reorganized Church has tried to maintain? or was it Joseph Smith, as all other branches of the Mormon Church have ever declared it to be? Take the utterances of Brigham Young as we find them in the *Journal of Discourses*, published in Salt Lake City, and other Mormon publications, and compare them with this revelation of 1843, and you will discover at a glance that Brigham Young could not have been its author; the language, the style and composition are not his. But on the other hand, compare this production with any of the acknowledged "revelations" of the prophet, especially that of 1841, (See Doc. and Cov., page 301,) and you will at once see that the language, the diction and style, are unmistakably peculiar to Joseph Smith. The style is his, the language is his, and the conception is his.

And besides this there was not a man in the entire church who possessed the cunning to devise such a system. The profound Orson Pratt was too philosophical, the verbose and somewhat scholarly Orson Spencer was too precise in the construction of his sentences, while the illiterate and self-willed Brigham Young was too abrupt in his manner to have given expression to the document. It is perfectly clear that neither of these men could have produced it. In fact Joseph once received a "revelation" challenging any man in the church to produce a revelation like one of his. Oliver Cowdery made the effort, resulting in an inglorious failure, and the experiment has never since been repeated.

Who does not know that a man possessing such absolute control over his people as that exercised by Joseph Smith could have extirpated the evil with a single stroke of his pen? Who is so blind as not to see that a "thus saith the Lord" from the prophet (in whom the entire people had unlimited confidence) condemning the system in terms as strong and positive as those employed to enjoin its observance, would at once have crushed the life out of the monster, and saved his people from ruin and shame? No, sir! it is impossible that Joseph and Hyrum Smith are innocent of this great crime against the womanhood of America, and the society of a cultivated and refined nation.

Hyrum Smith

(From a portrait painted in his forty-fourth year.)

your mother Emma Smith

(From a photograph taken in her seventieth year.)

your Husband until death Joseph Smith Jr

(From a portrait painted in his thirty-eighth year.)

CHAPTER XXXV.

SPRANG FROM THE SAME ROOT.

Sprang from the same root—Shedding innocent blood—Evil and obscene practices—Who was their author?—Fruit of the Mormon tree—History of the polygamy revelation—What Emma Smith says about it—Interviewed by her son—What her statement proves—Her testimony does not agree with that of Elder Marks—Brigham Young's testimony—A copy of the revelation preserved by Brigham—Published in 1852—The Laws and Fosters—Nauvoo Expositor destroyed—The prophet arrested—Affidavits of Ebenezer Robinson and wife—Hyrum Smith taught them polygamy.

NEARLY all the corrupt doctrines and murderous practices which later matured in Salt Lake City, including "blood-atonement," or human sacrifice, killing "apostates" and murdering defenseless Gentiles—such, for instance, as the wholesale murder at Mountain Meadows—are but enlargements upon the doctrines of this revelation. Every sin known to the catalogue of crime, except to commit murder "wherein ye shed *innocent* blood," should be forgiven, according to the terms of the "new and everlasting covenant;" and the leaders were to be the sole judges as to the meaning of the term "*innocent* blood." Nothing but this one sin could prevent a man who had entered into this "covenant" from "passing by the gods and angels," and "entering his exaltation" in the world to come.

The spirit of this "celestial law"—polygamy and eternal hatred of the Gentiles—permeated every branch and faction of the Mormon Church which sprang up immediately after the death of the prophet. Not only the "Brighamites," but the followers of James J. Strang, of Beaver Island, Lyman Wright, of Texas, and Sidney Rigdon, of Pennsylvania, were all filled to the point of saturation with the very essence of this abominable doctrine. All the evil and obscene practices which have combined to render Mormonism odious, and mark the very name as the synonym of all evil, are directly traceable to the authority of this hateful document.

Where did all these evil practices by different bodies, separated by thousands of miles, originate? Who was their author? Whence came this law common to them all? How came this perfect agreement between these different factions upon these peculiarities of Mormonism, only three years after the prophet's death? There can be but one answer, and that is, they had unquestionably sprung from the same fountain—they were the legitimate fruits of the Mormon tree, and the revelation of July 12, 1843. And this but illustrates the old proverb, "Actions speak louder than words." As to the authorship of this unique document, there hardly seems room for but one opinion. The careful reader can scarcely fail to detect the earmarks of Joseph Smith in almost every paragraph of this "law of celestial marriage."

The history of this remarkable document seems to be about as follows:

The "revelation" is said to have been written by William Clayton, Joseph's private secretary, as the words fell from the lips of the prophet, and was carefully copied, while the document was in the possession of Bishop N. K. Whitney, Joseph's particular friend. The original, it is claimed, was afterwards burnt by Emma Smith, the prophet's wife, who used the tongs in committing it to the flames, unwilling, as any pure woman would be, to have her fingers come in contact with the vile document.

This statement, however, if not even the existence of such a "revelation," Emma Smith denied a short time before her death, April 30, 1879, as may be seen by the following questions and answers:

Question, by President Joseph Smith to his mother: "What about the revelation on polygamy? Did Joseph Smith have anything like it? What of spiritual wifery?"

Answer. "There was no revelation on either polygamy or spiritual wives. There were some *rumors* of something of the sort, of which I asked my husband. He assured me that all there was of it, was that in a chat about plural wives he had said, 'Well, such a system might be, if everybody was agreed to it, and would behave as they should; but they would not; and besides, it was contrary to the will of heaven.' No such thing as polygamy, or spiritual wifery, was taught publicly or privately before my husband's death, that I have now, or ever had, any knowledge of."

Question. "Did he not have other wives than yourself?"

Answer. "He had no other wife but me; nor did he to my knowledge ever have."

Question. "Did he not hold marital relation with women other than yourself?"

Answer. "He did not have improper relations with any woman that ever came to my knowledge."

Question. "Was there nothing about spiritual wives that you recollect?"

Answer. "At one time my husband came to me and asked me if I had heard certain rumors about spiritual marriages, or anything of the kind; and assured me that if I had, they were without foundation; that there was no such doctrine, and never should be with his knowledge or consent. I know that he had no other wife, or wives, than myself, in any sense, either spiritual or otherwise." (Tullidge's History, pages 791, 792.)

Thus it will be seen that Mrs. Emma Smith, widow of the prophet, had no personal knowledge of the revelation on polygamy—she had heard *rumors* concerning the "revelation," which, her husband assured her, had grown out of "a chat about plural wives," in which he had remarked that "such a system *might be, if everybody was agreed to it*, and would behave as they should."

Mrs. Smith was a lady of more than ordinary mental endowments, and possessed a reputation for honor and integrity that won the respect and esteem of those who knew her best. It is but fair to presume, therefore, that she stated the facts as she understood and recollected them, but having attained her seventy-fifth year, and her health having been poor for several years before her death, it is but natural to conclude that her memory would be somewhat defective. That rumors of "polygamy and spiritual wifery" were afloat at the time of her husband's death she admitted; but that he had other wives than herself she did not believe. Of course it is just possible, if not indeed quite probable, that the exact truth was kept from her as far as possible, and that while the evil existed in fact, she was led to believe it existed only in theory—a mere "rumor."

Yet her statement proves, beyond all doubt, that there was some talk about this revelation on polygamy, or "spiritual wives," previous to the time of Joseph Smith's death, which is in perfect accord with the testimony of all who have ever said anything on the subject. When Mrs. Smith says that polygamy was not taught publicly, she states what is very probably true; but in saying it was never taught privately, she asserts what, in the very nature of the case, it was impossible for her to know; for the reason that it could have been privately taught while she would be totally ignorant of the fact. The most that can be affirmed of Mrs. Smith's statement, therefore, is that polygamy was not taught publicly, and that she firmly believed it had not been taught privately.

But how does this agree with the statements of others who had better opportunities to know what was privately taught in Nauvoo relative to this question?—that of Elder Marks, for instance, whose testimony we have already given. He was a man whose veracity was not to be questioned; and although a faithful member of the Reorganized Church, his testimony is never alluded to by any of its leading writers or speakers. Neither Joseph, Alexander nor David make any reference to it, although each of them is the author of a tract on polygamy. This fact may be regarded as very significant, indeed. It has the appearance of an evasion of the real issue. If Joseph Smith talked with Wm. Marks about polygamy, then polygamy had been taught, if not publicly, it was most certainly both taught and practiced secretly.

The testimony of the witnesses places the fact

beyond reasonable doubt that Joseph Smith knew polygamy existed, and the monster having got beyond his control he trembled for the possible results. We now wish to offer a little evidence produced from another quarter. Relative to the revelation in question, Brigham Young, in a discourse delivered in the Tabernacle, Salt Lake City, Aug. 29th, 1852, among other things said:

"You heard Brother Pratt state this morning that a revelation would be read this afternoon, which was given previous to Joseph's death. . . . The original copy of this revelation was burnt up. William Clayton was the man who wrote it from the mouth of the prophet. In the meantime it was in Bishop Whitney's possession. He wished the privilege to copy it, which Brother Joseph granted. *Sister Emma burnt the original.* The reason I mention this is because the people who did not know of the revelation suppose it is not now in existence. The revelation will be read to you. . . . This revelation has been in my possession many years; and who has known it? I keep a patent lock on my desk, and there does not anything leak out that should not." (Tullidge's History, page 565, 566).

Thus it will be seen that a copy of the original "revelation" (which is the common root from which all these polygamous branches of the Mormon Church simultaneously sprang), was received by Joseph Smith; written, as he uttered the words, by William Clayton; copied by Bishop Whitney, the prophet's particular friend; preserved under lock and key by Pres. Brigham Young, and publicly read by Apostle Orson Pratt in August, 1852.

The objection offered by the Reorganized Church,

that this document was not made public till after the removal of the church to Salt Lake Valley, eight years after the prophet's death; and that it was probably manufactured out of whole cloth by Brigham Young and his followers in order to justify their general practice of polygamy, is certainly not justified by the facts.

Not only have Brigham Young and other leaders declared that Joseph Smith was the author of the revelation on "celestial marriage," but various members of the "high council," the highest judicial tribunal of the church, swear that the very document in question was read by Hyrum Smith before them while that body was in session in Nauvoo, Illinois, Aug. 12, 1843. These affidavits, together with those of several women who were the polygamous wives of both Joseph and Hyrum Smith, will appear in their proper place.

It is not sufficient to meet the testimony of all these witnesses with a bare denial. In order to render their testimony invalid the alleged facts must be met by the testimony of other witnesses, equally competent, to establish other facts which, in their very nature, render the testimony of plaintiff's witnesses highly improbable, and prove the alleged facts set up in the petition or proposition of the plaintiff to be impossible. This the Reorganized Church has never attempted, and which, indeed, it may fairly be presumed it cannot do.

The only witnesses ever introduced by the Reorganized Church, namely, Mrs. Emma Smith and William Marks, have both testified to facts which confirm rather than disprove the declarations of

Brigham Young and others concerning the existence of polygamy at the time of the prophet's death.

I shall now introduce the testimony of other witnesses to prove that the so-called denials of Joseph and Hyrum Smith shortly before their death were mere subterfuges, behind which they hoped to shield their defenseless heads from the effects of the impending storm which was soon to break upon them. Just before the gathering of the mob at Carthage, which resulted in the violent death of the two leaders, there was another serious defection from the prophet, namely, the apostasy of the brothers, William and Wilson Law, the latter having been Major-General of the Nauvoo Legion, and the former a member of the "First Presidency," the highest quorum in the church; the Higbees, Fosters, and "other formidable foes who had been expelled from the church," as Mr. Tullidge states it. (See History, page 476.) Concerning these expelled apostates Mr. Tullidge further remarks:

"These sought to establish in Nauvoo an incendiary paper called the Nauvoo *Expositor*, the avowed purpose of which was to stir up the people of Illinois to bring Joseph Smith 'to justice for his crimes,' and expel the Saints from the State. It was like building the magazine of the enemy in the City of Refuge; and also after the first number of the *Expositor* the Nauvoo City Council declared the paper a public nuisance and dangerous to the peace of the commonwealth; and they thereupon ordered the office of the paper to be demolished by the marshal and his posse." (Ibid, page 476.)

It is perhaps needless to say that this patriotic

city council was composed entirely of Mormons, and that Joseph Smith was at the time himself mayor of the city of Nauvoo. (See Tullidge's History, page 484.) Complaint was made and warrants issued for the arrest of the prophet and others concerned in the destruction of the *Expositor* office, the writs being returnable at Carthage, the county seat. But Joseph, believing that greater safety was to be found among his brethren, swore out a writ of *habeas corpus*, and was tried before Daniel H. Wells, a particular friend of the prophet, but a deadly enemy to the Laws, the publishers of the *Expositor*. Concerning this trial Joseph says:

"At 2 P. M. we all went before Justice Wells at his house, and after a long and close examination we were discharged." (Ibid, page 482.)

That they were under these circumstances acquitted of this serious offense against the law of the State is not a matter of surprise, but certainly it does not speak well for the honor and integrity of the men engaged in the transaction. If they were innocent of the crimes charged by the *Expositor*, why did not the leaders openly invite a careful investigation of the charges? Why should it be thought necessary, simply because they had the power in their own hands, to suppress the freedom of speech and the liberty of the press in this wanton manner? To the unbiased, reflective mind there is but one answer to this question; they feared the consequences of further exposure by these men who stood so near to the prophet, and who therefore knew whereof they affirmed. These are the most probable reasons why the *Expositor* office was "demolished" and its press broken to pieces and thrown into the Mississippi river.

The reader will perhaps remember that the Laws and Higbees figured in the certificate concerning Dr. Bennett's "secret wife system," published some two years previously. If they were honest in their statements, they were probably ignorant of the existence of any such system at the time, and upon learning the *facts* later, became disgusted with the whole affair and left the church. On the other hand, *if they were not honest*, as Mormons usually declare, then they can not be believed under any circumstances, and their former testimony is rendered absolutely worthless.

It was at this exact time that Elder William Marks, of the Reorganized Church, declared that he talked with Joseph about *polygamy*, and that they must try and "speedily put it down," or it would ultimately ruin the church. This fact affords a clue to the probable cause of the apostasy of the Laws, Fosters, Higbees and others, and their consequent denunciation of the prophet through the columns of the *Expositor*.

That polygamy had been secretly taught by Joseph and Hyrum Smith for months prior to this rupture between these dissenters and the prophet, I shall now undertake to prove beyond the possibility of reasonable doubt.

Ebenezer Robinson and his wife Angeline, it will be remembered, were among the signers of the famous certificate already referred to, which appeared in the *Times and Seasons*, Oct. 1, 1842, (as quoted by Alexander H. Smith) some two years previous to the time of which we have just spoken. They were both baptized by Joseph Smith before their marriage, and were at a later day joined in marriage by the prophet. Mr. Robinson also became editor of the *Times and*

Seasons, the official organ of the church, and was therefore a man in whom Joseph reposed great confidence.

It may not be amiss to remark in this connection that some time in 1865 the writer, while performing ministerial duties in Decatur County, Iowa, became intimately acquainted with both Mr. Robinson and his wife, who were at the time faithful members of the Reorganized Church. We often talked about the early days of the church, and the closing scenes at Nauvoo. During some of these conversations Mr. Robinson repeatedly assured me that he knew more about those early days than he then wished to disclose, but that he intended at some future time to make a statement of *facts* as he knew them to exist. My efforts to have him confide his secret to me were unavailing, his only reply being, "You are a young man, and I do not wish to say anything that will tend to shake and possibly destroy your faith." And thus for the time the matter rested. Mr. Robinson was, however, true to his promise, and left the statement he had intended to make. Following are the affidavits of Mr. Robinson and his wife, made several years before their death.

"To WHOM IT MAY CONCERN:

"We, Ebenezer Robinson and Angeline Robinson, husband and wife, hereby certify that in the fall of 1843 Hyrum Smith, brother of Joseph Smith, came to our house at Nauvoo, Illinois, and taught us the doctrine of polygamy. And I, the said Ebenezer Robinson, hereby further state that he gave me special instructions how I could manage the matter so as not to have it known to the public. He also told us that while he had heretofore opposed the doctrine, he was wrong and his brother Joseph was right; referring to his teaching it.

"EBENEZER ROBINSON.
"ANGELINE E. ROBINSON.

"Sworn to and subscribed before me this 29th day of December, 1873.

[L. S.] "J. M. SALLEE, Notary Public."

Mrs. Robinson having died since the execution of the foregoing, and some question arising as to *how* and wherein the said Hyrum Smith (one of the first officers and leaders of the church) had given special instruction to Mr. Robinson, he was questioned in regard to the matter, whereupon he executed the following:

"TO WHOM IT MAY CONCERN:

"This is to certify that in the latter part of November, or in December, 1843, Hyrum Smith (brother of Joseph Smith, President of the Church of Jesus Christ of Latter Day Saints) came to my house in Nauvoo, Illinois, and taught me the doctrine of spiritual wives, or polygamy.

"He said he heard the voice of the Lord give the revelation on spiritual wifery (polygamy) to his brother Joseph, and that while he had heretofore opposed the doctrine, he was wrong, and his brother Joseph was right all the time.

"He told me to make a selection of some young woman and he would send her to me, and take her to my home, and if she should have an heir, to give out word that she had a husband who had gone on a mission to a foreign country. He seemed disappointed when I declined to do so.   E. ROBINSON.

"*Davis City, Iowa, October 23, 1885.*

"Subscribed and sworn to before me, a Notary Public in and for Decatur County, Iowa, this 24th day of October, A. D. 1885.

[L. S.]   "Z. H. GURLEY, Notary Public."

Copied from the Biographical and Historical Record of Ringgold and Decatur Counties, Iowa, at pages 543 and 544.

This, it seems to me, ought to be conclusive upon this point, and is absolutely unanswerable. Here are the sworn statements of two persons whose veracity has never been called in question, even among members of the Mormon Church, up to the time of making their statements; and I have never learned that their truthfulness and sincerity have been called in question even since the above affidavits were made.

Neither of these persons can justly be charged with any sinister motive in connection with this transaction, as they could gain nothing except possibly the ill will of the people of the Reorganized Church, by whom they were at the time surrounded. In view of the fact that Mr. and Mrs. Robinson were strong personal friends of Joseph and Hyrum Smith at the time the latter tried to lead them into polygamy, and that in spite of all this they lived and died in the faith, renders it highly probably that they state the exact truth concerning the relation which the prophet and patriarch sustained to polygamy.

I shall now present the testimony of many other witnesses upon this subject, which proves that Joseph and Hyrum Smith not only *taught* polygamy, but that they also *practiced* what they taught; and that "Joseph the Prophet" was the author of that nefarious document called the law of "celestial marriage."

CHAPTER XXXVI.

BEARDED THE LION IN HIS DEN.

Bearded the lion in his den—Alexander and David Smith in Utah—Deny that their father was in polygamy—Brighamites respond—Smith-Littlefield controversy—Positive proof that Joseph Smith had pural wives—Testimony of David Fullmer—Thomas Grover's letter—Certificate of Lovina Walker—Affidavit of Emily D. P. Young—Affidavit of Leonard Soby—What Z. H. Gurley says of Mr. Soby—Testimony of Mercy R. Thompson—She was sealed to Hyrum Smith—Her letter to President Smith—His view of the case—He accounts for the origin of polygamy—Summary.

AT a general conference of the Reorganized Church, held at St. Louis, Mo., April 6-11, 1869, Alexander H. and David H. Smith, sons of "Joseph, the seer," were associated in a mission to Utah. Young and full of zeal, they prosecuted their work with warmth and vigor. Confidently believing that their father was in no way responsible for the introduction of polygamy into the church, they bearded the lion in his den, challenging Brigham and the Utah authorities to produce the evidence they had to offer in support of the claim that Joseph Smith was a polygamist and the author of the revelation on celestial marriage. This called forth a response from the "Brighamites" in the form of numerous affidavits from persons whose opportunities were ample for knowing whereof they affirmed. Among these were women who declared that they had been the wives respectively of the prophet and patriarch at Nauvoo.

The controversy thus raised continued for years,

culminating in 1886 in a correspondence between President Joseph Smith, of Lamoni, Iowa, and Elder L. O. Littlefield, of Salt Lake City. The documents produced by Mr. Littlefield were later published in tract form entitled,

"CELESTIAL MARRIAGE.
"POSITIVE PROOF THAT JOSEPH SMITH HAD PLURAL WIVES."

From the above tract the following extracts are taken. These documents, with Mr. Littlefield's remarks thereon, were published in *The Utah Journal*, Logan, Utah, April 21 and April 24, 1886. In introducing the question, Mr. Littlefield says:

"In the History of Joseph Smith, under date of October 5, 1843, can be found the following:

"Gave instructions to try those persons who were preaching, teaching or practicing the doctrine of plural wives; for according to the law I hold the keys of this power in the last days; for there is never but one on earth at a time on whom the power and its keys are conferred; and I have constantly said that no man shall have but one wife at a time unless the Lord direct otherwise."

It may be a matter of interest to the reader to know that the Manuscript History of Joseph Smith (as written by himself) at the time of his death fell into the hands of the leaders, and was taken by them to Salt Lake City; and it is from this record the foregoing extract was taken by Mr. Littlefield. And how perfectly it harmonizes with both the text of the "revelation," and the statement of Elder Marks. No man but Joseph held the "keys of this power," and some were breaking over the rule and taking other wives without a "revelation" through the prophet; and because they were so reckless charges were to be preferred against them.

As to the genuineness of the revelation in question, the following is in point:

TESTIMONY OF DAVID FULLMER.

"Territory of Utah, } ss.
County of Salt Lake.

"Be it remembered on this fifteenth day of June, A. D., 1869, personally appeared before me, James Jack, a Notary Public in and for said county, David Fullmer, who was by me sworn in due form of law, and upon his oath saith, that on or about the twelfth day of August, A. D., 1843, while in meeting with the High Council, (he being a member thereof), in Hyrum Smith's brick office, in the City of Nauvoo, County of Hancock, State of Illinois, Dunbar Wilson made inquiry in relation to the subject of a plurality of wives, as there were rumors about respecting it, and he was satisfied there was something in those remarks, and he wanted to know what it was, upon which Hyrum Smith stepped across the road to his residence, and soon returned, bringing with him a copy of the revelation on celestial marriage, given to Joseph Smith, July 12, A. D., 1843, and read the same to the High Council, and bore testimony of its truth. The said David Fullmer further said that to the best of his memory and belief, the following named persons were present: Wm. Marks, Austin A. Cowles, Samuel Bent, George W. Harris, Dunbar Wilson, Wm. Huntington, Levi Jackman, Aaron Johnson, Thomas Grover, David Fullmer, Phineas Richards, James Allred and Leonard Soby. And the said David Fullmer further saith that Wm. Marks, Austin A. Cowles and Leonard Soby were the only persons present who did not receive the testimony of Hyrum Smith, and that all the others did receive it from the teaching and testimony of the said Hyrum Smith. And further, that the copy of said Revelation on Celestial Marriage, published in the *Deseret News* extra of September fourteenth, A. D., 1852, is a true copy of the same.   DAVID FULLMER."

"Subscribed and sworn to by the said David Fullmer the day and year first above written.

"JAMES JACK, Notary Public."

EXTRACT FROM THOMAS GROVER'S LETTER.

" The High Council, of Nauvoo, was called together by the Prophet Joseph Smith, to know whether they would accept the revelation on celestial marriage or not.

"The presidency of the Stake, Wm. Marks, Father Coles and the late Apostle Charles C. Rich, were there present. The following are the names of the High Council that were present, in their order, viz.: Samuel Bent, William Huntington, Alpheus Cutler, Thomas Grover, Lewis D. Wilson, David Fullmer, Aaron Johnson, Newel Knight, Leonard Soby, Isaac Allred, Henry G. Sherwood and, I think, Samuel Smith.

"Brother Hyrum Smith was called upon to read the revelation. He did so, and after reading it said: 'Now, you that believe this revelation and go forth and obey the same shall be saved, and you that reject it shall be damned.'

"We saw this prediction verified in less than one week. Of the Presidency of the Stake, William

Marks and Father Coles rejected the revelation; of the Council that were present, Leonard Soby rejected it. From that time forward there was a very strong division in the High Council. These three men greatly diminished in spirit day after day, so that there was a great difference in the line of their conduct, which was perceivable to every member that kept the faith.

"From that time forward we often received instructions from the Prophet as to what was the will of the Lord and how to proceed."

CERTIFICATE OF LOVINA WALKER.

"I, Lovina Walker, hereby certify that while I was living with Aunt Emma Smith, in Fulton City, Fulton County, Illinois, in the year 1849, she told me that she, Emma Smith, was present, and witnessed the marriage or sealing of Eliza Partridge, Emily Partridge, Maria Lawrence, and Sarah Lawrence to her husband Joseph Smith, and that she gave her consent thereto.
"LOVINA WALKER."

"We hereby witness that Lovina Walker made and signed the above statement on the 16th day of June, A. D. 1869, of her own free will and accord.
"HYRUM WALKER.
"SARAH E. SMITH.
"JOS. F. SMITH."

Joseph F. Smith, who verifies the foregoing certificate, is a son of the Patriarch Hyrum Smith, and cousin of Alexander and David, who were at the time missionaries to Utah.

AFFIDAVIT OF EMILY D. P. YOUNG.

"TERRITORY OF UTAH, } ss.
COUNTY OF SALT LAKE.

" Be it remembered that on this first day of May, A. D. 1869, personally appeared before me, Elias Smith, Judge of Probate for said county, Emily Dow Patridge Young, who was by me sworn in due form of law, and upon her oath, saith that on the eleventh day of May, A. D. 1843, at the city of Nauvoo, county of Hancock, State of Illinois, she was married or sealed to Joseph Smith, President of the Church of Jesus Christ of Latter Day Saints, by James Adams, a High Priest in said church, according to the law of the same regulating marriage, in the presence of Emma (Hale) Smith and Eliza Maria Partridge (Lyman.)   EMILY D. P. YOUNG."

" Subscribed and sworn to by the said Emily D. P. Young, the day and year first above written.

" E. SMITH, Probate Judge."

Mrs. Emily D. P. Young is identical with Emily Partridge mentioned in the certificate of Mrs. Lavina Walker, as the polygamous wife of Joseph Smith. She was Brigham Young's eighteenth wife, and concerning whom Mrs. Stenhouse says:

" When Joseph died, Brigham told his wives that they were at liberty to choose whom they would for husbands; . . . thus it was that Emily Partridge became Brigham's wife." (Tell it All, page 289.)

In a former chapter I have said that in all polygamous marriages the regular marriage ceremony, authorized in 1835, was employed, and Mrs. Young declares that she was " sealed " to Joseph by a "High Priest in said church, *according to the law of the same regulating marriage.*"

Owing to the aggressive methods of the missionaries of the Reorganized Church in Utah, and their constant denial that Joseph and Hyrum Smith ever sanctioned, much less authorized, the practice of polygamy, the "authorities" were active in the collection of such proofs as would establish the fact, and place it beyond reasonable doubt. In the mean time a controversy had grown up between President Joseph Smith, editor of the *Saints' Herald*, Lamoni, Iowa, and Elder L. O. Littlefield, through the Utah *Journal*, Logan, Utah, concerning which the editor of the Ogden (Utah) *Herald*, of Jan. 5, 1886, says:

"Our readers will remember that in the correspondence which passed between Elder Littlefield and Joseph Smith, Jr., of the Reorganized Church some time since, Mr. Smith challenged Elder Littlefield to give the names of parties who were present and heard the revelation on celestial marriage read before the High Council at Nauvoo."

Thus challenged, Mr. Littlefield presented the statements of David Fullmer and Thomas Grover, already given, adding thereto the sworn statement of Leonard Soby, a member of the High Council, which I now herewith submit as follows:

AFFIDAVIT OF LEONARD SOBY.

"Copy.

"STATE OF NEW JERSEY, } *ss.*
COUNTY OF BURLINGTON. }

"Be it remembered that on this fourteenth day of November, A. D. 1883, personally appeared before me, J. W. Roberts, a Justice of the Peace, county and State aforesaid, Leonard Soby, who was by me sworn in due form of law, and upon oath saith, that on or about the 12th day of August, 1843, in the city of

Nauvoo, in the State of Illinois, in the county of Hancock, before the High Council of the Church of Jesus Christ of Latter Day Saints, of which body and council aforesaid he was a member, personally appeared one Hyrum Smith, of the first presidency of said church, and brother to Joseph Smith, the president and prophet of the same, and presented to said council the Revelation on Polygamy, enjoining its observance and declaring it came from God; unto which a large majority of the council agreed and assented, believing it to be of a celestial order, though no vote was taken upon it, for the reason that the voice of the prophet, in such matters, was understood by us to be the voice of God to the church, and that said revelation was presented to said council, as before stated, as coming from Joseph Smith, the prophet of the Lord, and was received by us as other revelations had been. The said Leonard Soby further saith that Elder Austin A. Cowles, a member of the High Council aforesaid, did, subsequently to the 12th day of August, 1843, openly declare against the said revelation on polygamy, and the doctrines therein contained. LEONARD SOBY."

"Subscribed and sworn to by the said Leonard Soby, the day and year first above written.

"JOSHUA W. ROBERTS,
"Justice of the Peace."

A very interesting and significant episode connected with this affair, and which is not generally known, is thus presented by the Ogden *Herald:*

"Among the names given by Elder Littlefield [to President Joseph Smith] was that of Leonard Soby. The prophet of the Reorganized Church knew where

Mr. Soby resided, and instructed a member of his church in high standing to draw up an affidavit stating that Mr. Soby was not present at such meeting, and never heard the revelation read.

"The affidavit was drawn up under the instruction of Joseph Smith, Jr., and Mr. Gurley, who was something of a lawyer, called on Mr. Soby at his home in Beverly, New Jersey, and requested him to sign it. The affidavit stated that Mr. Soby was present at the High Council meeting referred to, but did not hear the revelation read. When Mr. Gurley requested Mr. Soby to sign the document, Soby objected, saying he was present at the meeting and heard the revelation, and could not sign an affidavit to the contrary. This considerably disconcerted his interlocutor, and Mr. Soby added: 'If you will draw up an affidavit setting forth that I was there and did hear the revelation, I will sign it for you.' But Mr. Gurley did not want that kind of testimony, and retired rather crestfallen, but wiser, and has since apostatized from the Reorganized Church." (From the Ogden, Utah, *Herald*, Jan. 5, 1886.)

Of Mr. Gurley's visit, Mr. Soby, in a letter to Mr. Littlefield, dated Jan. 21, 1886, remarks:

"The facts as published in the [Ogden] *Herald* are true, referring to the interview between Mr. Gurley and myself, and I refer you to him for a copy of my affidavit. Mr. Gurley is very much of a gentleman, and if you ask for it in my name he will not refuse." (Celestial Marriage, by Littlefield, page 3.)

Mr. Gurley, a personal friend of the writer, who is now an influential member of the Iowa General Assembly from the sixth district, furnished the copy of Mr. Soby's affidavit presented above, and in a personal letter speaks of his visit to Mr. Soby as follows:

"I talked with Mr. Soby carefully, and fully satisfied myself that he was honest and sincere. He had opposed polygamy, but finally concluded that he was wrong and Joseph right—just as Hyrum Smith declared, as set forth in Robinson's affidavit. Littlefield's statement that I retired *crestfallen* is *off*—not true. It is evidently confounded with another party."

Mr. Soby in his affidavit refers to the fact that Elder Austin Cowles refused to accept the revelation on celestial marriage, and at last "openly declared against the said revelation on polygamy and the doctrines therein contained." The writer is himself a witness to the the truthfulness of this portion of Mr. Soby's statement. While located in Decatur County, Iowa, in A. D. 1865, as a minister of the Reorganized Church, I made the acquaintance of "Father Cowles," as he was then called, and often visited at his house. As he stood aloof from all religious bodies, and knowing he was a man of prominence in church matters at Nauvoo while the prophet lived, we naturally talked on questions pertaining to the church; and he assured me that polygamy was the fatal rock upon which Mormonism was wrecked, and that he knew that Joseph and Hyrum were both "mixed up in it." But this I could not believe at the time, and attributed his declarations to the fact that he had apostatized. But under the light of more recent development it is perfectly apparent that the venerable old man knew what he was talking about.

With the introduction of one more witness I shall submit this question to the arbitrament of an enlightened and, as I believe, a just public.

TESTIMONY OF MERCY R. THOMPSON.

"SALT LAKE CITY, January 31, 1886.
"A. M. MUSSER,
   "Dear Brother:—

"Having noticed in the *Deseret News* an inquiry for testimony concerning the revelation on plural marriage, and having read the testimony of Brother Grover, it came to my mind that perhaps it would be right for me to add my testimony to his on the subject of Brother Hyrum reading it in the High Council. I well remember the circumstance. I remember he told me he had read it to the brethren in his office. He put it into my hands and left it with me for several days. I had been sealed to him by Brother Joseph a few weeks previously, and was well acquainted with almost every member of the High Council, and know Brother Grover's testimony to be correct. Now if this testimony would be of any use to such as are weak in the faith or tempted to doubt, I should be very thankful. Please make use of this in any way you think best, as well as the copy of the letter addressed to Joseph Smith at Lamoni.
   "Your Sister in the Gospel,
      "MERCY R. THOMPSON."

TESTIMONY AS TO HER MARRIAGE TO HYRUM SMITH.

"SALT LAKE CITY, Sept. 5, 1886.
"MR. JOSEPH SMITH,
   "Lamoni, Ill. [Iowa],
      "Dear Sir:—

"After having asked my Father in heaven to help me, I sit down to write a few lines as dictated by the Holy Spirit.

"After reading the correspondence between you and L. O. Littlefield, I concluded it was the duty of some one to bear a testimony which could not be disputed. Finding from your letters to Littlefield that no one of your father's friends had performed this duty while you were here, now I will begin at once and tell you my experience.

"My beloved husband, R. B. Thompson, your father's private secretary to the end of his mortal life, died August 27, 1841. (I presume you will remember him.) Nearly two years after his death your father told me that my husband had appeared to him several times, telling him that he did not wish me to request your uncle Hyrum to have me sealed to him for time. Hyrum communicated this to his wife (my sister), who by request opened the subject to me, when every thing within me rose in opposition to such a step; but when your father called and explained the subject to me I dared not refuse to obey the counsel, lest peradventure I should be found fighting against God, and especially when he told me the last time my husband appeared to him he came with such power that it made him tremble.

"He then inquired of the Lord what he should do; the answer was, 'Go and do as my servant hath required.' He then took all opportunity to communicate this to your uncle Hyrum, who told me that the Holy Spirit rested upon him from the crown of his head to the soles of his feet. The time was appointed, with the consent of all parties, and your father sealed me to your uncle Hyrum for time, in my sister's room, with a covenant to deliver me up in the morning of the resurrection to Robert Blaskell Thompson with whatever offspring should be the result of the union, at the same time counseling your uncle to build a room for me and move me over as soon as convenient, which he did, and I remained there as a wife the same as my sister to the day of his death. All this I am ready to testify to in the presence of God, angels and men.

"Now I assure you I have not been prompted or dictated by any mortal being in writing to you; neither does a living soul know it but my invalid daughter.

"God bless you, is the sincere prayer of your true friend. MERCY R. THOMPSON.

"P. S.—If you feel disposed to ask me any questions, I will be pleased to answer concerning blessings which I received under the hands of your late mother, by the direction of your father.—M. R. T. in *Deseret News*." (Littlefield's Celestial Marriage, pages 1 and 2.)

The testimony of the above named witnesses makes up the case so far as the question of polygamy is concerned, and includes the principal facts upon which the parties to the controversy depend in order to the establishment of their respective contentions, and from them the reader will be able to form conclusions for himself. The correctness of such conclusions will of course depend very largely upon the impartiality with which the evidence is weighed.

As may be expected, President Joseph Smith has not been an idle and disinterested spectator in this unique drama, but has been an active participant in the somewhat spirited contest between the rival churches of the Saints for supremacy. He has taken all the facts into consideration, and it cannot fail to be a matter of interest to the reader to know what disposition President Smith makes of the evidence presented above. While the conclusions are not, perhaps, such as others may form, yet it is but just and proper that they should be given here.

Referring to the visit to his mother and his interview with her upon the perplexing question of polygamy, and his father's relation thereto, President Smith, in his autobiography, thus states his conclusions:

"It will be seen that in view of her departure at so early a time after the statements made by my mother heretofore recorded, those statements may be regarded as her last testimony upon the subjects named. It may be as well, then, that I here state my convictions regarding the vexing question of polygamy.

"I believe that during the last years of my father's life there was a discussion among the elders, and possibly in practice, a theory like the following: that persons who might believe that there was a sufficient degree of spiritual affinity between them as married companions, to warrant the desire to perpetuate that union in the world to come and after the resurrection, could go before some high priest whom they might choose, and there making known their desire, might be *married* for *eternity*, pledging themselves while in the flesh unto each other for the observance of the rights of companionship in the spirit; that this was called spiritual marriage, and upon the supposition that what was sealed by this priesthood, before which this pledge was made on earth, was sealed in heaven, the marriage relation then entered into would continue in eternity. That this was not authorized by command of God or rule of the church; but grew out of the constant discussion had among the elders; and that after a time it resulted in the wish (father to the thought) that married companionship rendered unpleasant here by incompatibilities of different sorts, might be cured for the world to come, by securing through this means a congenial companion in the spirit; that there was but brief hesitancy between the wish and an attempt to put it into form and practice. That once started, the idea grew; spiritual affinities were sought after, and in seeking them the hitherto sacred precincts of home were invaded; less and less restraint was exercised; the lines between virtue and license, hitherto sharply drawn, grew more and more indistinct; spiritual companionship if sanctioned by a holy priesthood, to confer favors and pleasures in the world to come, might be antedated and put to actual test here—and so the enjoyment of a spiritual companionship in eternity became a companionship here; a wife a spiritual wife, if congenial; if not, one that was congenial was sought, and a wife in fact was supplemented by one in spirit, which in easy transition became one in essential earthly relationship. From this, if one, why not two or more, and plural marriage, or plurality of wives, was the growth. That so soon as the prophet discovered that this must inevitably be the result of the marriage for eternity between married companions, which for the time was perhaps looked upon as a harmless enlargement of the priesthood theory, and rather intended to glorify them in doing business for eternity and the heavens, he set about to correct it. But the evil had, unnoted by him, taken root, and it was too late. What had been possibly innocently spiritual became fleshly, sensual—devilish. He was taken away. The long train of circumstances burst upon the people. He and Hyrum placed themselves in the front of the impending storm and went down to death. That which in life they were powerless to prevent rapidly took the successive forms heretofore stated, and polygamy, after eight years of further fostering in secret, rose in terrible malignity to essay the destruction of the church. That my father may have been a party to the first step in this strange development, I am perhaps prepared to admit, though the evidence connecting him with it is vague and uncertain; but that he was in any otherwise responsible for plural marriage, plurality of wives, or polygamy, I do not know, nor are the evidences so far produced to me conclusive to force my belief." (Tullidge's History, pages 798, 799 and 800.)

In justice to President Smith I wish to state in this connection, that at the time the above was written (1880) all the facts developed in the *Littlefield-Smith correspondence* (1886) were perhaps not in his possession; but as eleven years have since elapsed, and these opinions have never been revised, it is quite fair to presume that they reflect the present views and convictions of the Prophet of the Reorganized Church, and as such they are here submitted.

In all Mormon literature I have never met with a statement by any writer where the probable manner in which polygamy was conceived, and the processes of its development are presented with greater clearness and force than is the above from the pen of President Smith. His view as to the manner in which the system was evolved is in perfect harmony with the facts as they are given in the preceding chapters relative to this subject; but the *manner* in which the system originated is of far less importance to Mormonism than is the question relating to the *authority* upon which it is based.

The conclusions reached by the writer are widely different from those stated by Mr. Smith in the closing paragraph of the statement above quoted. He seems to think the evidence quite insufficient to force the conviction that his father was in any manner "responsible for plural marriage, plurality of wives, or polygamy," while the writer's mind has literally been "forced" by the overwhelming character of the evidence presented upon this point.

SUMMARY.

The facts as we glean them from the circumstances of the case, and the testimony of credible witnesses, may be stated substantially as follows:

1. The conduct of the Mormon leaders at a time prior to August, 1835, had been such as to give rise to the charge of "fornication and polygamy."

2. That this belief on the part of those not connected with the church, instead of diminishing, was only intensified with the developments of the passing years.

3. That a "secret wife system" was gradually developed among the leaders, which came to light through the disclosures of General John C. Bennett in 1842.

4. These revelations were followed by others of a more startling character early in 1844, in strong charges of crime made by William Law, of the "First Presidency," and Major-General Wilson Law, of the Nauvoo Legion, through the columns of the *Expositor*.

5. That from 1842 to 1844 polygamy had been preached in various States by the elders of the church, thus showing it to be general.

6. Efforts were made by Joseph and Hyrum Smith to suppress the facts by making public denials— through the press—that such things were taught or practiced by the leaders, thus seeking to evade the charge that a "secret wife system," or polygamy, existed in Nauvoo.

7. That in order to seemingly support this view, and enforce it upon the public mind, several of these elders were "cut off," or threatened with expulsion, for teaching "polygamy and other false and corrupt doctrines."

8. That at the very time these notices and denials were published in the *Times and Seasons*, by the authority of Joseph and Hyrum Smith, they were both not only teaching the doctrine, but were actually practicing polygamy—Joseph having *five* and Hyrum *two* wives, as now appears by the testimony of the women themselves.

9. That the revelation on celestial marriage was presented to the members of the High Council, convened for that purpose by Joseph Smith, and was read by Hyrum Smith, in their presence, Aug. 12, 1844.

10. A copy of this document was preserved by Brigham Young, who had it publicly read by Orson Pratt in the Tabernacle at Salt Lake City, August, 1852, and was published in *The Deseret News* in September of the same year.

These are the facts as they appear from the records, and as they are proved by the great preponderance of the evidence in the case. What importance attaches to these facts? and how will they affect the Mormon Church? are questions worthy the consideration of the thoughtful student of the times.

Of one thing we may be quite sure, and that is, if Joseph Smith was the author of that "revelation" enjoining polygamy, it at once brands him as a wicked and unscrupulous impostor, and wholly unworthy of the respect and esteem of decent people. If he is the author of such an abominable document, how can any sane man repose the slightest confidence in any of his so-called revelations?

If the matters and things set forth in the testimony of these witnesses shall be esteemed as true, then it must in all candor be admitted that Joseph was an unblushing impostor, and as a consequence, Mormonism is a deception and a fraud. And if this be true, O, then, "what shall the harvest be?"

With the consciousness of having endeavored to fairly and honestly present the facts as I have been able to gather them, the question is submitted to the reader, and we leave it with him to decide as to whether Joseph Smith was or was not the author of Mormon polygamy.

CHAPTER XXXVII.

THE GATHERING.

The gathering—A new Jerusalem promised—Western Missouri the land of Zion—Independence the central spot—Temple to be built—Saints begin to gather—Established in Zion—A dark cloud arises—Driven from Jackson County—Zion in possession of the enemy—The redemption of Zion—How it is to be accomplished—A parable—Zion's camp—Baurak Ale—The Lord's warriors—Start for Zion—Meet a superior force—A narrow escape—A terrible storm—A new revelation—Army to disband—Wait for a little season—Cholera in the camp—Tried as Abraham—I will fight your battles—Shall find grace and favor in the eyes of the people—Let my army become very strong—Far West—The Mormon war—Resist the militia—Several killed—Exterminating order of Gov. Boggs—Joseph and the leaders arrested—Mormons driven from the State—The whole gathering scheme a failure.

THE fact that God had promised to gather the tribes of scattered Israel and restore them to their own lands seems to have been the germ from which sprang the gathering mania, so prevalent among the Saints of every class and name. The idea of gathering did not of course originate with the common people, but like every other doctrine and dogma of Mormonism, it had its origin in the brain of Joseph Smith. The earlier views of the prophet on this question were rather dim and shadowy; the first specific reference to the subject being in September, 1830, as follows:

"And ye [six elders] are called to bring to pass the gathering of mine elect [mentioned in par. 1], for mine elect hear my voice, and harden not their hearts; wherefore the decree hath gone forth from the Father that they shall be gathered into *one place* upon the face of this land, . . . for I will reveal myself from heaven with power and great glory, with all the hosts thereof, and dwell in righteousness with men on earth a thousand years, and the wicked shall not stand." (Doc. and Cov., page 115).

Thus it will be seen that the first idea was to gather to one place, and thus be ready to receive Christ at his appearing. Three months later, December, 1830, and while Sidney Rigdon was assisting the prophet in the work of "translating" (!) the Old and New Testament Scriptures, there was a slight enlargement upon the first idea of the gathering, as the following extract shows:

"And righteousness and truth will I cause to sweep the earth as with a flood, to gather out mine own elect from the four quarters of the earth *unto a place which I shall prepare; a holy city*, that my people may gird up their loins, and be looking forth for the time of my coming; for *there* shall be my tabernacle, *and it shall be called Zion, a new Jerusalem.*" (Doc. and Cov., page 133).

Three months later, in March, 1831, the prophet has further illumination upon the subject of the gathering. Joseph had now located in Kirtland, O., and P. P. Pratt, Oliver Cowdery, Peter Whitmer and a number of others, were doing missionary work in the far west, and had written very flattering reports of the country, especially that portion of Missouri immediately surrounding Independence, the county seat of Jackson county. These historic facts may serve to throw some very interesting side-lights upon the following " revelation."

"Wherefore, I the Lord have said, gather ye out from the eastern lands, assemble ye yourselves together, ye elders of my church; . . . and with one heart and with one mind, gather up your riches that ye may purchase an inheritance which shall hereafter be appointed unto you, and it shall be called the New Jerusalem, *a land of peace*, a city of refuge, *a place of safety* for the saints of the Most High God; and the glory of the Lord shall be there, and the *terror* of the Lord shall be there, insomuch that the wicked will not come unto it; and it shall be called *Zion*.

"And it shall come to pass, among the wicked, that every man that will not take up his sword against his neighbor, must needs flee unto Zion for safety. And there shall be *gathered unto* it out of *every nation under heaven;* and it shall be the only people that shall not be at war one with another. And it shall be said among the wicked, Let us not go up to battle against Zion, for the inhabitants of Zion are *terrible*, wherefore we cannot stand." (Doc. and Cov., pages 155 and 156.)

Just how much truth there is in this boastful revelation will appear further on, but this shows the general trend of the prophet's mind. A "New Jerusalem" must be established as a refuge, or a "place of safety" for the saints, but just *where* the "city of refuge" was to be located, the prophet was not yet ready to announce; but it was not long deferred, however, for in June, *just three months* from the date of the last revelation on the gathering (it seems remarkable that these attacks were periodical—three months apart), Joseph, the next day after the first general conference at Kirtland, Ohio, received a "revelation," commanding him, with others, to go to

Independence, Mo., where also the next conference was to be held. Following is what the Lord is represented to have said about the matter:

"Wherefore, verily I say unto you, let my servant Joseph Smith, Jr., and Sidney Rigdon, take their journey as soon as preparations can be made to leave their homes, and journey to the land of Missouri. And inasmuch as they are faithful unto me, it shall be made known unto them . . . the land of your inheritances." (Doc. and Cov., page 167.)

Accordingly, Joseph and Sidney, in company with a number of the leading men, "took their journey, and journeyed" to the "land of Missouri," where they arrived about the middle of July. Delighted with the country, and encouraged by the prospects of the future, the prophet soon received the following "revelation:"

"Hearken, O ye elders of my church, saith the Lord your God, who have assembled yourselves together, according to my commandments, in this land, which is the land of Missouri, which is the land which I have appointed and consecrated for the gathering of my saints: wherefore this is the land of promise, and the place for the city of Zion. And thus saith the Lord your God, if ye will receive wisdom here is wisdom. Behold the place which is now called Independence, is the center place, and the spot for the temple is lying westward upon a lot which is not far from the courthouse; wherefore it is wisdom that the land should be purchased by the saints; and also every tract lying westward, even to the line running directly between Jew and Gentile. And every tract bordering by the prairies, inasmuch as my disciples are enabled to buy lands. Behold this is wisdom, that they may obtain it for an *everlasting inherit-ance.*" (Doc. and Cov., page 174.)

The same revelation goes on to appoint Sidney Gilbert as an agent to buy all the land in the " regions round about," and also to engage in the mercantile business, to supply goods to the people, "and thus provide for my saints." By the same revelation a printer was appointed, and thus was " my servant William W. Phelps *planted* in this place, and established as a printer unto the church."

Manifesting that energy and push which have ever characterized Mormon colonies, they were soon comfortably located in the land of Zion, which was " consecrated and dedicated for the gathering of the saints." The temple lot was dedicated in August, and the saints were looking forward in great hope, much encouraged by this " glimpse of the future," as the prophet expressed it, " which time will yet unfold to the satisfaction of all."

The Saints soon began to gather from the eastern country and settle upon these fertile lands, till in a short time their numbers were swollen to hundreds if not to thousands. Zion was now established, and the Saints were happy in the thought that a city of refuge had been provided for them—so that, when " the overflowing scourge " should pass through the land, they would be safe from all harm—it should pass over them and not hurt them.

Time passed, and the Saints continued to gather upon "the promised land," settling principally in Jackson, Clay, Ray and other adjacent counties in western Missouri. Their hopes were bright and expectant, their prophet having assured them of success. A dark and ominous cloud had appeared upon the horizon, which was destined soon to eclipse the rising sun of their expected glory and cast a dark shadow over the bright spirit of their dreams. The rapid influx of so large a number of undesirable citizens (undesirable, perhaps, because of their peculiar religious views, and the "pluck and plod" which bring material prosperity), created, on the part of the people of Missouri, a strong feeling of opposition to the "newscomers," which soon ripened into a thorough hatred of everything Mormon.

Retaliation was the inevitable result of this exhibition of envy and malice, and which, in its turn, only seemed to further intensify the feeling of their enemies, who finally, by mob force, drove every Mormon from Jackson county in November, 1833, and later, under the "exterminating" order of Governor L. W. Boggs, they were in a body expelled from the State.

While the Mormons, and more especially the leaders, were doubtless responsible for a liberal share of these troubles, yet for this flagrant outrage upon the rights and liberties of free American citizens, there cannot be offered even the shadow of excuse. The plea that the Mormons had violated the laws of the State cannot be offered in justification of so grave an offense against the cause of humanity, and the peace and dignity of the State of Missouri. If the Mormons had violated the laws of the State, as their enemies charged, why not try them for their offenses, and if found guilty, punish them according to the provisions of the law they are charged with having violated? To say they could not be convicted, if guilty, cannot be entered as a plea in abatement of the offense, for certainly if the State had the power to expel the entire Mormon citizenship from the State, it must have possessed the power to enforce its laws against the individual transgressor.

It matters not what their peculiarities, or how absurd may appear the tenets of their religion, they were American citizens, amenable to the laws of the country, and as such should have been protected in their rights of citizenship. A great nation, a sovereign State and a large-minded, liberty-loving people can well afford to deal justly, even with "Mormons." The scenes of Independence and Carthage can never again be repeated in the United States, and well for the honor of a great nation that it is so.

The thoughtful reader will have observed that the plans of the prophet had been frustrated, and the dream of his fancy shattered. Something must be done to redeem Zion from the grasp and dominion of the enemy. The city of refuge must be built, and a "place of safety" prepared for the Saints. Soon the time should come when a desolating scourge should be poured out upon the inhabitants of the land; earthquake, famine and pestilence were to waste the inhabitants of the earth, and every nation should be at war with another. The Saints alone should be at peace, and every man who would not take up the sword against his neighbor would "flee to Zion for safety." This beautiful dream of the Saints had vanished, and their hopes were shattered. Something must be done to avert the calamity and save the failing faith of the people.

The prophet, equal to the emergency, soon finds a way out of the difficulty—*Zion must be redeemed.* Another "revelation" was now in order, and it was not long delayed. Only a few weeks after the Saints had been driven from Jackson County the following revelation was received, showing the reason why this affliction was permitted to come upon them:

"Verily I say unto you, concerning your brethren who have been afflicted and persecuted and cast out from the land of their inheritance, I, the Lord, have suffered the affliction to come upon them, wherewith they have been afflicted in consequence of their transgressions. . . . Therefore they must needs be chastened and tried, even as Abraham. . . Verily I say unto you, notwithstanding their sins, . . . I will not utterly cast them off; and in the day of wrath I will remember mercy. I have sworn, and the decree hath gone forth by a former commandment which I have given unto you, that I would *let fall the sword* of mine indignation *in behalf of my people;* and even as I have said *it shall come to pass*. . . . Therefore let your hearts be comforted concerning Zion, for all flesh is in mine hands: be still and know that I am God. Zion shall not be moved out of her place, notwithstanding her children are scattered, they that remain and are pure in heart *shall return* and come to their inheritances, *they and their children*, with songs of everlasting joy, to *build up the waste places of Zion*." (Doc. and Cov., pages 165, 166.)

Latter Day Saints boast of the literal fulfillment of Joseph Smith's prophecies, and point with confidence to this fact as one of the strongest proofs of the authenticity of his prophetic mission. In view of this I wish to call attention to three distinct promises in the above which utterly failed in their accomplishment, namely:

1. That God would let fall his sword *in behalf of the Latter Day Saints.*
2. That although they had been driven from their lands and *scattered,* they should "*return to their inheritances.*"
3. That both "*they and their children*" should return with songs of joy and "*build up the waste places of Zion.*"

Not one of these predictions ever came to pass, although every effort was put forth by Joseph Smith and the leaders to accomplish the work, as we shall presently see. Zion must be redeemed, but *how* was this much desired end to be accomplished? Like all other great questions in Mormonism, this was promptly settled by "revelation." Joseph then proceeds to solve the problem by means of a parable. He represents the Lord as saying:

"And now I show unto you a parable, that you may know my will concerning the redemption of Zion. A certain nobleman had a spot of land, very choice [Jackson County]; and he said unto his servants, Go ye into my vineyard, even upon this very choice piece of land, and plant twelve olive trees; and set watchmen round about them, and build a tower, that one may overlook the land round about, . . . that mine olive trees may not be broken down when the enemy shall come to spoil and take unto them the fruit of my vineyard. Now the servants of the nobleman went and did as their lord commanded them; and they planted the olive trees, and built a hedge round about, and set watchmen, and *began* to build a tower." (Doc. and Cov., page 267.)

But these servants did not complete the work assigned them, for while they were questioning the methods of their lord, "the enemy came by *night* [just as the mob did at Independence] and broke down the hedge, and the servants of the nobleman arose and were affrighted and fled [just as the Mormons did]; and the enemy destroyed their works and broke down the olive trees." (Ibid, page 268.)

Having thus lost their possessions, how were these "servants" to get them back again? This perplexing question was to be settled in the following business-like manner:

"And the lord of the vineyard said unto one of his servants [Joseph], Go and gather together the residue of my servants [the churches in the East], and take all the strength of mine house, which are my *warriors*, my young men, and they that are of middle age also, among my servants, who are the strength of mine house, save only those whom I have appointed to tarry; and go ye *straightway* unto the land of my vineyard [Jackson County] and *redeem my vineyard*, for it is mine, I have bought it with money. Therefore get ye straightway unto my land; *break down the walls of mine enemies*, throw down their tower, and *scatter their watchmen;* and inasmuch as they gather together against you, *avenge me of mine enemies;* that by and by I may come with the residue of mine house [the remainder of the church] and possess the land." (Ibid, page 268.)

This arrangement seems to have met with general approval, and so measures were at once inaugurated to carry out the plan and put the expedition in motion. No sooner was it discovered by this astute "seer" that the plan suggested by the parable met with the approval of both leaders and people than another "revelation" was forthcoming designating the "servant" of the parable who was to "gather together the residue of my servants," to go up and redeem Zion.

"Behold, I say unto you, the redemption of Zion must needs come by *power;* therefore I will raise up unto my people a man who shall lead them *like as Moses led the children of Israel,* for ye are the children of Israel and of the seed of Abraham; and ye must needs be *led out of bondage by power,* and with a stretched out arm. . . .

"Verily, verily I say unto you, that my servant Baurak Ale [Joseph Smith] is the man to whom I likened the servant to whom the lord of the vineyard spoke in the parable which I have given you.

"Therefore let my servant Baurak Ale say unto the strength of my house, my middle aged, gather yourselves together unto the land of Zion; . . . and inasmuch as mine enemies come against you to drive you from my goodly land, . . . *ye shall curse them;* and whomsoever ye curse I will curse; and ye shall avenge me of mine enemies; and my *presence* shall be with you, even in avenging me of mine enemies, unto the third and fourth generation of them that hate me." (Ibid, page 277.)

It will be very interesting to note in what a signal manner the latter day "Moses," "my servant Baurak Ale," failed in every essential particular. Not a promise made in any of these "revelations" concerning the redemption of Zion has ever had even the semblance of fulfillment, as we shall see.

This same revelation from which the above is quoted contains another promise which utterly failed. It is this:

"But verily I say unto you, that I have *decreed* a

decree which my people *shall realize*, inasmuch as they hearken from this very hour unto the *counsel* which I, the Lord their God, shall give unto them. Behold they *shall*, for I have decreed it, begin to prevail against mine enemies *from this very hour*, . . . and they shall *never cease* to prevail until the kingdoms of the world [the United States with the rest] are subdued under my feet.

"But verily I say unto you, *I have decreed* that your brethren, which have been scattered, *shall return* to the land of their inheritances and build up the waste places of Zion, . . . no more to be thrown down." (Ibid, page 276.)

That they "hearkened" unto the counsel of "my servant Baurak Ale," all subsequent Mormon history abundantly attests. Sidney Rigdon, Parley P. Pratt, Lyman Wright and others, were commanded to go into the "eastern countries"—meaning the eastern States—and gather up companies to go and redeem Zion. They were to continue till they had secured "*five hundred*," if possible, and if not, then *three hundred;* "and if ye cannot obtain three hundred, seek diligently that peradventure ye may obtain *one hundred*. But verily I say unto you, a commandment I give unto you, that ye shall not go up into the land of Zion until you have obtained *one hundred* of the strength of my house. . . . Pray earnestly that my servant Baurak Ale may go with you and preside in the midst of my people." (Ibid, page 278.)

The officers sent out soon raised *two hundred* choice men—*twice* the number which was necessary to assure their success under the provisions of this revelation, as may be seen from the following:

"Parley P. Pratt, on this subject writes as follows:

"'It was now the first of May, 1834, and our mission had resulted in the assembling of about *two hundred* men at Kirtland, with teams, baggage, provisions, *arms*, etc., for a march of one thousand miles, to carry some supplies to the afflicted and persecuted Saints in Missouri, and to *reinforce and strengthen them*. . . . This little army was led by President Joseph Smith [*Baurak Ale*] in person. It commenced its march about the first of May.'" (Smith's History, vol. 1, page 456).

Concerning the preparations for this expedition we also have the following:

"Joseph continues:

"'May 5. Having gathered and prepared clothing and other necessaries to carry to our brethren and sisters who had been robbed and plundered of nearly all their effects; and having provided for ourselves horses and wagons, and *firearms,* and all sorts of *munitions of war* of the most portable kind for self-defense, as our enemies were thick on every hand, I started with the remainder of the company, from Kirtland, for Missouri.'" (Ibid, page 454.)

Thus we see the people were obedient to the counsel which had been given, and according to the terms of the revelation, were entitled to success. This army, a list of whose names appears in Smith's History, Vol. 1, page 462-464, is known in Mormon history as "Zion's Camp."

The army continued its march (on foot) till they reached the western part of the State of Missouri, about the middle of June. As we might naturally expect, a body of over two hundred armed men from another State marching to a given point for the avowed purpose of reinstating, by force of arms if necessary, their friends who had been expelled from their homes in Jackson County, created great excitement among the inhabitants of the State, and finally resulted in armed opposition to their further progress. On the evening of June 19th Joseph's army "encamped on an elevated piece of ground between two brances of Fishing River." Concerning what occurred here, "my servant, Baurak Ale," has this to say:

"As we halted and were making preparations for the night, five men armed with guns rode into our camp and told us we should see hell before morning, and their accompanying oaths partook of all the malice of demons. They told us that sixty men were coming from Richmond, Ray County, and seventy more from Clay County, sworn to our utter destruction." (Ibid, page 464.)

Some two hundred others were ready to leave Jackson County to join with these to prevent the further progress of Joseph's army. The Clay and Ray County contingents were just on the west bank of the river awaiting reinforcement from Jackson County, expecting, it would seem, to make an attack on Zion's Camp either that night or early the next morning; and, according to the Mormon account of the affair, commenced a "cannonading" while the sun was yet "one hour high." (Page 465.)

Just about sunset, however, a terrific hailstorm arose and beat upon both parties in a frightful manner. The rainfall was unprecedented; and the next morning the stream was impassable for either army. With everything drenched, and water-soaked ammunition, the would-be combatants could do nothing more than hurl epithets and vile imprecations at the enemy from the opposite bank of the swollen river.

The storm was by the Mormons regarded as a providential interposition, while the Missourians looked upon it as a very unfortunate affair, as it prevented them from carrying out their purpose to "kill Joe Smith and his army." Thus far "Zion's Camp" had acted in good faith; and believing, as they did, that the Lord had "decreed a decree" to the effect that they were to "break down the tower, and scatter the watchmen" of the enemy, and restore their afflicted brethren to their "inheritances in Zion," they did not for one moment doubt that it would be accomplished. But "my servant Baurak Ale" knew that the hope was vain. He had not dreamed of meeting such resistance as that which lay just across the river.

Prompted by the soundness of the old proverb that "discretion is the better part of valor," the prophet concluded it would not do to undertake to enforce his measures against such odds. Besides this, he had sent a delegation to request the Governor, Daniel Dunklin, to furnish him a "sufficient military force," to "reinstate the exiles and protect them in the possession of their homes in Jackson County." But this the Governor refused to do. (See Smith's History, Vol. 1, pages 471, 472.)

Knowing it would be madness to attempt to reach Independence under such circumstances, the "seer" was not long in devising another means of escape from the difficulty in which his audacity had placed him. The next morning after the storm the "camp" moved to a little prairie some five miles distant, to a more "secure place, where they could defend themselves from the rage of their enemies."

Something must be done; the enemy was upon them, and the Lord had not appeared to defend them. The "Moses," who was to redeem modern Israel from bondage, unlike his great predecessor, was about to be vanquished, and "Israel" was already on the retreat. A happy thought occurred to "Baurak Ale." He would give the people of Israel another revelation explaining a matter concerning which they never before had received an intimation, namely, that all this sacrifice of time, money and life—for many of them died—was only a trial of their faith,—that the Lord had never intended to redeem Zion by means of this expedition. The following extracts from a document known as the "Fishing River revelation," will serve to show the extreme lengths to which deception and fraud may drive the unscrupulous. Here is the manner in which the prophet meets the present difficulty:

"Verily I say unto you, who have assembled yourselves together that you may learn my will concerning the redemption of mine afflicted people. Behold, I say unto you, were it not for the transgressions of my people, speaking concerning the church, and not individuals, they might have been redeemed even now; but, behold, they have not learned to be obedient to the things which I have required at their hands."

Then complaint is made that they were "not united according to the union required by the law of the celestial kingdom,"—and that they did not "impart of their substance, as becometh saints;" and that they must "learn obedience, if it must needs be by the things which they suffer." But Joseph was very particular to inform them that he did not speak " concerning those who are appointed to *lead* my people, who are the *first elders of my church.*" O, no! not these; it was upon the common people who would not give their hard-earned dollars to the leaders, that the blame of this inglorious failure must now rest. Shame!

"Therefore, in consequence of the transgression of my people, it is expedient in me that mine elders should *wait* for a little season for the redemption of Zion."

Can any man of common sense be made to believe that an all-wise God did not understand the frame of mind that existed in these people at the time this expedition started from Ohio, only a month before, just as well as he did after this defeat of Joseph Smith's plan? It seems incredible that men of ordinary intelligence could be so blind. And yet such was the strength of this delusion that men of fair, yes, of even more than ordinary intellectual powers, were made to roll the deception under the tongue as a sweet morsel. It is simply astonishing. Again:

"For behold, I do not require at their hands to fight the battles of Zion."

And yet had not they been commanded to do the *very thing* that they are now informed they are not required to do? Had not the "strength of mine house"—the young and strong, "my *warriors*," been armed and equipped, only a few weeks before, *for that very purpose?* Had not these same confiding "warriors" been assured by a former "revelation" that God would go before them, just as he had gone before the Israelites, in order to assure their success? Had not the decree previously gone forth that Zion should be redeemed with *power*, and with an *outstretched arm* under the leadership of their Moses?

And yet when the trying moment came, when this modern Moses should have stretched forth his arm for the deliverance of the oppressed of his people, he slinks away behind the wicked subterfuge of another so-called revelation, and lays the blame of his ignominious failure upon a people who were in no way responsible for his folly. The blasphemous document thus continues:

"For as I said in a former commandment, even so I will fulfill, *I will fight your battles.*"

Never, in all the history of Mormonism, was there a better opportunity offered for this boastful god of the Saints to fight their battles than this very occasion afforded. Why, instead of a scourge of cholera being poured out upon the camp of Zion, did it not fall upon these ungodly Gentiles, who, according to their version of the affair, had not only robbed and plundered their innocent brethren, but were now standing with drawn swords ready to slay the prophet and devour the "residue of his people?" Why *wait* for a little season before executing his wrath upon these "mine enemies?" O, consistency, thou art indeed a jewel!

"Behold, the destroyer have I sent forth to destroy and lay waste mine enemies."

When was this destroyer sent forth among these enemies? *Where* did he operate? And *whom* did he destroy? Will some wise men among the Saints answer these pertinent questions? I have studied closely every phase of Mormon history as it relates to the difficulties both in Missouri and Illinois, and I have never yet been able to find a single footprint of the fell monster. He has never yet appeared, and it is now too late in the day for his appearance, and the statement is thus shown to be irredeemably false.

"And not many years hence they shall not be left to pollute mine heritage, and to blaspheme my name upon the lands which I have consecrated for the gathering together of my Saints."

Sixty-three years have passed—almost the full number allotted to man—and yet Zion is not redeemed; these "enemies" still "pollute" the lands, and still the Saints are waiting. With all these facts staring them in the face, how can any intelligent Latter Day Saint look forward to the time when Zion shall be redeemed, with even the shadow of reason upon which to rest his hope? Instead of the inhabitants of Missouri having been laid waste by the destroyer, instead of there being not one left to pollute the land of Zion, the lands are all occupied, great cities, whose population is numbered by the scores of thousands, have sprung up all over the country, and where there was one man then there are a hundred now. Such are Joseph Smith's prophecies and their fulfillment, and such the foundation upon which the hope of the Saints must forever rest, so far, at least, as the "redemption of Zion" is concerned. But to proceed:

"Behold, I have commanded my servant Baurak Ale to say unto the strength of my house, even my *warriors*, my young men and middle-aged, to gather together for the redemption of my people, and throw down the towers of mine enemies, and scatter their watchmen; but the strength of mine house have not hearkened unto my words; but inasmuch as there are those who have hearkened unto my words, I have prepared a *blessing* and an *endowment* for them, if they continue faithful. I have heard their prayers, and will accept their offering; and it is expedient in me that they should be brought thus far, *for a trial of their faith.*"

What a weak, pitiable excuse! What a shameless subterfuge! And yet it seems to have satisfied the majority of these warrior dupes—yes, *dupes;* and I use the word advisedly, and after much careful consideration of all the facts—for they followed the "counsel" of "my servant Joseph" to the very letter.

Those who had no families were required to remain, while those who had left their families in the East were to "tarry for a season," subject to the counsel of their leader. Following these instructions the camp of Zion was in a short time disbanded. The prophet, however, did not wish the impression to prevail, neither with the warriors nor the "residue of mine house," that the expedition had failed, or that the determination to redeem Zion had been abandoned; and so the "revelation" carefully provides for this contingency as follows:

"Talk not of judgment, neither boast of faith, nor of mighty works [the very things that rendered the Mormons odious to the people]; but carefully gather together as much in *one region* as can be consistently with the feelings of the people: and behold, *I will give you favor and grace in their eyes,* that you may rest in *peace* and *safety,* while you are saying unto the people, execute judgment and justice for us according to law, and redress us of our wrongs."

Thus what they failed to accomplish by force they were now to endeavor to bring to pass by stealth. I wish in this connection to call attention to two promises in the above extract which utterly and irredeemably failed:

1. The Saints were to find "grace and favor" in the eyes of the people, and,

2. They were to "rest in peace and safety" while they were asking for redress.

How faithfully the god of the Saints fulfilled these promises will appear as we proceed. The revelation continues:

"Now, behold, I say unto you, my friends, in this way you may find favor in the eyes of the people, until the army of Israel becomes very great."

Yes, that was the idea; they were to "lift up an ensign of peace, . . . and make proposals of peace," and thus secure the good will of the people. In the meantime God was to "soften the hearts of the people," as he had softened Pharaoh's heart, "until my servant Baurak Ale and Baneemy [Sidney Rigdon] whom I have appointed, shall have time to gather up the strength of mine house; . . . and after these lands are purchased I will hold the armies of Israel guiltless in taking possession of their lands, . . . and of throwing down the towers of mine enemies that may be upon them, and scattering their watchmen, and avenging me of mine enemies to the third and fourth generation of them that hate me. But firstly, let my army become very great."

This self-appointed Moses had discovered that his army of "warriors" were wholly unequal to the task they had undertaken to perform, and therefore counseled that they quietly disperse and settle in "the regions round about," and wait till Joseph and Sidney could return and gather up a sufficient reinforcement, and *then* they would "throw down their towers and scatter their watchmen," and in this manner Zion should be redeemed from possession and control of the enemy. But all this was but a cunning devise of the prophet to extricate himself from the difficulties in which his rash act had involved him.

While "Baurak Ale and Baneemy" were gathering up the "strength of mine house," all the lands in Jackson County were to be purchased; and soon after the promised endowment which was to take place in the Kirtland temple, they should have power "to accomplish all things pertaining to Zion." This revelation concludes as follows:

"And all things shall work together for your good; therefore be faithful, and behold, and lo, I am with you even to the end. Even so. Amen." (See Doc. and Cov., pages 285-288.)

It will be borne in mind that the Lord is represented in this revelation as having brought these people thus far "for a trial of their faith," and that he had "accepted their offering," and would therefore be with them "even to the end." As to how well this promise was kept, and in what a satisfactory (?) manner the god of Joseph was with these poor deluded people, I shall permit the prophet himself to relate. The ink was scarcely dry upon the paper containing these blasphemous promises and declarations till cholera broke out among them in a virulent form. Concerning this matter Joseph says:

"About this time Brothers Thayer and Hayes were attacked with cholera, and Brother Hancock was taken during the storm. I called the camp together and told them that in consequence of the disobedience of some who had been *unwilling to listen to my words*, but had rebelled, God had decreed that sickness should come upon them, and that *they should die like sheep with the rot;* that I was sorry, but could not help it." (Smith's History, Vol. 1, page 246, 247.)

They removed a short distance to fresh quarters, but still the dread disease continued. Joseph further says:

"June 24. This night the cholera burst forth among us, and about midnight it was manifest in its worst form. Our ears were saluted with cries and moanings and lamentations on every hand; even those on guard fell to the earth with their guns in their hands, so sudden and powerful was the attack of this terrible disease. At the commencement I attempted to lay on hands for their recovery, but I quickly learned by painful experience that when the great Jehovah decrees destruction upon a people, makes known his determination, man must not attempt to stay his hand. The moment I attempted to rebuke the disease, that moment I was attacked; and had I not desisted, I must have saved the life of my brother by the sacrifice of my own, for when I *rebuked* the disease *it left him* and seized me." (Smith's History, Vol. 1, page 479.)

Please stick a peg here, as we shall advert to this a little further on.

How utterly absurd is all this! and how completely incompatible with the promise of the revelation given them only forty-eight hours before. God was to be with them *to the end;* but instead of this they were now dying " like sheep with the rot," and all, forsooth, because some of them seemed unwilling to bow to the mandates of this autocrat.

"When the cholera made its appearance," continues Joseph, " Elder John S. Carter was the first man who stepped forward to rebuke it, and upon this was *instantly seized* and became the first victim in the camp." (Ibid, page 480.)

The impression is sought to be made that God had sent this terrible scourge upon the " camp " for disobedience to the words of their Moses. Joseph Smith, the autocrat, never lost an opportunity to impress the thought upon the minds of his dupes that he was the chief Mogul of Mormonism, and that his word was supreme.

The next morning after the cholera appeared, the " camp " was divided into small bands, in the hope to thus stay the ravages of the " destroyer," but it continued unabated for four days, during which time there were sixty-eight cases and *fourteen* deaths.

The careful reader will doubtless have observed that neither the prophet nor any of his followers possessed the power to " rebuke " the disease, although they several times attempted to do so. Joseph assured them that it was *the hand of God* upon them, and that no earthly power could stay it; but one of his apostles, Heber C. Kimball, in relating the *facts* as they came within his experience, says:

" From that time the destroyer ceased, having afflicted us about four days. Sixty-eight were taken with the disease, of which number fourteen died, the remainder recovering, as we found out *an effectual remedy for the disease*, which was, by dipping the person afflicted into cold water, or pouring it on him, which had the desired effect of stopping the purging, vomiting and cramping. Some of the brethren when they were seized with the disease and began to cramp and purge, the fever raging upon them, desired to be put into cold water, and some stripped and plunged themselves into the stream and *obtained immediate relief*. This led us to try the experiment on others, and *in every case* it proved highly beneficial and *effectual* where it was taken in season." (Smith's History, Vol. 1, page 486.)

Apart from other considerations, the above quotation might be regarded as of but little importance; but when considered in its relation to what Joseph Smith had declared to them when the scourge first appeared, it becomes a matter of some consequence. He had told them that God sent this disease among them, and that no human means could avail to stay the hand of the destroyer. And so when the faithful John S. Carter stepped bravely forward to "rebuke the disease," with prayer and the laying on of hands, he fell like Dagon before the ark of God, becoming "the first victim in the camp," and thus emphasizing the words of the prophet.

But when some poor sufferer, out of sheer desperation, threw himself into the stream which flowed by the camp, its waters proved a veritable Bethesda. All who plunged beneath its waves were saved—were healed. Thus were the waters of Rush Creek potent to do what the combined efforts of prophet and apostles had failed to accomplish, namely, to stop the ravages of the plague which God had sent among them, and which Joseph had said *could not be stayed*.

Who that is not blinded by the grossest superstition can fail to see that this whole affair was but the merest sham, a most transparent fraud? Yet these superstitious followers of the fictitious Moses clung with characteristic tenacity to the delusive hope that Zion would, in the near future, be redeemed, and that they and their children would return to Zion with songs of everlasting joy.

Viewing this question from the higher standpoint of reason and common sense, it is a matter of astonishment that Latter Day Saints of ordinary intelligence can any longer believe that they shall ever be able to possess what they vaguely conceive to be "the land of Zion." At the time when Joseph set this scheme on foot, all these lands could have been purchased at about Government price, $1.25 per acre; whereas, they are now worth anywhere from $40 to $100 per acre. If they could not purchase these lands *then*, how can they do so *now?*

The "camp," however, carried out their instructions and returned to Kirtland, to receive their "endowments" and wait till the army had become *very strong*. They patiently waited, but waited in vain. Instead of finding "grace and favor in the eyes of the people," the hatred engendered by the attempt of their leaders to invade the State with an armed force only grew stronger with the passing years.

After the Saints had been driven from Independence, and after the failure of Joseph and his "warriors" to reinstate them, a new city called Far West became the headquarters of the church in the West, and to this place and vicinity the prophet urged his people to gather. Over five hundred left Kirkland at one time (May 18, 1838) for the promised land, while many gathered from Canada, Ohio and other States, to Far West.

This unprecedented influx of Mormons again aroused the suspicions of the people of Western Missouri, and in a very short time almost the entire State rose in arms against them; and then followed what is known in history as "the Mormon war."

The first demonstrations of violence, it seems, appeared in Davies and Caldwell Counties, in October, 1838. Mobs had gathered and threatened to drive the Mormons from their homes. A company of Saints was raised and sent to Davies County to protect their brethren. The mob was dispersed, leaving a small cannon in possession of the Saints.

From this time forward the situation became more and more serious, till the Governor of the State ordered out the militia to quell the disturbance. This small force was under the command of Captain Bogart. A party of sixty Mormons, under the command of Apostle David W. Patten, was sent out to meet what they supposed to be a mob. A battle ensued in which Captain Patten and two of his men were killed, while the militia lost but one man. About the same time another event occurred at Haun's Mill, on Shoal Creek, some twenty miles below Far West, which greatly exasperated the Latter Day Saints.

This is known in Mormon history as the "Massacre of Haun's Mill," which was doubtless a brutal piece of butchery. News of these engagements soon reached the ears of Governor L. W. Boggs, who, having been informed that the Mormons had resisted Captain Bogart's militia with an armed force, issued, on the 27th of October, 1838, to General Clark, what is known in the annals of Mormonism as "Gov. Bogg's order of extermination." As this unique document is almost invariably represented by Mormon writers to be *unconditional*—that is, the Latter Day Saints had no choice except as between *expulsion* from the State, or *death*—I will here quote that portion of the Governor's order which relates to extermination, as follows:

"Headquarters Militia,
City of Jefeerson, Mo., Oct. 27, 1838.

"Sir: Since the order of the morning to you, directing you to cause four hundred mounted men to be raised within your division, I have received by Amos Rees, Esq., and Wiley E. Williams, Esq., one of my aids, information of the most appalling character, which changes the whole face of things, and places the Mormons in the attitude of open and avowed defiance of the laws, and of having made war upon the people of this State. Your orders are, therefore, to hasten your operations and endeavor to reach Richmond, Ray Co., with all possible speed. The Mormons must be treated as enemies, and must be *exterminated*, or driven from the State, *if necessary, for the public good.* Their outrages are beyond all description.

. . . .

"Instead, therefore, of proceeding, as first directed, to reinstate the citizens of Davies in their homes, you will proceed immediately to Richmond, and there operate *against* the Mormons. Brigadier-General Parks, of Ray, has been ordered to have four hundred men of his brigade in readiness to join you at Richmond. The whole force will be placed under your command. L. W. Boggs,
"Governor and Commander-in-Chief."

"To General Clark." (Tullidge's History, pages 242, 243.) (Italics in the above are mine.)

Thus it will be seen that Governor Boggs had ordered General Clark to proceed to Davies County, and reinstate the Mormon citizens who had been driven from their homes by a lawless mob, but who, upon being informed that Captain Patten had actually attacked the State troops under command of Captain Bogart, changed the order, and directed the forces of the State to be employed against the Mormons, who, by their act of firing upon the militia had placed themselves in the attitude of rebellion against the State of Missouri. Perhaps no Governor of any other State would, or could, have done less.

It will also be observed that the order issued to General Clark does not provide that the Mormons should be "exterminated" *if they did not leave the State;* but rather that they must be exterminated, or driven from the State, "*if necessary for the public good.*"

The prophet and many of the leaders were, at the time of these occurrences, at Far West, Caldwell, Co. On Oct. 30, the State troops marched upon the city of Far West, under command of General Lucas, and encamped for the night about a mile distant. The Caldwell militia were under the command of Colonel Hinkle, a Mormon. The Mormons "threw up temporary fortifications of wagons, timber, etc.," says Joseph Smith, and "the militia of Far West guarded the city" through the night.

Next day (31st) General Lucas was reinforced by about 1,500 men.

About 8 o'clock, A. M., Gen. Lucas sent a flag (presumably a flag of truce) towards the city, which was met by Col. Hinkle and others, when, it seems, negotiations were entered into between Gen. Lucas and Col. Hinkle for the final settlement of the Mormon troubles.

As to the character of this agreement the prophet states it as follows, although upon what authority he does not say:

"Colonel Hinkle went out to meet the flag, and secretly made an engagement, 1st, To give up their [the church's] leaders to be tried and punished; 2nd, To make an appropriation of their property— all who had taken up arms—to the payment of their debts and indemnity for damage done by them; 3rd, That the balance should leave the State, and be protected out by the militia, but be permitted to remain under protection until further orders were received from the Commander-in-chief; 4th, To give up the arms of every description, to be receipted for." (Tullidge's History, page 244.)

Relative to what transpired later in the day, Joseph thus continues:

"Towards evening I was waited upon by Colonel Hinkle, who stated that the officers of the militia desired to have an interview with me and some others, hoping that the difficulties might be settled without having occasion to carry into effect the exterminating orders which they had received from the Governor. I immediately complied with the request, and in company with Elders Rigdon and Pratt, Colonel Wight and George W. Robinson, went into the camp of the militia. But judge of my surprise, when, instead of being treated with that respect which is due from one citizen to another, we were taken as prisoners of war, and were treated with the utmost contempt." (Ibid, pages 244, 245.)

We do not wish to appear irreverent, but I cannot forbear giving expression to the thought that, had "Joseph, the seer," been as apt at reading the future as he was at seeing the past, he might have been able to see the trap into which he and the leaders were about to fall. But this he could not do, with all his boasted powers of prophecy. He was as blind as the willing dupes who followed him "into the camp of the militia," and so into the custody of the law, and behind the bars of Liberty jail.

This was the beginning of the end, so far as the gathering of the Saints to the "Land of Zion" is concerned.

The stipulations entered into between General Lucas, representing the State of Missouri, and Colonel Hinkle, on the part of the Mormons, was ultimately carried out, and the Saints, under the leadership of Brigham Young, left the State the following spring, and settled in Western Illinois.

For the part Colonel Hinkle performed in this matter, and especially the delivery of the leaders to the authority of the State to be tried for their offenses, he has ever been regarded as the Benedict Arnold of the Mormon Church. As to whether his act was honorable or otherwise, the reader will judge for himself.

Joseph and Hyrum Smith, with a number of other prominent men of the church, were committed to the Liberty, Clay Co., jail, to await the action of the Grand Jury. In the following April the prisoners were removed to Davies County, where they were regularly indicted for "murder, treason, larceny, arson and burglary."

Upon a change of venue the prisoners were taken to Boone County and confined in jail to await their trial upon the foregoing charges. But they were never tried. The guard under whose care the prisoners were placed one night got beastly drunk, and taking advantage of the opportunity thus afforded, they all escaped, and at once made their way to Illinois, where they found a safe retreat among their friends.

The redemption of Zion was now abandoned as a forlorn hope. The dream of the prophet had vanished, and the hopes of an expectant people were sadly disappointed.

Zion still languishes, for the inhabitants thereof were made desolate. The "enemy" still "pollutes" the land, and the "Temple of the Lord" is still unbuilt. Under such circumstances of disappointment and failure in the past, upon what can the Saints build their hopes for the future?

Every promise concerning Zion and her redemption has resulted in disastrous and hopeless failure, and every prophecy remains unfulfilled. Still they look forward to the time when they can sing as they never sang before,

> "Then gather up for Zion,
> Ye Saints throughout the land,
> And clear the way before you,
> As God shall give command;
> Though wicked men and devils
> Exert their power, 'tis vain,
> Since He who is eternal
> Has said you shall obtain."

To ordinary mortals, viewing the facts as they exist in history, it is a wonder that the people do not forever abandon such mischievous and hurtful doctrines. But not so. The Saints still cling to their faith, and sing, and hope, and pray for the redemption of Zion, and the establishment of the "New Jerusalem." O, vain faith! delusive hope!

CHAPTER XXXVIII.

PROPHECIES OF JOSEPH SMITH—WERE THEY FULFILLED?

Prophecies of Joseph Smith—Were they fulfilled?—The rebellion of South Carolina—President Jackson and the Nullifiers—The great rebellion—War of 1861-5—The prophecy analyzed—Unfulfilled—Letter to R. N. E. Seaton—Bloodshed, famine and earthquakes—A desolating scourge—Letter to John C. Calhoun—Dire things predicted—The prophet grows eloquent—The whole prediction a failure.

PERHAPS there is nothing connected with the peculiarities of Mormonism in which the average Latter Day Saint has greater confidence than that all the prophetic utterances of Joseph will be literally fulfilled. The reason which they offer in justification of this belief may be found in the fact that they believe some of the most striking and remarkable among his many predictions have already had circumstantial and complete fulfillment.

It is with a view to determine the accuracy of this claim that we shall now turn our thought to this question.

The first prophecy of a general character to which I shall invite the reader's attention is that which relates to our late civil war, which is said to have been given Dec. 25, 1832. Upon careful consideration of the surrounding circumstances, I have observed that every so-called revelation of the prophet was suggested by some incident growing out of the environments. For instance, that which he received commanding him, in company with others, to go to

Independence, Missouri, grew out of the flattering reports of Parley P. Pratt and others concerning the wonderful fertility and beauty of the country and the great natural advantages which it offered to the persecuted Saints in the East. The fact that Independence was a most beautiful location for a city suggested the "revelation" concerning the location of Zion, and the place for the temple. In like manner, the defeat of "Zion's Camp" by the prompt interference of an overpowering force of the wicked Gentiles prompted the "Fishing River revelation," and so on through the whole list.

The revelation we are now about to consider was suggested by one of the most remarkable incidents in American history, namely, the threatened dissolution of the American Union by the famous nullification act of the legislature of South Carolina, in November, 1832. The whole country was in a state of unusual excitement. President Jackson took prompt measures to suppress the nullifiers, and the Government made preparations to invade South Carolina, and the State made preparations to defend. War was imminent, and everybody expected trouble. Confident that civil war would be the final result of all this activity, and wishing to appear as the Daniel of the dispensation, Joseph promptly received the following revelation:

"Verily, thus saith the Lord concerning the *wars* that will shortly come to pass, beginning with the rebellion of South Carolina, which will eventually terminate in the death and misery of many souls. The days will come that wars will be poured out upon *all nations, beginning at that place;* for behold, the Southern States shall be divided against the Northern

States, and the Southern States will call on other nations, even the nation of Great Britain, as it is called, and they [Great Britain] shall also call upon other nations, in order to defend themselves against other nations; and thus war shall be poured out upon *all* nations. And it shall come to pass after many days, slaves shall rise up against their masters, who shall be marshaled and disciplined for war. And it shall come to pass also that the remnants who are left of the land will marshal themselves, and shall become exceeding angry, and shall vex the Gentiles with a sore vexation; and thus, with the sword and by bloodshed, the inhabitants of the earth shall mourn; and with famine, and plague, and earthquakes, and the thunder of heaven, and the fierce and vivid lightning also, shall the inhabitants of the earth be made to feel the wrath and indignation and chastening hand of an Almighty God, until the consumption decreed hath made a full end of all nations; that the cry of the saints and of the blood of the saints shall cease to come up into the ears of the Lord of Sabbaoth from the earth, to be avenged of his enemies. Wherefore stand ye in holy places, and be not moved until the day of the Lord come; for behold, it cometh quickly, saith the Lord. Amen." (Smith's History, Vol. 1, pages 262 and 263.)

The Saints maintain that this rather remarkable prediction has had a very striking fulfillment. Whether this claim is justified by the facts of subsequent history remains to be seen. It by no means follows that because two or three points in this prediction have seemingly had a partial accomplishment the prophecy is authentic, and therefore divine.

In order to get at the exact truth concerning this

prophecy we must take into consideration all the
material facts and circumstances under which the
prediction was made, and also the details of its fulfillment. As already intimated, South Carolina was
at the time in a state of rebellion, and active preparations for war were being made on the part of both
the Federal Government and the State of South
Carolina. Everybody expected that civil war, with all
its attendant horrors, would be the inevitable result;
and in the event of war it was the general belief
among statesmen that the entire South would support
the action of South Carolina by joining in the conflict. The question of slavery had been agitated to a
degree that produced great bitterness in the minds of
the Southern people, and a spirit of general discon-
tent in the feelings of the Negroes of the South.

Under such circumstances it will not be difficult to
perceive that any man of ordinary information and
intelligence could have predicted the results of a war
between the North and South. Before we proceed to
analyze this remarkable production I wish to call
attention to a somewhat pertinent fact connected
with it.

It will doubtless be remembered that the Elders of
the Reorganized Church reject the revelation on
polygamy because it was kept from the general public, and was not published till 1852, by the authority
of the Church at Salt Lake City. If this objection be
valid, then it will apply with equal force in case of
the revelation now under consideration. This
prophecy never saw the light of day till it appeared
in "The Pearl of Great Price," published in Liver-
pool, England, in 1851, only one year after the revelation on "celestial marriage" appeared in "*The*

Deseret News, at Salt Lake City. Where is the *proof* that Joseph Smith ever received such a revelation as that predicting the civil war? If the document be genuine, why did it not appear in the book of Doctrine and Covenants, authorized by the act of a General Assembly at Kirtland, Ohio, in 1835? The prophet himself was the chairman of the committee that made the selection of the more important of his revelations which should compose the book. This "revelation and prophecy" concerning the civil war has ever been considered one of the most important of all Joseph's Smith's revelations. Why was it kept from the public for so many years? Why did it not appear with the other revelations in 1835, published less than three years after it is said to have been received? One of two answers must be the correct one: either the revelation *did not exist* at that time, or else the committee regarded it as a complete *failure*, and accordingly *suppressed* the remarkable document. The latter reason is probably the true one, and affords the solution of the whole question.

As a matter of fact, no man can be found, so far as I am able to learn, who either saw the revelation, or even heard of it, till it appeared in "The Pearl of Great Price." (See Smith's History, Vol. 1, page 262.)

I state these things for the purpose of calling attention to the fact that the genuineness of this document is by no means established, and that its authenticity must be regarded as very doubtful. By waiving all technicalities, let us deal with the document on its merits, that we may determine how much of it, if any, has been fulfilled, and how much has failed; and in order to do this I shall separate and number the propositions.

1. South Carolina should rebel, (had rebelled, in fact) and war between the States should follow.

2. The Southern States should call upon Great Britain for assistance.

3. Great Britain should call upon other nations, in order to defend herself against other nations, and thus become seriously involved in war.

4. This action should result in the formation of alliances, both offensive and defensive, between all the great powers of earth.

5. And wars should *thus* be poured out upon *all nations*, beginning at the rebellion of South Carolina.

6. "And it shall come to pass after many days that slaves shall rise up against their masters, who should be marshaled and disciplined for war."

7. "The remnants who are left of the land," were to become "exceeding angry and vex the Gentiles with a sore vexation."

8. During these perilous times the Saints should stand in holy places,—that is, in Zion (Independence) and her "stakes," (other places of safety—See Doc. and Cov., pages 153 and 266) and *should not be moved.*

9. "And thus with the sword and by bloodshed, the inhabitants of the earth shall mourn;" and famine, pleague and earthquakes, and the thunder of heaven, and fierce and vivid lightning should never cease "until the consumption decreed" of God had made a "*full end of all nations.*"

10. The final consummation of all things was at hand, when Christ should "come quickly," in power and great glory.

If this prophecy was uttered with reference to the rebellion of South Carolina in November, 1832, as it most assuredly was, then not one word of it ever came to pass. But if, as the Saints now maintain, it had reference to the secession movement of 1861, then some of the things mentioned may be said to have come true. For instance, the Southern States followed South Carolina out of the Union, and war between the States was the result, thus fulfilling proposition No. 1.

In the next place the Southern States, through their commissioners, called upon Great Britain for assistance. This may be regarded as *fulfillment No. 2*.

Thus it will be seen that out of the ten events which were to transpire in regular sequence, as the result of the rebellion of South Carolina, only *two* have had even an approximate or apparent fulfillment, namely, the secession of South Carolina, and the war between the States.

Latter Day Saints claim, however, that the proposition which says "*slaves* shall rise up against their masters," was also fulfilled. But this is not true. The negroes of the South did not rebel against their masters; neither were they marshaled and disciplined for war, as the prophecy declares. After the famous emancipation proclamation of Abraham Lincoln there were no more "slaves" in the South—they were all now freed men. These freed men rushed to the support of the government, and were enlisted into the Union army. But no *slave* ever rose against his master, and no *slave* was marshaled and disciplined for war. This may, therefore, be set down as *failure No. 1*.

Great Britain did not become involved in consequence of the war between the States, and did not call upon other nations, as the prophecy declared she would do. This is *failure No. 2.*

No alliances between the great powers were formed as a result of the South Carolina rebellion, and hence *failure No. 3.*

Through these alliances, offensive and defensive, the prophecy declares that war should be *poured out upon all nations*, immediately following the rebellion of South Carolina. Nothing of the kind occurred, and hence *failure No. 4.*

In the next place the "remnants,"—and that may mean anything, possibly the shattered and demoralized Southern armies,—were to "vex the Gentiles with a sore vexation." Nothing of the kind was ever known to have occurred, and that makes *failure No. 5.*

The Saints were to stand in holy places, that is, they should occupy their "inheritances in Zion," and were not to "be moved." But as they were driven from Independence (Zion) and from Jackson County, in November, 1833, and all other Mormons from the State in 1839, this may be regarded as *failure No. 6.*

By means of war and bloodshed; by famine, plague and earthquake, God would continue to destroy the inhabitants of the earth, until he had made a "*full end of all nations.*"

Not a nation—not even the Turkish empire—has been destroyed. No nation on the earth has come to an abrupt or untimely end, and hence *failure No. 7.*

The final consummation of all things does not appear imminent, and the Lord has not appeared to take vengeance upon the ungodly; and things move along about as of yore, and thus we record *failure No. 8*.

With these stubborn facts staring them in the face, how can the representatives of the Saints look an intelligent audience in the face and affirm that this prophecy has had literal and circumstantial accomplishment!

It takes not divine inspiration to declare that *war* would be the result of any attempt upon the part of South Carolina, or of all the Southern States combined, to overthrow the Federal Government. But one of the remarkable features of this prophecy is the entire omission of any reference to several of the most important events connected with the late war. It says nothing about the formation of the Southern Confederacy, nor does it intimate that the greatest rebellion of any age was crushed, and the States brought back into the Federal Union.

While it declares that slaves would rise against their masters, it is as mute as a sphynx upon the question of emancipation,—not a word about the shackles falling from the limbs of four millions of slaves, by the single stroke of the immortal Lincoln's pen.

Not a word about any of these things, and yet they are the most important events connected with the great civil war growing out of the rebellion of South Carolina.

Thus it will be seen that this prophecy of which Latter Day Saints are wont to boast, only guessed with reasonable accuracy, *two* points, while it utterly failed in *eight;* besides omitting to mention *three* of the most important events connected with the subject. The prophecy thus remains unfulfilled, and the time is now past when its accomplishment can be regarded as among the possibilities of the future.

So confident, however, was the prophet that war would be the result of the attitude of South Carolina in 1832, that he made it the basis of another prophecy on January 4, 1833. In a letter to Mr. R. N. E. Seaton, of Rochester, N. Y., the editor of a leading newspaper published in that city, Mr. Smith says:

"And now I am prepared to say, by the authority of Jesus Christ, that not many years shall pass away before the United States shall present such a scene of *bloodshed* as has not a parallel in the history of our nation; pestilence, hail, famine, and earthquakes will sweep the wicked of this generation from off the face of the land, to open and prepare the way for the return of the lost tribes of Israel from the north country. The people of Lord . . . have already commenced gathering together to Zion, which is in the State of Missouri; therefore I declare unto you the warning which the Lord has commanded me to declare unto this generation. . . . Repent ye, repent ye, and embrace the everlasting covenant, and flee to Zion before the overflowing scourge overtakes you, for there are those now living upon the earth whose eyes shall not be closed in death until they see all these things, which I have spoken, fulfilled." (Smith's History, Vol. 1, page 262.)

Thus it may be seen that the prophet still believed in his prediction of December 25, and that war would follow that particular rebellion, until a scene of bloodshed and carnage, which has no parallel in the history of our nation, should be the result. But this, like most of his prophecies, proved a complete failure, as the history of those times abundantly shows.

The difficulties which then existed were finally settled by the adoption of Henry Clay's Compromise Tariff Act of 1833. The Government forces were withdrawn, and the dark war-cloud that hung over the nation like a pall was thus dissipated, and peace again restored. The prophecy was a failure, and the prophet himself seems to have lost his faith as to its accomplishment, and hence, the revelation did not appear in the Book of Doctrine and Covenants, which was published a short time afterwards.

But even if we give it the broadest possible scope and allow that the second rebellion of South Carolina was the time referred to, as claimed by its advocates, when the predicted calamities should begin, even then it must be regarded as a failure.

The prophecy contained in the Seaton letter is but an abridgement of that of Dec. 25, 1832, with a few points more clearly stated. It is certainly true that, following the rebellion of 1861, there was presented a scene of "bloodshed" which has no parallel in the annals of the country; but when you have said this, all has been said that can in truth be declared with respect to the fulfillment of this prophecy. Not another item in the prediction has had even the semblance of accomplishment.

The "overflowing scourge," soon to overtake the wicked inhabitants of the land, did not materialize, and Mr. Seaton thought it wholly unnecessary to "flee to Zion" for safety. "The people of the Lord," who were then gathering to Zion, were driven from their homes in less than a year from the time the prediction was uttered. Pestilence, hail, famine and earthquakes did not "sweep the wicked of this generation from off the face of the land," and the "lost tribes of Israel" have not returned from "the north country" in the regions of the pole.

All these things were to transpire in their regular order, immediately following the rebellion of South Carolina; but all of which are only rendered conspicuous by their absence, thus marking the prophecy as a poor, miserable failure. Further comment upon this document appears useless; and I therefore pass to the consideration of another of Joseph's prophecies.

In a letter addressed to John C. Calhoun, of South Carolina, dated at Nauvoo, Ill., Jan. 2, 1844, may be found what is perhaps the most remarkable and striking of all the prophecies delivered by this eccentric and impulsive man. He had, in a previous communication, asked the renowned South Carolina statesman what would be his rule of action relative to the Latter Day Saints, who had been expelled from the State of Missouri, should he be elected President of the United States. To this inquiry Mr. Calhoun returned the following reply:

"But as you refer to the case of Missouri, candor compels me to repeat what I said to you at Washington, that, according to my views, the case does not come within the jurisdiction of the Federal Government, which is one of limited and specific powers." (Smith's History, Vol. 1, page 451.)

To this Joseph made a lengthy and characteristic reply. Among other things the prophet says:

"If the General Government has no power to reinstate expelled citizens to their rights, there is a monstrous hypocrite fed and fostered from the hard earnings of the people. A real 'bull-beggar' upheld by sycophants. And although you may wink to the priests to stigmatize, wheedle the drunkard to swear, and raise the hue and cry of 'Impostor! false prophet! G---- d---n old Joe Smith!' yet remember, if the Latter Day Saints are not restored to all their rights, and paid for all their losses, according to the known rules of justice and judgment, reciprocation and common honesty among men, that God will come out of his hiding place and vex this nation with a sore vexation; yea, the consuming wrath of an offended God shall smoke through the nation with as much distress and woe as independence has blazed through it with pleasure and delight. . . .

"In the days of General Jackson, when France refused the first installment for spoliations, there was power, force and honor enough to resent injustice and insult, and the money came. And shall Missouri, filled with negro drivers and white men stealers, go 'unwhipped of justice' for tenfold greater sins than France? No! verily no! While I have power of body and mind—while water runs and grass grows— while virtue is lovely and vice hateful, and while a stone points out a sacred spot where a fragment of American liberty once was, I or my posterity will plead the cause of injured innocence until Missouri makes atonement for all her sins, or sinks digraced, degraded, and damned to hell, 'where the worm dieth not, and the fire is not quenched.'" (Tullidge's History, pages 455, 456.)

The fulfillment of this remarkable prophecy is made contingent upon the action of the General Government. If the United States should take the matter in hand, and reinstate the expelled Latter Day Saints to their possessions in Missouri, the nation should escape the pending calamity. But if the

Federal Government failed to do this, then "the consuming wrath of an offended God" should *smoke through the nation* with as much *distress and woe* as "independence had ever blazed through with pleasure and delight."

The government did not even attempt to restore the Saints, and yet the consuming wrath of God failed to smoke through the nation. The old flag still floats to the breezes of every clime, and the nation has not yet been "consumed." But instead, she stands to-day as one of the greatest powers on the earth.

So much, then, for this great flourish of trumpets by the Modern Seer.

Besides this national woe—this consuming wrath—there was also to be a special dispensation of divine wrath visited upon the State of Missouri. This great State, "filled with negro drivers and white men stealers," should not go "unwhipped of justice" for her great sin in thrusting the Saints from their homes. "No! verily no!" She, too, must suffer for her individual transgressions. She must make atonement for driving an innocent people from their homes. Either Joseph or his posterity should continue to plead the cause of an injured people till Missouri had made ample restitution, or till she should sink "disgraced, degraded, and damned to hell."

In the following June Joseph was killed by a mob in Carthage jail, and could, therefore, no longer plead the cause of his people. Thus sixteen years passed away, and no voice was heard to plead the cause of the exiled Saints. At the end of that time, however, or in 1860, the eldest son of the murdered Seer took his father's place at the head of the Reorganized Church, but still no pleading voice was heard. And up to this date the son has never been known to petition either the State of Missouri or the General Government to restore the Mormon people to their lost inheritances in Zion.

It is likewise a well-known fact that neither the State of Missouri nor the Federal Government has ever put forth the slightest effort to make the restitution this vengeful revelation demands, and yet they both stand as living witnesses of the vanity and presumption of the prophet, and the absolute unreliability of his prophetic utterances.

The United States of America stands to-day as the peer of the most advanced nation on the globe, while Missouri takes high rank among the sisterhood of States, and has been neither disgraced, degraded, nor "damned to hell," as the vindictive prophet declared she should be, but, in her imperial majesty, she stands erect to pronounce the prophecy a failure, and its author a fraud.

CHAPTER XXXIX.

CONCLUSION—A LETTER TO ELDER T. E. L.

A letter to Elder T. E. L.—Modern revelation—Apostles and prophets—Church organization—Its various officers—Two Priesthoods—"Those abominations"—Early Christians—A charge repelled—Those idolatrous Israelites—No new revelation necessary—The "basic idea of Mormonism"—An important question—The New Testament a perfect guide—Five pointed questions—Six reasons examined—The Bible a detector—A mere srcapping of incidents—The whole system wrong—Conclusion.

OTHER topics might be discussed with propriety, and possibly with profit, but as we have examined many of the more important questions connected with Mormon theology, it will perhaps be sufficient to close this volume with a letter to a prominent Elder of the Reorganized Church, to which no reply was made. Following is the letter:

DEAR BROTHER:—
Your communication of recent date came duly to hand, and its contents have been carefully considered. In the opening paragraphs of your letter you express the thought that I seem to "confess, at least in part, the faith of the Saints" concerning God's revealments to man at the present day. Then so let it be; for I am very glad the "Saints" have some things in common with all Christian people which I am able to endorse.

I am quite aware it is the "faith of the Saints" that any person may receive a revelation for himself, but while this is true, it is likewise a fact that *all* are alike prohibited from receiving revelation *for the benefit of the church*. This divine prerogative is confined to the "Prophet, Seer, Revelator and Translator," Joseph Smith, "for he receiveth them even as Moses." So says the "Doctrine and Covenants."

MODERN REVELATION.

It is hardly necessary for me to say that I most heartily disbelieve this whole revelation business, and for the best of reasons. I have seen too much of it. Too many gross errors and glaring absurdities, not to mention the "grosser crimes," have been authorized through its exercise for me to repose the least confidence in it. The "grosser crimes" of Utah, including polygamy and murder; the abominations of Strangism on Beaver Island, including polygamy, wholesale theft, highway robbery and foulest murder; the gross absurdities of "Baneemyism," and the unblushing obscenity of Rigdonism, all had their origin in pretended revelation.

In view of these facts I repeat the question, Of what possible benefit is this professed revelation to the world? In answer to this question I undertake to say that no good, but much evil, has resulted, and nothing else can reasonably be expected.

I prefer a system of religion with moral, spiritual and intellectual advancement as its leading characteristics, with no revelation but the Bible, to a system that claims so much in the way of new revelation, whose tendencies are in the opposite direction, and whose fruit has ever been evil. "A tree is known by its fruits."

APOSTLES AND PROPHETS.

Respecting a church organization with inspired apostles and prophets, you ask: "But why not apostles and prophets to-day?" Now, Bro. Lloyd, let us try to take a fair, sensible, honest view of this matter, as I am fully assured you are capable of doing, if only you can rise above sectarian prejudice, and for the time, at least, lay aside pre-conceived opinions.

And in order to get the question fairly before your mind, allow me to present a proposition for your consideration. It is this: In the original and Biblical sense of the word you have neither an *apostle* nor a *prophet* in the church.

It is true you have what you are pleased to call apostles, but they are not such in the proper sense of that term, and no proof can be adduced to support the claim. And further, there is no class of ministers in your organization *designated and known* as "prophets." Please note this carefully. This, you know, is a fact not to be questioned for one moment. Take any work extant recognized by the church as authoritative, and run over the list of officers, or what is termed "the order of the priesthood," from the "First Presidency" down to the deacon, and the office of "prophet" does not appear.

For proof of this you are referred to "Presidency and Priesthood," by Apostle W. H. Kelley, and "Manual of the Priesthood," by Chas. Derry, president of the "High Priest's Quorum." In neither of these works can be found the office of *prophet*.

As to the church organization of which you boast, and which is claimed to be strictly Biblical, allow me to say it is wholly unauthorized. No such organization as that which you claim for the church is known to the New Testament, or the Old either, for that matter. I speak advisedly while making this declaration, knowing whereof I affirm.

"See that ye make all things according to the pattern," is the watchword of all Latter Day Saints, and I intend to hold them strictly to a rule of their own choosing respecting their form of church government.

CHURCH GOVERNMENT.

W. H. Kelley, in his "Presidency and Priesthood," on pages 53 and 83, gives the list of officials in the church as follows:

1. "The First Presidency," consisting of one "chief apostle and Melchizedek high priest," and two "counselors" or "assistants."
2. The quorum of twelve apostles.
3. The (a) seventy elders.
4. The elders.
5. Bishops ["the presiding bishop and his two counselors," called the (b) "Bishoprick"]?
6. (c) Priests.
7. Teachers.
8. Deacons.
9. High Priests.
10. (d) Evangelists.
11. (e) Pastors.

Here we have eleven distinct offices presented by Mr. Kelley as necessary to the complete organization of the Church of Christ, and that they constitute the organic structure of the body he represents.

It is quite needless, perhaps, for me to remind you that some of these offices are not once mentioned in the entire history of the New Testament Church.

Prominently among these are the "First Presidency." Neither Christ nor his apostles knew anything whatever of a "First Presidency."

Mr. Kelley, in rendering his list, totally ignores an office in his church second only in dignity to that of the "First Presidency," namely, that of "Patriarch." Why he did so we are left to imagine. No hint can be found in the New Testament Scriptures of the existence in the church of such a thing as a Patriarch.

Not a word about a "Bishoprick," consisting of a "presiding bishop" and his two "counselors." No mention—not even a *hint*—in all the Bible of a "Quorum of High Priests." Nothing said about the office of "priest" in the Church of Christ. Not a syllable about the "High Council in Zion," nor yet of the "High Council in the *stakes* (!) of Zion." Not a word about any of these things; and yet you urge them as a part of the organic structure of the church. And while you do this you say exultingly to the entire religious world, "See that you have all things according to the divine pattern, *as it is laid down in the Bible.*" Truly may we exclaim, "O consistency, thou art indeed a jewel."

Now, my dear brother, no one knows better than do you that in all God's word there can be found no support whatever for such a wild vagary. Not a scrap of history, either sacred or profane, can be produced that even so much as remotely hints at such an organization as that which you seek to maintain.

No man in the history of the Mormon Church has entered upon this difficult task with as much painstaking labor as has W. H. Kelley in his "Presidency and Priesthood;" and yet his effort is devoid of a single *fact*, either of Scripture or history, that, when fairly construed, even tends to support his position. With respect to the *two priesthoods*, namely, "the Melchizedek and the Aaronic," being in the church, his every argument is based upon *assumption*, pure and simple.

You may think this a broad, and perhaps groundless, assertion, yet I make it after having carefully read his book, and know whereof I speak, and do not fear successful contradiction.

In closing your argument on "apostles and prophets," you say: "Surely no one, reading its pages [meaning the Bible], can intelligently claim its support for a disbelief in the necessity now, for apostles and prophets."

If this be true, then why do you not have in the church a class of ministers specifically denominated *prophets* as set forth in 1 Cor. 12: 28, but purposely omitted by Mr. Kelley in his list of officers?

You have a class of ministers called "apostles," but where are your "prophets" in the same specific sense? You know perfectly well that you have none. This being true, and having several offices, with their respective incumbents, wholly unknown to the New Testament, and hence unauthorized by it, what becomes of your boasted claim of having a strictly Biblical church organization,—a house built according to the pattern? If you lack one member, you come short of the pattern. If you have several members not included in the structure of the original body, then you overreach the pattern, which is equally objectionable. But when it is considered that your system *lacks* in one direction and *over-*

reaches in the other, then there can be but one conclusion, and that is, *the structure is not made according to the pattern*, and hence must be *wrong*. I see no possible way of escape from this conclusion.

"THOSE ABOMINATIONS."

Under this head you ask:

"But why should these trouble you, when you confess it to be due to a departure from the light of modern revelations?"

These abominations do not trouble me in the least, but you seem to overlook the point I most wish to make, namely, that if the modern "revelation" has not the power to so influence and impress men as to restrain them from the commission of such abominations, of what possible good can such a revelation be to the world? That is the vital point.

I am not a little surprised, I confess, at your effort to apologize for this latter day abomination, by asserting that the Christians were chargeable with similar offences. Upon this point you ask:

"Shall we say that the revelation of Jesus is chargeable with *abominations among Christians*, only a few years after Jesus ascended?"

In answer to this charge allow me to suggest that it may be well for you to *prove* that Christians, generally, were guilty of the abominations you charge upon them, before you make it the ground of an apology for this latter day abomination.

I deny the charge most emphatically, and declare that it cannot be maintained. That their enemies charged them with immorality and crime is conceded; but that they were guilty as charged, Christians everywhere deny.

The rule by which I may desire to test so-called modern revelation is equally applicable to the revelation made by Jesus Christ. If the religion revealed by Jesus was not, and is not, sufficient to restrain the evil tendencies of human nature and elevate man to a higher plane of life, then it is not the religion that will redeem a fallen race.

You have but to compare the present advanced state of the world, intellectually, morally and spiritually, with the conditions which existed at the time the revelation was made, to convince you of its divine origin.

Sixty-seven years have now transpired since the dawn of "revelation's holy light," as announced by Joseph Smith. Compare the results of this sixty-seven years with the corresponding period of time beginning with the introductory work and revelation of Jesus Christ, and we must say the divinity of the revelation of Jesus is made to appear, and in comparison with whose grandeur and glory the pretended revelation of Joseph Smith sinks into contemptible insignificance. We must determine the value of a system by the amount of good it accomplishes. Look at *results*, not theories.

THOSE IDOLATROUS ISRAELITES.

Your reference to the idolatry of the children of Israel, while Moses was in Mount Sinai receiving the Law, is wholly inadmissible as an apology for the abominations growing out of Mormonism, and cannot be forced into service as an excuse for the utter failure of Joseph Smith's new revelation. These Israelites, for four hundred years, had been kept in bondage and in ignorance, and were comparable only to the freedmen of the South at the time of their emancipation from the bondage of slavery. Will you, in order to make out a case, place the followers of Joseph Smith on a level, morally, intellectually and spiritually, with these ignorant slaves of both ancient and modern times? Surely it must be a desperate case that requires such a mode of defense.

No, Bro. L——, this will not do. The *truth* explains the situation far better; and the truth is, there was no potency in the modern revelation for good, and hence its failure.

On the third page of your letter you seek to evade the force of my remarks in the arraignment of the "old church" by saying:

"The facts of the case, when fully considered, will vindicate the great mass of the people; *for not one in ten was guilty.*"

Suppose we examine a few of the facts connected with this matter.

At the time of Mr. Smith's death, in 1844, the church, it has ever been claimed by Latter Day Saints, numbered 200,000 souls. Of this number, according to your figures, 20,000 only were guilty. This leaves 180,000 who stand "vindicated." Take from this number the entire membership of the Reorganized Church, which, in round numbers, is about 25,000 (and this, you will doubtless concede, is quite liberal, as many of this number must be new converts), and we have a balance of 155,000. Where shall we look for these Saints, 155,000 strong, who stand "vindicated" by your mode of argument? Where, except under the domain of the Utah Church, can this number be found? Can you account for them?

Again: If only ten per cent were guilty, as you assert, why was it declared in what is known as the "Revelation of 1841," written by Joseph Smith, that if the church did not complete the temple at Nauvoo, Ill., within a given time, they should "be rejected as a church with your dead, saith the Lord your God?" The Reorganized Church has ever maintained that when Joseph Smith publicly announced, just before his death, that there should be "no more *baptisms for the dead*" in the Mississippi River, the *entire church* was rejected of God. How can you justify this wholesale condemnation of both the living and the dead, if not one in ten was guilty?

So far as the moral character of the people of the Reorganized Church is concerned, I have only to remind you that whatever of moral excellence they may possess is due, not to the "distinctively Mormonic Canons," but rather to the divine excellence of the early "Christian Canons," as we have them in the New Testament Scriptures.

NO NEW REVELATION NECESSARY.

That during a period of some four thousand years—from Adam to Christ—God did graciously reveal his will to man in various ways, is readily and frankly conceded; but this fact does not afford a sufficient reason for believing that he will ever continue to do so. To my mind this reason is insufficient. The conclusion is not warranted by the premise. If men were justified by the works of the Law, then your argument would appear to possess the elements of consistency. But Paul assures us that "man is not justified by the works of the law, but by faith in Jesus Christ, . . . Christ having redeemed us from the curse of the law; for by the works of the law shall no flesh be justified." (Gal. 2: 16; 3: 13.)

When Christ came into the world he made a revelation of God's will to man, by the provisions of which all flesh might be justified before him.

The divine law thus revealed, James assures us, is the "perfect law of liberty" (Jas. 1: 25.) The Gospel law, then, is a perfect law; and if perfect it contains every necessary provision for man's redemption. Peter assures us that this revelation of God's will to man contains "all things that pertain unto life and godliness." (2 Pet. 1: 3.)

This cannot be said of any revelation given to man previously to this time. But here we have a law which contains everything necessary to life; everything necessary to godliness, and hence, everything necessary to man's salvation. It follows, then, as a logical sequence, that if everything necessary to the salvation of a fallen race was given through Jesus Christ, there can be no possible need for a subsequent revelation.

Any additions to this perfect law would only mar and destroy its beauty; and that is just what Joseph Smith's revelation has done.

Referring to my illustration, you say: "That little 'constitution' argument fails to meet the case," but you do not attempt to show, by analyzing it, wherein it "fails."

"BASIC IDEA OF MORMONISM."

Again: You say "the basic idea of Mormonism remains unshaken and unmoved." I presume you mean the "basic idea" remains "unshaken" in the minds of those who still endorse it. Nothing more.

The same may be said of Mohammedanism or of Buddhism. It does not follow that, because "the basic idea" of a system may remain "unshaken" in the minds of its devotees, the principle involved in such "basic idea" is necessarily correct.

You seemingly wish to impress upon my mind the fact of God's immutability, a point never brought in question, and has nothing to do with the questions in controversy. No Christian doubts that God is unchangeable, and that he commands and he revokes. It is very illogical, as well as unscriptural, to say that what God did sometime in the remote past he will always continue to do. For example, he once placed his people under the severe training of a "schoolmaster"—the Law—but this is no just ground for believing he would always retain the old Jewish pedagogue. But, quite to the contrary, we have the fact clearly established that Christ is the "end of the law," and hence Paul says "we are *no longer* under the schoolmaster," but under grace.

Hence it does not follow that because God revealed his will to man, especially endowed, *before* Christ, he will ever contiuue to do so *after* the "perfect law of liberty" was given.

AN IMPORTANT QUESTION.

This brings me to the consideration of a question you propound which I consider directly to the point, and very important. It is this:

"If it was ever the purpose of God to suspend the function of revelation, and so be unlike all the precedents established during the previous four thousand years, why did he make *special promises* through

Jesus Christ, *pledging continuous revelation* to his people?"

This question reminds me of an incident said to have occurred in the schoolroom. The professor was hearing a class in natural philosophy, and presented the following hypothetical question: "Suppose a tank filled with water weighs 375 pounds. Why is it that if a fish weighing seven pounds be put into the tank it does not increase its weight by just so many pounds?" Various reasons were assigned, but no two pupils could agree as to *why* the weight was not increased by the addition of a seven-pound fish. Finally the professor said:

"You have failed to consider a very important matter connected with the solution of this question. It is imperative that you first determine that the weight is *not* increased by the addition of the fish, and then you may be able to say *why* it is not."

Accordingly, allow me to suggest that you first *prove* that God made "special promises" through Christ, "pledging *continuous revelation* to his people," and then I will try to tell you *why* he did so. All the answer I deem it necessary to make at present is to state that no "special promise" can be found in the sayings of Christ, and no such "pledge" has ever been made by him.

It is my habit, as you are doubtless aware, to state my points of objection without ambiguity; and so, if I am in error in this matter, it will be the easiest thing in the world to show it by pointing to chapter and verse wherein the "special promise" and the divine "pledge" are made. And I repeat it, and do so knowing every passage upon which you rely for support, that no scriptural proof can be adduced in support of your position upon this point.

THE NEW TESTAMENT A PERFECT RULE.

I wish now to call attention to a paragraph in your letter which is, to say the least, very remarkable. Referring to the Old and New Testament Scriptures, you say:

"The writings of the Old Testament are only in part. . . . The New Testament is, at best, but a *scrapping* of incidents and ideas, but a compilation of a few epistles and letters, and the book of John's visions."

When your missionaries go out upon their missions to preach the "everlasting Gospel" to the nations of the earth, they hold up the Bible to the world as the *rule* of faith and practice, the *standard* by which they must be governed, the "*banknote detector*" by which all spurious theological coins may be detected. And it seems a little strange that you should now find it necessary to recede from this position and aver that the New Testament is, at best, but fragmentary and incomplete. But why should I wonder that you boldly assert on page nine of your letter that the "New Testament *is not all-sufficient* upon these great questions," when it is a well known fact that you but voice the sentiment of the entire church upon this point?

To say the New Testament is, at best, but fragmentary, and therefore a very imperfect guide, is to charge both Jesus and his disciples with incompetency and unfaithfulness in the discharge of duties divinely imposed. And this, to my mind, is the worst possible phase of agnosticism.

Now I am fully convinced that the New Testament, as a rule of Christian faith and practice, is all-sufficient—that whatsoever is not contained in it is not necessary. This rule holds good as to both doctrine and church organization. A doctrine that cannot be clearly established by its authority is wholly useless, if not absolutely hurtful.

A church organization that cannot be sustained by clear, unmistakable proofs from the New Testament Scriptures, is unworthy of serious consideration, and should be rejected.

It will not do, Bro. L——, to say that Christ gave an imperfect law, and that the disciples failed in the discharge of their duties, and that God waited eighteen hundred years to correct the blunder through Joseph Smith. This is asking too much of men endowed with an ordinary degree of common sense.

FIVE POINTED QUESTIONS.

On page ten of your letter you begin your answer to my five pointed questions. In answer to the question, "What valid reason can be given for believing God ever gave a revelation to Joseph Smith?" you make the following reply:

1. The claim is not unreasonable.
2. It is not anti-Scriptural.
3. It is in harmony with "all Scriptures."
4. It is in fulfillment of ancient prophecy.
5. Joseph Smith's prophecies have had direct fulfillment.
6. The gifts of the Holy Spirit have followed the word preached.

In answer to the above allow me to suggest that the "reasons" given are but so many assertions unsupported by the necessary proofs; and with a bare denial I might, with all propriety, let the matter rest where it is.

But I will go a little further, and reply:

1. The claim is unreasonable, because *no single additional truth*, either moral or spiritual, has been given, as you admit.

2. It is unscriptural, because Mr. Smith's system, in organization and doctrine, is at variance with the Bible.

3. No scriptural proofs can be adduced in its support.

4. No "ancient prophecy" points to Joseph Smith or his pretended revelation.

5. No prophecy of Joseph Smith has ever had "direct fulfillment"—not even that concerning the "rebellion of South Carolina."

6. From a forty years' experience, and careful observation, I know of no "spiritual gifts" to have "followed the word preached."

It is true I have witnessed what enthusiasts called the "gift of tongues," the "interpretation of tongues," the "gift of prophecy," the "gift of healing" and other "gifts," but none that I believe were, in fact "spiritual gifts," in the Biblical sense of that term. Judging from the light of my own experience and observation, as well as from the experience of scores of others with whom I have been associated during the past thirty or forty years, I have become perfectly satisfied that the miraculous things claimed are "rather fanciful than true." *Never*, in all my experience, have I been permitted to witness *one single miracle*. Not one.

I have seen what credulous persons were pleased to

call such, but nothing which ever appealed to my cool, sober second thought—to my intelligence—as a genuine miracle. To be candid with you and honest with myself, I have no reason to believe in the existence of anything miraculous, in the proper sense of that term, as connected with the Reorganized Church.

These six reasons, then, are valid only to those who have previously endorsed Mr. Smith's claim to prophetic powers, but have no weight whatever in convincing unbelievers, and hence are valueless.

In answer to my second question, namely, What principle of truth, necessary to man's salvation, did Joseph Smith advance that did not already exist? You refer me to Nos. 1, 2, 3, 4 and 5 of pages 7, 8 and 9 of your letter. Upon a careful examination of the numbers the fact appears that *not a single new truth appears*.

The new revelation, instead of presenting a new thought, or a new truth, simply takes part in a controversy on questions made plain in the Bible. For example.

No. 1. On the question of "water baptism," takes the side of *immersion*. The Baptists had decided this point in the same way hundreds of years before Joseph Smith was born. There is nothing new in this.

No. 2. The laying on of hands in confirmation is nothing new. Others have practiced this for centuries. The Roman Catholic and Episcopal Churches practice it, as do also the Six Principle Baptists. So no new light can be claimed on this point.

No. 3. The only point presented in this paragraph is, that somebody must be *authorized* to minister in Gospel ordinances. Every church in existence, whether Catholic or Protestant, believes the same. But Joseph Smith claims that this authority can be conferred only through his revelation. This you believe also; and I am frank to confess this may be considered something new, and the only new thought so far discovered.

No. 4. Deals with the Eucharist, but no new thought is evolved. The new "revelation" does not determine the day of the week upon which the Eucharist shall be celebrated, nor how often it shall occur.

No. 5. In this something new—absolutely new—is presented, and I am frank to confess it. It deals with *church organization;* and such an organization as that presented by Joseph Smith and promulgated by all Latter Day Saints never had an existence till he originated it.

Christ and the apostles never dreamed of such a system—never authorized it. No subsequent history even so much as hints at anything of the kind. Yes, that is something new.

As I have already shown, the entire system is at variance with the Bible "pattern," and must therefore be rejected as grossly erroneous, and offensive to the great Master Builder.

THE BIBLE A DETECTOR.

Your entire argument is directed against the generally received opinion that the New Testament Scriptures are a sufficient rule for the government of the church and the salvation of man. In fact, you unhesitatingly declare the "New Testament is not all-sufficient." Upon this point I am fully aware you represent the real sentiment of your church. But does it not seem like duplicity for your leading men, both in their published works and in their sermons, to hold up the Bible as being the *only means* by which to detect error and false doctrine, when it is perfectly clear that they do not themselves, in their hearts, believe what they say?

I cannot better illustrate this than by quoting from Apostle Wm. H. Kelley in his "Presidency and Priesthood." Speaking of what he calls "a money test," or detector of counterfeit coins, he says:

"When every mark and figure on a coin or bill tendered in exchange harmonizes with the detector, it is pronounced good money. But if there is any thing found on the coin or bill *not to be found in the detector*, or if there is something *left out* of the coin or bill that is found in the detector, it is rejected as spurious.

"The New Testament contains the history of the formation of the primitive church; hence it is the test or detector by which all church organizations claiming to be true are to be tried. . . . Then, friend, seeker, take the New Testament in your hand as your *guide and test*, by which to try systems, and start out and make search throughout Christendom, and see how many churches may be found that will answer to the pattern as being the church of Jesus Christ. Do not lose sight of the detector, or you will be in danger of being imposed upon by something man-made and spurious." (Pages 49, 50.)

Why this seemingly earnest exhortation to take the New Testament as a "guide and test" when starting out in search of the truth, when the ministry of your church are united in declaring it to be an insufficient and unreliable guide—"a mere scrapping of incidents," as you phrase it?

As well may you start out to detect spurious coins and bills with a fragmentary and imperfect detector in your hand, as to start out to detect frauds and spurious religions with an imperfect Bible in your hand. In either case your "detector" would utterly fail to detect.

I do not speak flatteringly when I say a man of your intelligence and powers to analyze cannot fail to see that there must be something radically wrong with either your logic or your facts; and I do not hesitate to say the trouble is with your facts. *Your whole system is wrong.*

I think I understand just why such appeals as that quoted from Mr. Kelley's book are made. He, with all others making the appeal, well knows that other churches do not have "apostles and prophets" in their organic structure, in the specific sense in which you employ the term, and claiming to have them in your church, attention is called to the fact, and much stress laid upon this "detector" rule in order to catch the unwary and captivate the credulous.

This method is misleading, because it does not present the whole truth. Many facts are kept in the background, and come to light only after the investigator has committed himself to the system. In this connection I repeat with emphasis that no such church organization as that which you represent, with its "two priesthoods" and numerous officials, is known to the Bible, and cannot be sustained by the authority of Christ and his apostles. I make this declaration with all confidence, knowing whereof I affirm, and am prepared to meet the issue.

www.ingramcontent.com/pod-product-compliance
Lightning Source LLC
Chambersburg PA
CBHW032002300426
44117CB00008B/873